Presidential Primaries
and Nominations

Presidential Primaries and Nominations

William Crotty
Northwestern University

John S. Jackson III
Southern Illinois University
at Carbondale

A division of Congressional Quarterly Inc.
1414 22nd Street, N.W., Washington, D.C. 20037

Library of Congress Cataloging in Publication Data

Crotty, William J.
  Presidential primaries and nominations.

  Includes index.
  1. Presidents—United States—Nomination.
I. Jackson, John S., 1940-   . II. Title.
JK521.C76 1985   324.5′4   84-17662
ISBN 0-87187-260-9

Pat, Molly, and Bob Crotty
Jeff and Jill Jackson

Preface

Few collective decisions made by any people in any nation can rival the importance of the choice made every four years by the American people when they elect a president. Closely linked to that momentous decision are the events that lead to the selection of candidates by the two major parties. Our choice of the president in the general election, the choice between a Democrat and a Republican, has been much studied; the research constitutes a rich tradition in American political science. Somewhat less well documented are the prenomination and nomination stages of the presidential elections. This book comprehensively addresses the process of presidential selection from the declaration of candidacies through the parties' national conventions, focusing on how the nominating system has changed in recent decades and what the consequences of the changes have been.

In viewing the development of the current nominating system, we refer to the prereform, reform, and postreform eras. We define the period before 1968 as the prereform era, which was characterized by a nominating system dominated by party elites; 1968 witnessed upheaval that led to the transformation of the presidential nominating system. In 1968 to 1976, the reform era, new national party rules were put into place, establishing a mixture of rank-and-file and party elite participation in the process—the mixed system we refer to throughout the book. The postreform period, beginning in 1976, has been characterized by the dominance of primaries in the system and by a general acceptance of the national parties' role in the nominating process. Although incremental changes continue to be made, the postreform nominating system has remained largely intact.

We are more sanguine about the new nominating system than are many recent academic, journalistic, and political observers; we view the system as the latest manifestation of forces and philosophies that have contended for ascendancy throughout American history. Nonetheless, we present here a balanced account of change and reaction to change over the past few decades, including why change has occurred and how critics have reacted.

In this book we analyze the presidential nominating process—its origins, how it operates, its strengths, and its weaknesses. Chapter 1 traces the historical evolution of our nominating system, showing how individual processes originated and how reform impulses led to changes. In Chapter 2 we examine the latest major round of reforms, viewing these as a continuation of earlier impulses. Several of the most important characteristics of the current nominating system—consequences of the reform era, such as the centralization of party power and the influence of the media—are the focus of Chapter 3. That chapter also presents party change in the context of U.S. social and economic circumstances. The first three chapters constitute Part I of the book.

Part II, the next five chapters, is the core of the empirical material of the book. Chapter 4 develops the empirical evidence available relevant to the questions of who participates and what and whom they represent as it applies to primaries, caucuses, and national conventions. Chapter 5 examines the characteristics of the delegates: who they are personally and politically and how representative they are both of the voters and of the candidates. Chapter 6 considers the influence of candidate image and ideology on how voters decide for whom they will vote and looks at how candidates use image, ideology, and positioning to develop campaign strategies for the nomination and general election races. Chapter 7 turns to the costs of running for the presidential nomination and briefly reviews the history of the regulations governing nominating campaigns. Chapter 8 discusses the national conventions, how they are organized, how they decide, and what their impact is on the candidates' prospects for the general election.

In the concluding chapter, Chapter 9, which constitutes Part III of the book, we review the criticisms of the present system, provide our own assessment of the current system, and review some of the proposed reforms and changes for the future.

Throughout the book we have relied on the valuable research of other scholars of the nomination process. Our own previous research and publications are also relevant, since we have long been working on party reform, the national conventions, and presidential nominations. In addition, we have done original research for this book, and the results are first published here.

We are grateful to the many individuals and institutions who have contributed to this book. On the early drafts we received valuable advice from John H. Aldrich of the University of Minnesota, John F. Bibby of the University of Wisconsin, Milwaukee, and Milton C. Cummings of Johns Hopkins University. For the data in Chapter 4 we have relied in part on the Inter-University Consortium for Political and Social Research. The data for the *American National Election Study, 1980,* were originally collected by the Center for Political Studies of the Institute for Social Research, the University of Michigan, for the National Election Studies, under the overall direction of Warren E. Miller; Maria Elena Sanchez was director of studies in 1980. The data were collected under a grant from the National Science Foundation. Neither the original collectors of the data nor the Consortium bear any responsibility for the analyses or interpretations presented here.

At Southern Illinois University, the Office of Research Development and Administration and the Department of Political Science have helped sponsor John Jackson's research over the years. Jill Vaughn assisted in the typing of the manuscript. William Crotty is grateful for the assistance of Lucille Mayer, Ann Busool, Rose Martinelli, Carole Schwartz, and Evelyn Manley. Both authors also wish to thank Rhodes Cook of Congressional Quarterly and the staff at CQ Press, especially Joanne D. Daniels, director; Nola Healy Lynch, developmental editor; and Patricia M. Russotto, project editor.

William Crotty
John S. Jackson III

Contents

Preface   vii

Part I: Overview of the Nominating System

1. **An Introduction to the Nominating System**   3
   The Context of Presidential Nomination   3
   The Cycle of Reform   7
   The Old Party System   21
   Conclusion   22

2. **Reforming the System**   27
   Democratic Party Reform   27
   Republican Party Reform   44
   The Consequences of the Reform Era   49
   Conclusion   51

3. **Presidential Nomination in the 1980s**   55
   The Centralization of Party Processes   55
   The Dominance of the Primaries   62
   Social Instability and the Nominating System   69
   The Influence of the Media   74

Part II: Studies of the Nominating System

4. **The Voters: Participation and Representativeness**   83
   Representativeness of Primary Voters   85
   Caucuses versus Primaries   95
   Conclusion   97

5. **A Profile of the National Convention Delegates**   103
   The Theory of Representation   104
   The Representativeness of the Delegates   106

Ideology   116
Issues and Issue-Based Ideology   123
Conclusion   136

6. **Voting Behavior and Candidate Strategy**   141
   Voting Behavior   141
   Candidate Strategy   149
   Conclusion   156

7. **Financing the Prenomination Campaign**   159
   Introduction   159
   Sources of Funding   164
   Expenditures   171
   The State of Campaign Financing   179
   Proposals for Change in Campaign Financing   185

8. **The National Conventions**   187
   The Nature of the Conventions   187
   The Functions of the National Conventions   188
   Setting Up the Conventions   189
   The Media at the Conventions   192
   The Delegates at the Conventions   193
   The Candidates at the Conventions   199
   Selection of the Vice Presidential Candidates   201
   The Importance of Party Unity   204
   Revitalizing the National Conventions   206

Part III: Future of the Nominating System

9. **Where Do We Go from Here?**   213
   The Candidates and the System   214
   Proposals for Further Reform   220
   Conclusion   230

Appendix   235

Index   243

Part I—

Overview of the Nominating System

An Introduction to the Nominating System

1

The Context of Presidential Nomination

The selection of presidential nominees is a critical point—some would contend the *most* critical point—in the process of democratic governance in the United States today. In the twentieth century, especially since the New Deal period, the federal government has become increasingly involved in the domestic affairs—in the social, economic, and political life—of the nation. In foreign affairs, since World War II the United States has taken on the role of world superpower. People have come to expect the government to resolve the difficulties faced by modern society, and they now recognize the importance and power of the president in both domestic and foreign affairs. The president, as the chief executive, sets the major agenda for the rest of the government and propels the system toward that agenda. It follows that the way we choose our presidents has an impact on the quality of life, perhaps on the potential for continuing life, for all of us.

The presidential nominating system, the single most important responsibility of the political parties, has thus become a natural focus of attention. Many segments of the polity are actors in the process of selecting presidential nominees: party organizations, party elites, voters, the media, and the candidates themselves. In Figure 1.1 we provide an overview of the presidential nominating process, beginning with the strategic political environment—the state of the economy, relations with other nations, environmental and energy concerns, the influence of the media, and so on. Interrelated with this are the candidates and the

3

Strategic Political Environment

The state of the economy
Foreign and military conditions
Domestic conditions
The media
The public opinion polls
Partisan distribution
Interest group distribution

Candidates

Incumbent or not
In- or out-party in the White House
Image
Positions on the crucial issues
Relative position vis-à-vis other candidates
Party strength of the candidate
Group strength of the candidate
Resources available
Staff and organization
Stamina and time for campaigning

Procedural Rules of the Nominations

Primaries versus caucuses
Timing of the primaries/caucuses
Geographical location of the primaries/caucuses
Rules governing campaign finance
National party rules versus state and local rules
Court decisions

National Convention

Level of conflict
Outcomes of credentials and rules fights
Rules regarding delegate freedom
Media coverage
Candidate and staff work
Interest group activities
Actions of candidates

Nomination

Figure 1.1 Overview of the Presidential Nominating Process

abilities, personal qualities, experience levels, policy commitments, and campaign themes they bring to the contest. The strategic political environment and the types of candidates vary greatly from election year to election year.

Within this broad context the parties choose their nominees according to their internal procedural rules and processes. The rules address both the legal criteria for the selection of delegates to the conventions and the political processes involved in delegate selection (and thus in selection of nominees). Among the most important dimensions of the rules setting are the number, timing, geographical distribution, and basic mixture of the state-level primaries and caucuses. That mixture has been subject to change since the late 1960s. In addition, the funding available for individual campaigns determines not only where and, to a degree, how effectively a candidate will contest the party's primaries and caucuses, but also what kind of hearing he will receive from the mass media and the American public.

Following the primaries and caucuses, each party's delegates meet for the national convention. The convention officially chooses the nominees for president and vice president, adopts the national statement of party policy (the platform), and attends to that year's party-related business. The rules governing the deliberations and formal organization of the national convention (which differ somewhat by party) can be influential in deciding among the candidates supported by competing interests. Most recent conventions, however, have nominated the candidate who emerged as a clear front-runner in the preconvention caucus and primary contests. The smoothness of the candidate's course through the preconvention primaries and caucuses and the strength of the consensus for his candidacy at the convention affect the prospects for both the candidate and the party in the general election campaign.

The processes for selecting the presidential nominees of the two major political parties have been a focus of contention in recent years. Although the parties and the nominating system have been examined numerous times in the past, the debate has taken on an urgency that was not always evident in earlier periods. Two factors largely account for the recent activity. First, the social and economic fabric of the United States has undergone profound change in recent years, to which the nation's political institutions have had to respond. Second, and closely related, the current presidential nominating system reflects the legacy of the reform movement of the late 1960s and early 1970s. Those reforms, which were themselves a response to the changing environment (Chapter 2), resulted in a power struggle between the groups that had held the balance of power in the earlier system and those that had become newly active in presidential nominating politics.

The issues involved in reform of the presidential nominating system today are much the same as they have been since the framing of the Constitution: How much democracy can the system bear and how should mass participation be institutionalized? The reforms enacted during the late 1960s and early 1970s, particularly in the Democratic party, have largely accomplished their goal of opening the nominating process to constituencies that previously were virtually excluded: minorities, women, and issue-oriented citizen-activists. At the same time, the change in the balance of power reduced the influence of the controllers of the earlier system: party professionals, public office holders, and the leaders of some interest groups, such as the labor unions.

In the 1980s the parties and their observers started evaluating the effects of the reforms, good and ill. Some have advocated a return to the prereform system, with its perceived advantages of strong party organizations and effective presidents; these people are unhappy with their parties' recent nominees, and they point to the further democratization of the processes as one source of the system's problems. Others have defended the reforms at all costs and see any changes as an attack on their hard-won gains. A compromise school of thought, with which the present authors identify, has attempted to accommodate both the positive elements of the old party values and the legitimate demands made by the broader constituencies to which the parties must appeal. One participant in Democratic party reform, former North Carolina governor Terry Sanford, has expressed his reservations about the advisability of democratizing reforms:

> The danger of democracy is not that democracy is dangerous, but that we somehow bring ourselves to believe that the democracy of the town hall can be extended to nationwide decisions. The danger of democracy thus becomes a danger that we will lose democracy in our attempt to gain more of it. . . .
>
> We pick our president . . . by participatory disorder that knows no equal in American society.[1]

Not every critic of the system would agree with Sanford that participatory democracy is the cause of the perceived failures. There is no way of turning back the clock and seeing what kinds of nominees and presidents we might have had in the absence of the reforms or to what extent the party system might have deteriorated if the democratizing impulse of the late 1960s and early 1970s had been ignored. But few would disagree with the statement that the parties have not achieved the perfect balance between means and ends, between the mixture of elements in the nominating system and the candidates selected. In addition, as the critics are now pointing out, there may well be a link between the nominating system, the presidents selected, and their ability to govern.[2] For these reasons we are now entering an era of reaction to the reforms, a period of rethinking and some reforming of the reforms.[3]

The cycle of reform and reaction to reform is not a recent phenomenon. As we will show in the remainder of this chapter, reforms have been a continuing part of the American political experience. From the colonial era forward, Americans have experimented with institutional changes and otherwise tinkered with the political system to improve it or to respond to problems and criticisms. Nowhere are the experimentation and tinkering more evident than in adjustments to the electoral system.

Changes in nominating practices were often directly related to changes in the social and political environment of the nation. The emergence of new groups resulted in different patterns of political power. The new power distributions forced changes in the old procedures of nomination to better reflect the realities of a nation in transition. Westward expansion, the Industrial Revolution, a growing population, the rise of the cities, divisions between city and countryside, regional problems, waves of immigrants, the emancipation and enfranchisement of the slaves, women's suffrage, and the emergence of new economic elites have all been backdrops for reform.

The Cycle of Reform

To understand presidential nomination in the United States today and to put the recent reforms of the nominating system into perspective, it is important to realize the extent to which today's issues reflect patterns that have reappeared from time to time throughout American history. Repeatedly, new electoral procedures and processes were incorporated as attempts to adapt to changes in the political environment. In this section we sketch the history of U.S. nominating processes, showing how each was added in response to a need for reform until the current mixed system—which includes vestiges of all the earlier systems—had evolved.

The Need for Parties

In the American colonial period and in the early years of the United States, during the *pre-party era,* which lasted into the 1790s, running for office was in principle very simple: any voter who wanted to could become a candidate. After deciding to enter a race, the candidate's road to election followed a generally predictable course. The campaign consisted of garnering support among the voters and political leaders through personal contact, the support of newspaper editors, and advertising in circulars and newspapers. Personal qualities and community status were usually the most important ingredients for success. The process was highly paternalistic and informal and was characterized by aristocratic indulgence. As political scientist Edward McChesney Sait has written:

> Candidates were self-announced or, more usually, brought forward by a group of influential persons after some sort of "parlor caucus"; and even when mass-meetings were called for the purpose of making local nominations, they ... probably did no more than ratify the proposals that were laid before them. The voters, themselves a very limited body according to our present democratic notions, accepted as a matter of course the leadership assumed by men of wealth and social prominence, the landed proprietors and members of the learned professions.[4]

The self-nominating system was the most democratic one conceivable at the time, considering the elitist nature of American politics and the low regard political leaders had for mass democracy. In a small population the elite—the voters, candidates, and officeholders—dealt directly with each other. Candidates and officeholders had to depend on face-to-face relationships with constituents; broader, mass relationships were the exception in a world where communication was rudimentary, travel was difficult, and the weather could cause true hardship.

In local and state nominations, as in most governmental processes, practices varied according to region. The southern states had the most extreme form of self-nomination. There, more than in any other region, the candidate's presentation of himself to the electorate—usually as one of a crowded field and subject to little party influence or discipline—was the foremost element. In New England an entirely different approach prevailed. Candidates were discussed and chosen at town meetings or by informal groups of community leaders. Individuals so selected did not even campaign. The South and New England were not inclined to dissatisfaction with their procedures, which were quite in keeping with the regions' views of government in general.

The self-nominating system was not structured to account for the interests of competing groups. There were broad divisions in the population—over the role of the federal government, for example. But there were no organized means of uniting voters with commonly shared views behind candidates who would represent them and be accountable to them. Issues and policy views were difficult to identify, and organized opposition was impossible. It had become impractical to count on the good intentions of those who actively participated in the political process. Ensuring that elected officials remained accountable to their constituencies for their actions became a formidable problem. Controversy erupted in the 1790s, as Joseph Charles explains:

> Each side, as the divisions grew wider, came to regard the other as traitors to the common course of their earlier years. . . . How to administer machinery newly set up, what concrete meaning, in unforeseen contingencies, to give to words which no longer meant the same thing to all: these were the new problems which weakened old ties and sharpened earlier differences. . . .
>
> Men who felt the future of republicanism depended upon the operation of a government based on a document so full of compromises as our Constitution were bound to divide on practical questions. . . . The fundamental issue of the 1790's was no other than the form of government and what type of society were to be produced in this country.[5]

The earliest effort to organize a party in the modern sense was made by the supporters of James Madison and Thomas Jefferson. Jefferson's party, the Democratic-Republican party (also known as the Republicans and as the Jeffersonians), was a forerunner of today's Democratic party. Their opponents were the Federalists. By 1796, significant competition had developed between these two groups. The Federalists had elected John Adams as the second president of the United States in 1796 and had dominated the administration of George Washington before that.

The embryonic party structure developed by the Democratic-Republicans allowed them to mobilize their forces for capturing public office; they elected Jefferson to the presidency in 1800. It also provided a form of representation, previously unavailable, for the party's base to assert itself in successively higher government councils. The use of emerging forms of party organization provided the Democratic-Republicans with an overwhelming superiority in political combat. In fact, William N. Chambers, one of the leading authorities in the field, has called that party the first truly modern political party in the world, for two reasons: their strong organizational ties between leaders and followers and their mass appeal.[6] The Federalists made weak attempts to mobilize grassroots support and structure a permanent political organization, but their elitist principles, though dominant among the most powerful national leaders, worked against strong grass-roots party organization. The coalition of local committees that united behind Jefferson's presidential candidacy in 1800 dislodged the incumbent Federalists with impressive speed. By 1816 the Federalists were no longer capable of effectively contesting presidential elections. Their leadership and ideology were too elitist, and their organization had never developed adequately at the mass base.[7]

When the Democratic-Republicans developed as the first major party in the 1790s and early 1800s, they needed some vehicles to achieve representative and broadly consultative party nominations. The principal method adopted to realize these ends was the caucus, a political form with roots extending well back into the colonial period.

The Development of the Caucus System

As the fledgling parties developed, the term *caucus* came primarily to designate any group of party members who would gather to nominate their party's candidates for public office. Most often the party's legislative caucus would meet to nominate candidates for governor and other state offices. The party caucus was a natural outgrowth of the Committees of Correspondence used to organize and direct the Revolutionary War. The elected representatives, who presumably spoke for the party's electorate and held its interests foremost, were in a logical position to decide nominations. Besides, in that era mass participation in the nominating system would have been logistically difficult and considered undesirable. In short, the caucus was a practical solution to a sensitive problem, and it did contain the basic elements of representation.[8]

The caucus assumed its most famous form in the congressional caucuses held from 1800 to 1824, which took over the functions of nominating presidential candidates for that era. The Federalists first used a secret congressional caucus, made up of Federalist party members then serving in Congress, to select John Adams as the party's presidential nominee in 1800. Adams, the incumbent, eventually lost the election to Thomas Jefferson. The caucus method of selecting a presidential candidate was not congenial to the Federalists, who distrusted even this much organization. The Democratic-Republicans ridiculed the process at first, but they later adapted the caucus to suit their own ends with little embarrassment. The congressional caucus remained the primary means of nominating presidential candidates from 1800 to 1824.[9]

The congressional caucus and the caucus system in general had its merits, but it also had severe structural drawbacks. It was, in fact, removed from and not directly representative of party sentiments at the grass-roots level, since districts that did not elect party members to Congress had no say at all in party presidential nominations. The caucus was cliquish and contained elements of elitism that eventually spelled its doom as the presidential nominating procedure.

The beginning of the end came with the 1824 election, when the congressional caucus rejected the presidential candidacy of a frontier hero and popular favorite, Andrew Jackson, in favor of a less adventurous choice, William Crawford. Crawford finished fourth in a four-man field in the general election. Not for the last time, a disastrous candidacy had dramatized the party's lack of responsiveness to its base and had forced party changes. Jackson denounced "King Caucus" and went on to win the presidency on his own in the 1828 election, breaking the monopolization of the office by the competing aristocracies of Virginia and Massachusetts. His election ushered in a vigorous era of democratic expansion and reforms, one of which was the replacement of the national-level nominating caucus by the national nominating convention.

National Conventions for Presidential Nominations

A *convention* is a body of elected or appointed representatives selected to represent their constituents at a higher level party meeting. Currently, party conventions are held at county, congressional district, state, and national levels. The first national convention was held in 1831 by the Anti-Masonic party to nominate its candidate for president. In 1832 the Jacksonian Democrats (successor to the Democratic-Republicans) adopted the idea and met to renominate Jackson in their first national convention. The forms instituted for conducting national convention business—from the committees on credentials and the platform to the procedures for nomination—were to prove remarkably durable. The basic structures for national convention operations and decision making have changed little to this day.[10] The Democratic party has held a national nominating convention every four years since 1832.

At their inception, the national conventions were hailed as a significant democratic innovation that helped establish popular control over presidential nominations. They provided organizational structure for the parties at a national level, and they enabled lower party organizations and even the mass party members to have some representative voice in national party affairs, including the most important of their collective decisions, selecting presidential candidates.

Representative bodies such as conventions were a familiar form of governance, of course, with state legislatures and the Congress being central to the nation's democratic system. State and local parties adopted the idea of having small party groups elect delegates to a larger convocation as early as the 1790s. Eventually, by about 1840, state party conventions replaced legislative party caucuses as the principal party nominating vehicles for statewide offices.[11]

Disillusionment followed the early enthusiasm for national party conventions. In the period immediately after the Civil War, corruption was rampant in the federal and many state and local governments. This was the era of the Robber Barons, when corrupt public officials helped big business and other special interests grow rich at the public's expense. The late nineteenth and early twentieth centuries also witnessed the growth of great urban political machines and their party bosses.

By the turn of the century criticism of the political parties was widespread. The spoils system, the awarding of jobs, contracts, and political favors to supporters, was the rule, not the exception. The public participated in nominations for public office only at the lowest levels. There were few laws governing convention and other presidential nominating procedures, and those that were on the books were not enforced. Observers found that some groups used physical force to gain or prohibit entry to convention deliberations and to control the proceedings. Delegates were often raucous and uniformed. Excessive powers were concentrated in the presiding officers, and there were no means of challenging convention decisions. These abuses threatened the foundations of democratic government. They "ranged from brutal violence and coarse fraud to the most refined and subtle cunning, and included every method that seemed adapted to the all-important object of securing the desired majority and controlling the convention."[12]

Yet the convention had not outlived its original usefulness for the party, both as a nominating process and as a tool for maintaining party organizations. Moreover, professional politicians, who held the reins of party and elective power, were not inclined to change a system that served their needs so well. But deservedly or not, conventions had in many respects become the symbol of all the political extravagances of the age.[13] By the early 1900s the search for a new nominating system was under way. Although the national convention was not abandoned entirely as a method of nominating presidential candidates, its use was considerably modified in the early decades of the twentieth century. The agent of change was the Progressives.

State Primaries in the Progressive Era and Beyond

The Progressives, part of a reform movement popular during the first two decades of the twentieth century, had an idealized conception of what a democracy should be and how it should operate. They believed in breaking the concentration of political power held by party leaders, primarily the urban party bosses associated with the early political machines. This meant "depoliticizing" the political process and making it more efficient, accountable, and, in a business sense, economical. To achieve these ends, the Progressives championed, among other things, the direct election of U.S. senators, the city council-manager form of urban government, nonpartisan elections, the statutory regulation of political parties and campaign finances, recall and referendum elections, and the primary. The last was intended to open the nominating process to all voters, thus breaking the hold of the political boss over candidate selection.

The primary was considered a bold step in the evolution of the nominating process toward a more open, participatory system. Bypassing the party organizations and leaders and the political boss and his machine, the primary placed the ultimate power over nominations in the hands of the party's electorate. For the first time, the electorate could vote directly on the question of who was to be the party's nominee for a particular office in the general election.

In time, the primary also opened internal party selection processes—once left to the discretion of party leaders—to control by the state. This occurred in two ways. First, since primaries are elections, such factors as the date, ballot forms, voter qualifications, delegate and presidential nominee filing regulations, and the like were determined, at least in part, by law in virtually every state. Second, as primary elections came to be perceived as the quasi-governmental functions they are, the federal courts in particular, despite an initial reluctance to involve themselves deeply in party affairs, began to rule against the primaries' most obvious abuses. The main targets were, most significantly, racial discrimination and, to a lesser extent, corrupt election practices outlawed by the state. The effect was to extend to voters in primary elections the same fair procedure protections implicit in general elections. State intervention of this nature was a new and generally welcome development that served to better protect the interests of those participating in the presidential nominating process.[14]

Evolution and Development of the Primary. The local use of the primary reaches back to the 1840s. The primary was first instituted, according to most historians, by the Democratic party of Crawford County, Pennsylvania. Although county Democrats dropped the primary as a nominating tool in 1850, it was resurrected by the newly created Crawford County Republican party in 1860.[15] From that date on, it enjoyed a more or less continuous use in a scattering of local party contests until its adoption by a number of states in the early 1900s as the vehicle for selecting delegates to presidential nominating conventions. Statewide primaries were first introduced during the 1890s, and by 1917 all but four states had some type of primary set up to nominate candidates for state or local offices.

There was a slight lag in the application of the primary method to presidential selection. Wisconsin in 1905 established by law a primary for the direct election of national convention delegates; this can be regarded as the first presidential primary. The law was enacted as a result of a division within the state's Republican party. Such factional division, leading directly to innovative political forms, is likely to occur in the majority party; at that time the Republicans were the majority party, in Wisconsin and in the nation. In 1904 the state Republican party had selected two separate slates of nominees for state office and two national convention delegations. As it happened, the convention seated one delegation, the Taft Regulars (or anti-La Follettes); but a year later the state supreme court ruled that the Progressive Republicans (the La Follette faction) had been the legally chosen delegation. Battles such as these between the Progressive and Regular factions were to become a familiar aspect of Republican politics nationwide and contributed to the party's loss of the presidency to Woodrow Wilson in 1912.

Pennsylvania (in 1906) and South Dakota (in 1909) subsequently adopted primaries to elect national convention delegates. The early primaries were generally used to choose national convention delegates; less often, through complex mechanisms, voters could indicate presidential preference in a primary, but in a way that would not commit convention delegates to that choice. (Many presidential primaries today retain that two-part character, that is, they can be either delegate selection primaries or presidential preference primaries— the "beauty contests"—or both.)

In 1910, through a voter initiative, Oregon adopted a primary system that represented the beginning of presidential primaries as they are familiar to us. The Oregon law allowed voters to register their preferences for president and vice president and to choose the national convention delegates directly. This model rapidly became popular with other states as well.

One Oregon newspaper immediately recognized the importance of the primary: "This popular vote [in the primary] . . . 'may readily become the beginning of a great change. It may grow historic, for it may be the inauguration of popular selection by the many of presidential candidates.' " [16]

By 1912, 15 states had provided for presidential primaries in some form. The bitter delegate battles at the Republican national convention of that year between the Roosevelt Progressives (later the Bull Moose party) and the Taft Regulars led 9 more states to adopt presidential primary laws over the next four years.

By 1916, however, this early primary movement had peaked. Rejection of the primary concept came as abruptly as had the movement for its adoption. Alabama legislated a presidential primary in the years after 1916, but it was voided as unconstitutional. Minnesota, Iowa, Vermont, and Montana reverted to convention systems of delegate selection in presidential contests. The primary movement faded, the enthusiasm that marked its inception blunted by the realities of its operation. (Table 1.1 shows the numbers of primaries held in each party from 1912 to 1984 and gives the percentage of convention delegates selected through primaries.)

The intentions of the Progressives were laudable, and many of the reforms they instituted helped establish the content for the contemporary operation of the political processes. Ultimately, though, primaries brought the idealistic supporters of political reform face to face with the realities of democratization. The reformers were not prepared to witness the maturation process of a mass democratic system, which often includes unpleasant side effects. The experience led to the disillusionment with the primary system that brought its growth to a standstill in the period between 1920 and 1968.

1920-1968: Limited Use of the Primary. Until the late 1960s primaries served at best as an alternative road to the nomination. Under the right conditions, depending on the field of candidates and the circumstances of a given election year, primaries could be influential in testing a candidate's appeal and in helping eventually to determine the party's presidential nominee.[17]

Primaries could be especially significant when the nomination was open—that is, when the president was of the other party or did not seek reelection, when there was no obvious heir apparent in the president's party, and when there was no single commanding figure in the race. In the following paragraphs we mention several elections in which the primaries did help a candidate win his party's nomination.

Herbert Hoover and Al Smith won commanding victories in their respective parties' primaries in 1928 and, after previous failures, captured their parties' nominations. In 1932 Franklin Roosevelt beat Al Smith, who had been the 1928 Democratic standard bearer, in three of

Table 1.1 Presidential Primaries, 1912-1984

Year	Democratic party			Republican party			Total	
	Number of primaries	Votes cast	Delegates selected through primaries	Number of primaries	Votes cast	Delegates selected through primaries	Votes cast	Delegates selected through primaries
1912	12	974,775	32.9%	13	2,261,240	41.7%	3,236,015	37.3%
1916	20	1,187,691	53.5	20	1,923,374	58.9	3,111,065	56.2
1920	16	971,671	44.6	20	3,186,248	57.8	3,193,415	51.2
1924	14	763,858	35.5	17	3,525,185	45.3	4,289,043	40.4
1928	17	1,264,220	42.2	16	4,110,288	44.9	5,374,508	43.5
1932	16	2,952,933	40.0	14	2,346,996	37.7	5,299,929	38.8
1936	14	5,181,808	36.5	12	3,319,810	37.5	8,501,618	37.0
1940	13	4,468,631	35.8	13	3,227,875	38.8	7,696,506	37.3
1944	14	1,867,609	36.7	13	2,271,605	38.7	4,139,214	37.7
1948	14	2,151,865	36.3	12	2,635,255	36.0	4,787,120	36.1
1952	15	4,909,225	38.7	13	7,801,413	39.0	12,710,638	38.8
1956	19	5,832,592	42.7	19	5,828,272	44.8	11,660,854	43.7
1960	16	5,686,664	38.3	15	5,537,967	38.6	11,224,631	38.5
1964	17	6,247,435	45.7	17	5,935,339	45.6	12,182,774	45.6
1968	15	7,535,069	40.2	15	4,473,551	38.1	12,008,620	39.1
1972	22	15,993,965	65.3	21	6,188,281	56.8	22,182,246	61.0
1976	30	18,884,000	76.0	30	9,724,000	71.0	28,608,000	73.5
1980	35	19,538,438	71.8	34	12,785,184	76.0	32,323,622	73.7
1984	25	17,814,392	62.1	30	—	71.0	—	66.1

Note: 1984 data include 5 states holding nonbinding presidential preference polls and based on unofficial results for primaries held after May 15th.

Source: Congressional Quarterly's Guide to U.S. Elections (Washington, D.C.: Congressional Quarterly Inc., 1975). The percentage of delegates selected by party for the years 1912-1976 was computed by F. Christopher Arterton and are contained in F. Christopher Arterton, "Campaign Organizations Confused the Media Political Environment," in *Race for the Presidency,* ed. James David Barber (Englewood Cliffs, N.J.: Prentice-Hall, 1978), 7. For 1980, see *Congressional Quarterly Weekly Report,* June 5, 1980, 1870-1873; for 1984, see *Congressional Quarterly Weekly Report,* February 11, 1984, 252 and June 16, 1984, 1443.

the four major primaries in which they faced each other; Roosevelt outpolled Smith 3 to 1 in the total party vote. The victories established his credibility as a campaigner and made it easier for his party's national convention to reject Smith, and with him any commitment to a replay of the 1928 race.

In 1952 Dwight Eisenhower was a popular hero of World War II but was not active in politics. Indeed, both parties had considered nominating him for president, but no one was sure which party he identified with. Eisenhower strategists employed the primaries as a successful wedge against the seemingly assured convention nomination of the conservative Robert Taft, who was known as "Mr. Republican" and widely supported by organization regulars.

Sen. John F. Kennedy needed the primaries in 1960 to prove his vote appeal and, in particular, to demonstrate that despite his Catholicism he could receive Protestant support. His Wisconsin and, even more significantly, his West Virginia primary wins showed him to be a formidable campaigner. His victories moved him into a lead he was able to convert into national convention support from the party bosses in the big states. In the same year Richard Nixon beat back any threat Gov. Nelson Rockefeller of New York might have posed to his presidential nomination by a consistently strong demonstration of his party support in the primaries.

Thus, success in the primaries could, under the right conditions, be of limited strategic importance in the fight for the nomination. During this era the primaries served the functions of forcing the party leaders to pay attention to particular candidates and of giving the candidates an opportunity to test their public appeal. Along the way, scores of would-be contenders were eliminated by their failure to impress either voters or party bosses by respectable showings in strategically critical primary contests. But while primary victories were sometimes a necessary condition for achieving party support, they were never sufficient to gain a nomination. For a variety of reasons, candidates had difficulty translating primary votes into national convention support. Often the presidential preference vote and the actual selection of delegates took place in separate elections. In addition, most of the national convention delegates were not selected in primaries at all, and most of the delegates selected in primaries were not bound to honor the voters' choice. There was no definite way to determine which candidates individual delegates would support at the convention. The laws and party rules governing delegate selection varied markedly from one state to the next. Potential presidential contenders faced a morass of legislative and administrative requirements within each primary state that made such an indirect appeal for a party's nomination attractive only to those who had no realistic alternative.

Political scientist Thomas Marshall has called the entire period of 1832-1968 the *brokered convention system* of nominations. His characterization is intended to emphasize the centrality of the convention decision and the relative independence party leaders had in deciding who the nominees would be during this long stretch of American history.[18]

Problems with the Primaries. A number of factors contributed to the stagnation the primary movement experienced from the 1920s to the 1960s. Primaries, in their early incarnation, weakened the party system but ultimately could not break the control exercised by party bosses over the presidential nominating process. Primaries also encouraged factionalism within the parties, and the different primary systems adopted by the states often left political parties unable to define eligibility for voters in primary elections. Voter participation in the process was much lower than anyone believed it would be, and the system still could not ensure selection of high quality presidential candidates. The high cost of campaigning also inhibited the spread of primaries.

Overall, primaries tended to weaken the structure of traditional party organizations. This was not accidental. The Progressives and other primary advocates never really appreciated the role of political parties within a democratic society. Then, as now, parties acted as representative agencies linking the views of party members and the mass public with those of party candidates and officeholders. The people who gain the most from such representation are those who are normally the least influential in government decision making, the unorganized voters. Without strong parties, such people have few effective vehicles through which to promote their interests and to express their political views. In a real sense parties serve as the great equalizers of American politics, providing the mass public with a counterweight to the power of interest groups and the influence of money.

Primaries also invited factionalism, encouraging party splits and prompting numerous candidates to campaign for office. Primary elections made the development of coherent policy stands difficult; they rewarded the colorful and even the demagogic, anyone who could attract (by any means) a distinctive bloc of political support. A candidate could win a primary with just a plurality of votes and therefore did not have to represent a majority of the primary voters. Furthermore, the individuals who chose to vote in primaries may not themselves have been representative of the broader party constituency, thus doubly diluting the significance of a plurality victory.[19] And primaries favored anyone who could consistently deliver a bloc vote, a factor that, ironically, increased the influence of the political boss.

Not surprisingly, the old-line party regulars never liked the primary idea. It represented an implicit threat to their control of the parties and elective office holders. The party's electorate, while usually apathetic, could on occasion be unpredictable as well. A popular candidate or a particularly intense factional fight within a party could attract an unexpectedly large primary turnout, potentially undermining party leaders' influence. When given the chance, party regulars were only too happy to return to the more manageable, less public nominating practices of earlier times.

Although primary outcomes were intended to reflect the views of the party's supporters, such was not always the case. The influence of party members could be diluted by the influx of independents and members of the opposition party. In some cases, the inclusion of nonparty members in party decision making served to reemphasize the irrelevance of the minority party, a result that increased the gap between the two parties and hindered efforts at party building by the weaker of the two major parties.

Some states (including Wisconsin) legislated *open* primaries, in which voters could vote in the primary they preferred without passing any test of party loyalty; however, they could vote in only one party's primary contests on any given election day. Other states adopted an extreme form of open primary, called the *blanket primary*, in which individuals could vote in different party contests at various levels, choosing among Democratic contenders for one set of offices, Republicans for others. And in California, a state that has a tradition of being inhospitable to party organizations, the same candidate could run in both Republican and Democratic primaries, making it possible to win both parties' nomination (as Earl Warren did repeatedly for the state's governorship in the 1940s); in such a case the general election race is almost irrelevant. The party, as a consequence, itself exercised little control over who could or could not participate in its decision-making processes.

In other states the primaries were *closed* to all but declared party members, that is, those who were willing to pass some sort of test of party identification. In some cases, the standards were leniently applied and the effects were approximately the same as for an open primary. In others, they were stringent to the point of excluding groups of party supporters and recent converts. Illinois and Mississippi until the 1970s required a person to be registered as a party member for approximately two years prior to the primary as a condition for participation. Such requirements kept participation to a minimum—as the state parties intended.

Voter participation in the primaries was well below what anyone had expected. Proponents of primaries had overestimated public interest in the outcomes of primary contests and misjudged the level of public indifference to elections. The broader electorate did not share the idealistic, middle-class political values of the reformers. Turnouts in primaries of between one-third and a little better than one-half of the vote cast in the presidential elections were common.[20]

Primary elections hurt the minority party's turnout even more than the majority party's. Minority parties, for example, often drew supporters to their primaries at a rate as much as 30 percent lower than the majority party did to theirs.[21] The average turnout for the second party in 12 primary states analyzed in the 1968 election year was about one-third of those eligible. States in which one party dominated political life proved to be the exception to the general trend toward low primary turnout because the real issues of who would hold state and local elective office were basically decided in these elections. Presidential nominees would appear on the same ballot, so turnout would be relatively higher in those states.

Not only were the goals of high levels of participation not achieved, but the quality of candidates for elective office did not appear to be substantially improved through primary nominations. Ballots were long, particularly when presidential primaries were held simultaneously with primaries for a wide variety of state and local nominations. Even the most motivated primary voter had difficulty in intelligently choosing from among the many candidates for each level of public office.[22]

Cost proved to be another factor that worked to discredit the primaries. State laws regulating primary expenditures highlighted for the first time the high costs of seeking political office. The media and the public felt these costs were excessive and began to associate primary nominations with large campaign expenditures.

In spite of their drawbacks, presidential primaries have always enjoyed a good deal of appeal and legitimacy in American political culture. They are easily understood and intuitively appealing to the mass public. They fit nicely within the demands and outlook of the mass media. These factors, coupled with a radically changing social environment, contributed to a second period of growth in the use of primaries after 1968. In fact, as we will see in Chapter 2, primaries have become a fixed part of the American political process; they have become the dominant method of nominating candidates for elective office at all levels below the presidency.

The Old
Party System

The political situation we have been describing, which remained virtually unchanged from the Progressive era through the New Deal period and into the 1960s, is generally known as the *old party* system. In this prereform era the party elite and dominant party factions tightly controlled the presidential nominating practices in both parties. The object was to name a candidate and settle on party policy positions that represented the interests of the influential elements within the parties' coalitions. In practice, the presidential candidate of the Democratic party represented some combination of the interests of organized labor; liberals; minorities, especially blacks; ethnic groups; religious groups, predominantly Catholics and Jews; big cities; the industrial Northeast and Midwest; and, in a paradoxical balancing act that continually strained the party, the conservative South. The Republican candidate had to prove acceptable to the business community and certain other monied interests; the party's moderate and extremely conservative factions; small towns and rural areas; the Great Plains and mountain states; and small states, which had disproportionate power within the party.

The party's base, the rank-and-file party members, had a limited and indirect role in presidential nominations. With a few notable exceptions (Oregon and Wisconsin, for example), the states did not permit primary voters or party caucus participants a direct means of choosing which individuals would represent the state party at the national convention or of deciding which presidential candidate the state delegation should endorse. Under this system, the primaries were essentially either advisory, indicating which candidates might have the most grass-roots support within a state, or tactical, demonstrating to the party bosses a candidate's potential to fund and run a campaign or to attract certain voters. The caucus/convention systems were basically restricted to party pros and, with a few exceptions (such as Minnesota), provided limited opportunity for grass-roots party members to participate.

Most of the delegates to the national conventions were party professionals and officeholders. There was little room for, or attention paid to, the rank-and-file party members, who might have chosen different nominees or been concerned about different policy matters. Those who held the balance of power under the old party system assumed that interest group leaders among the party elite reflected their constituents' needs and that bargaining among the party elites was the best possible method for directing these interests into the national party arena. Furthermore, this elite bargaining was thought to be the most likely way to ensure success for the party in the general election. But in fact whether the party's nominee actually reflected the interests of the grassroots membership depended on the perceptions and vision of the party leaders and the bargaining ability of the various factions. In turn, the relationship between the leaders of the factions and their constituencies was informal, indirect, and often unclear.

The system worked reasonably well as long as the party coalitions enjoyed a relatively high degree of cohesiveness and the party policies appeared to reflect the interests of their major factions. As American society began to polarize in the 1960s and the parties' coalitions began to fragment, the old party system and its traditional nominating practices proved a less satisfactory vehicle for settling policy differences and resolving internal party bickering. The matter came to a head in the mid-1960s and had its most profound effect upon the Democratic party.

Conclusion

Two main themes emerge from a review of the history of presidential nomination. First, the system became increasingly more structured, more formalized, and more tightly regulated. In earlier years such regulation was instituted in an effort to avoid corruption within the system; concern later shifted to providing adequate and equitable safeguards for those who participated. Second, successive reforms have resulted in a greater democratization of the process, making it more accessible and responsive to greater numbers of people.

The self-nominating system, which was characterized by personalism and informality, gave way in the 1790s to rudimentary experimentation with electoral structures designed to unite voters with commonly shared views about government. The earliest of these efforts were closely associated with the Democratic-Republicans, the forerunners of today's Democratic party and the first national, truly modern political party. The move of the less organization-conscious Federalists to counter their opponents by linking their national representatives to similarly mobilized grass-roots support led to the inauguration of the party system. Both fledgling groups were attempting to systematize and coordinate voter participation. This development, as with all reforms of political consequence, combined different degrees of necessity, pragmatism, and a sophisticated calculation of political advantage.

The congressional caucus later replaced the highly personalistic and elitist nominations of the early 1790s. National conventions for the purpose of making presidential nominations appeared by the 1830s and were plagued from the beginning by abuses and corruption. In the early twentieth century, largely as a result of the Progressives' efforts, direct primaries partly replaced state-level conventions as the means of choosing delegates to the parties' national conventions.

The Progressives brought radical changes to the nominating system, introducing the state into the parties' candidate selection process for the first time as regulator of primary elections and protector of voting rights. In time, the primary system left some of its advocates as frustrated as they had been with state-level convention nominations. The defeat of the reformers' hopes at this point led to a long period of neglect that would last until the contemporary reform era began in 1968.

Since primaries were first introduced there have been philosophical differences between their supporters and opponents, disagreements that run through the evaluations of many of our institutions. Those who favor strong and effective parties tend to disapprove of primaries and prefer more limited, internal party processes such as caucuses for presidential nomination; those who favor broader within-party democracy prefer primaries as the means of selecting presidential candidates.

The primary system did undercut the cohesiveness of party organizations. Consequently, it was also attacked by those who wished for more responsible parties. In this context, though, the larger, and continuing, question is whether a responsible party system is possible in a nation that is so large and diverse and characterized by a fragmented governmental structure.[23]

Each of the different nominating procedures—and, indeed, the party structure itself—was a manifestation of adaptation to change in response to the larger political environment. The impulses to realize more fully the promise of a democratic society and to better control public officials led to experimentation with particular party and electoral forms; ironically, the same impulses eventually dictated their improvement or their replacement.[24] As the original institution became subject to abuse, newer and more democratizing procedures were introduced to correct the excesses and return the system to the assumptions underlying its original design. The impetus for reform has usually grown within the context of factional dissatisfaction in the majority party. Not surprisingly, reforms have often been followed by some degree of backlash from those who have lost power, usually whoever were the party regulars of the time. There is a degree of circularity (as well as progression) to the movements, which is especially noticeable from the early 1900s. From this period on, the changes advocated have settled into a more predictable pattern—the imposition of tighter regulations on existing forms or the substitution of one device for another (for example, a primary for a statewide caucus/convention system).

Through it all, the often tacit assumptions underlying the need for and the functioning of these prenomination processes have remained much the same. The difficulty has been in the performance. In this respect, voters have persistently been frustrated over their inability to hold public and party officials accountable; when they feel left out, voters tend to perceive the nominating system and its decisions as illegitimate. The problems of reconciling participation with party control have worsened as the nation has grown. The disillusionment that fueled the continual efforts to improve the operation of party mechanisms for leadership selection and accountability appear far from spent; the impulse for reform and counterreform continues.

NOTES

1. Terry Sanford, *The Danger of Democracy* (New York: Westview, 1982), 100-101.
2. Nelson Polsby, *The Consequences of Party Reform* (New York: Oxford University Press, 1983). For a more detailed treatment of the history and implications of party reform, see William Crotty, *Political Reform and the American Experiment* (New York: Thomas Y. Crowell, 1977), from which parts of this chapter are adapted.
3. James W. Ceaser, *Reforming the Reforms: A Critical Analysis of the Presidential Selection Process* (Cambridge, Mass.: Ballinger, 1982).
4. Edward McChesney Sait, *American Parties and Elections* (New York: Century, 1927), 238.
5. Joseph Charles, *The Origins of the American Party System* (New York: Harper and Row, 1961), 6. This book is a particularly good discussion of the development of the two-party system. See also Richard Hofstadter, *The Idea of a Party System* (Berkeley: University of California Press, 1969).
6. William N. Chambers, *Political Parties in a New Nation* (New York: Oxford University Press, 1963).
7. Ibid.
8. Sait, *American Parties and Elections*, 241-242.
9. See Noble E. Cunningham, Jr., ed., *The Making of the American Party System 1789 to 1809* (Englewood Cliffs, N.J.: Prentice-Hall, 1965), 123-132.
10. See Richard C. Bain and Judith H. Parris, *Convention Decisions and Voting Records*, 2d ed. (Washington, D.C.: Brookings Institution, 1973); and Paul T. David, Ralph M. Goldman, and Richard C. Bain, *The Politics of National Party Conventions* (Washington, D.C.: Brookings Institution, 1960).

11. Sait, *American Parties and Elections*, 242-260; George D. Luetscher, *Early Political Machinery in the United States* (1903; reprint, New York: Da Capo Press, 1971); and Charles E. Merriam and Louise Overacker, *Primary Elections* (Chicago: University of Chicago Press, 1928), 1-2.
12. Merriam and Overacker, *Primary Elections*, 5.
13. For an assessment of the strengths of the convention system, see Herbert McClosky, "Are Political Conventions Undemocratic?" *New York Times Magazine*, August 4, 1968, 10-11, 62-68.
14. Merriam and Overacker, *Primary Elections*, 23-39.
15. Theodore W. Cousens, *Politics and Political Organization in America* (New York: Praeger, 1942), 364-365. A good bibliography of the early works on the subject can be found in this book. For a view different from that found in Cousens from an official of the county concerned, see Ernest Hempstead, "Forty Years of Direct Primaries," in *Primary Reform* (Ann Arbor: Michigan Political Science Association, 1905), 31-54.
16. Quoted in Louise Overacker, *The Presidential Primary* (New York: Macmillan, 1926), 12. This book is the most complete source for the developments of the presidential primary in its early phases. The quotation is from an Oregon newspaper that in turn quoted with obvious approval the original commentary from an Alabama newspaper on the merits of the practice when it had been developed in that state.
17. On the history of primaries in presidential nominations, see Gerald Pomper, *Nominating the President* (New York: Norton, 1966); and James W. Davis, *Presidential Primaries: Road to the White House* (Westport, Conn.: Greenwood Press, 1980).
18. Thomas R. Marshall, *Presidential Nominations in a Reform Age* (New York: Praeger, 1981).
19. The most influential statement of this point of view can be found in V. O. Key, Jr., *American State Politics: An Introduction* (New York: Knopf, 1956). Key's *Southern Politics* (New York: Random House, 1949) represents the most penetrating analysis of primaries in one-party states. More recent analyses of related problems include: Austin Ranney, "Turnout and Representation in Presidential Primary Elections," *American Political Science Review* 66 (March 1972): 21-37; Austin Ranney and Leon Epstein, "The Two Electorates: Voters and Nonvoters in a Wisconsin Primary," *Journal of Politics* 28 (August 1966): 598-616; and Ranney, "The Representativeness of Primary Electorates," *Midwest Journal of Political Science* 12 (May 1968): 224-238.
20. Overacker, *The Presidential Primary*, 143.
21. Louise Overacker, "The Operation of the State-Wide Direct Primary in New York State," in *The Direct Primary*, ed. J. T. Salter, Annals of the American Academy of Political and Social Science (Philadelphia, 1923), 146.
22. For a more recent example of the same type of criticism, see Roy Reed, "New Voter Form Stirs Mississippi," *New York Times*, August 7, 1972, 21.
23. See Committee on Political Parties, American Political Science Association, *Toward a More Responsible Two-Party System* (New York: Rinehart, 1950). The report originally appeared as a supplement to *American Political Science Review* 44 (September 1950). For a more recent assessment, see David H. Everson, *American Political Parties* (New York: New Viewpoints Press, 1980).
24. See Luetscher, *Early Political Machinery*, for one statement of the impulses guiding successive changes.

Reforming the System | 2

The history of the nominating process in the United States has in a sense been the history of reforms. As we have seen, different processes have been tried by the parties and the states in their efforts to suit their needs. The system has become a kind of juggling act as the interests of grass-roots party members, party organizations, states, and the population at large have sometimes conflicted in attempts to obtain the at times contradictory goals of being able to enforce the accountability of officeholders and of achieving the widest possible democratic participation.

In the past, as one institution became subject to abuse, another, more democratic procedure was introduced to correct the excesses and refocus the system on its original goals. In the twentieth century the changes have settled into a fairly predictable pattern, resulting in either the imposition of tighter regulations on existing forms or the substitution of one institution for another (for example, caucus for primary). The latest cycle of reform and counterreform has depended on changes in party rules more than in nominating institutions. As we examine in this chapter the reform and postreform eras and their legacy in contemporary party practices, we will concentrate on rules changes in the Democratic party, where most of the reforms were initiated.

Democratic Party Reform

The Democratic party, as the majority party of the 1960s and as the more heterogeneous coalition, was the focus of pressures for political change in the reform era. Society was undergoing rapid and radical change; specific manifestations of the social unrest and demands on the political system can be seen in the era represented by the 1964 and 1968 conventions.

Background

The 1964 Convention.   The seeds of the reform era were planted during the Democratic National Convention of 1964, held in Atlantic City, New Jersey. There was no real controversy over who the nominee would be; President Lyndon B. Johnson, who had succeeded John F. Kennedy upon his assassination in 1963, was assured of renomination. But other events of that convention foretold a major transformation in the presidential nominating system. The civil rights revolution that was sweeping the nation, championed by the Johnson administration and the Democratic party, served as the backdrop to the dramatic events.

The official delegation from the state of Mississippi to the 1964 convention was an all-white group of party leaders and regulars. This delegation was challenged by the Mississippi Freedom Democratic Party (MFDP), an integrated group of both black and white activists who were loyal to the national Democratic party and who were active in the civil rights movement in their state. The MFDP called on the Democratic party to live up to its civil rights ideals, and they demanded all the seats held by the segregationist delegation, which had been duly selected under Mississippi law. In the negotiations that ensued, Minnesota Sen. Hubert H. Humphrey, who would become Johnson's vice presidential candidate during that convention, engineered a compromise between the two groups. The compromise provided that two of the MFDP delegates would be seated and that the rest would be treated as "honored guests." More significantly, and little noted at the time, the convention passed resolutions outlawing racial discrimination in the delegate selection process and asserting the national party's right to require compliance. These resolutions were incorporated into the call to the 1968 Democratic convention, and they have become the core of the rules changes that transformed the powers of the national party as it expanded and solidified its control over the delegate selection process.

Social Unrest and Pressure on the Party.   In its influence on the Democratic party and the reform era, the civil rights movement was augmented by two other major social and political movements of the 1960s and 1970s: the protest over the war in Vietnam and the movement for equal rights for women. People associated with these three national movements focused much of their energy on the political process in general and on the presidential nomination process in particular as a way to put an end to policies they found offensive in foreign and domestic affairs, and as a way to overcome the historic disadvantages of blacks and women and achieve for them some measure of permanent political power. Certain other trends, such as the increased role of television in national political life, augmented these movements. But the protest movements themselves stimulated an upheaval in American politics.

1968: Watershed Year. In American political life and presidential politics 1968 was the year of Vietnam. The nation and the Democratic party were deeply divided over the war in Vietnam and over the conduct of the Johnson presidency. In the spring Johnson announced his withdrawal from presidential politics after suffering an embarrassingly poor showing against Sen. Eugene McCarthy in the New Hampshire primary and facing a likely repeat in the Wisconsin primary. In April the Rev. Martin Luther King, Jr., was assassinated in Memphis, where he was to lead a civil rights march; in June Sen. Robert Kennedy was assassinated in California the night of his victory in that state's Democratic presidential primary.

In the spring of 1968 McCarthy and Kennedy—insurgent candidates who hoped to end the Vietnam War and redirect the policies of the Johnson administration—did well in the primaries. Vice President Humphrey, heir apparent to the Johnson administration, delayed the announcement of his candidacy until the filing dates had passed for all the primaries. He thus avoided any test of his political strength or of the appeal of the Johnson administration's policies. Humphrey's decision also deprived the party's rank and file of any direct say in his nomination. Yet Humphrey easily won the Democratic party's nomination at the national convention with 67 percent of the delegate vote. Many Democrats wondered how the party's primary voters could have been so blatantly ignored.

The problems the insurgents encountered in working through the system, as the protesters and demonstrators of that period were constantly urged to do, proved formidable. In effect, they found that nominations under the old party system were effectively closed. The presidential nominating system was unresponsive to what seemed to them to be significant elements within the party. Indeed, the party membership had only a relatively small role in making nominations and in formulating (or influencing) party and national policy.

The testimony of one individual who attempted to be heard in a local party caucus in Missouri that year indicates the type of problems encountered:

> I received notice of the meeting the day before it was to occur. I arrived at the meeting over a quarter of an hour early.... At five minutes before the appointed hour, I found the door to be locked and several others of my associates unable to gain admittance. Upon gaining admittance ... I found that a temporary chairman ... had begun the meeting early. He had proclaimed himself permanent chairman without taking a vote or allowing other nominations for the position. He had appointed a nominating committee without asking for any further nominations to that committee, or calling for a vote. He then asked for a vote on the report from the nominating committee on the subject of delegates to the county convention, without reading the names on the list. A vote was taken without asking for the "no" votes.... Having obtained a less-than-majority response of "yes" 's, [the chairman] then struck me in the jaw and knocked me down, escaping with the list and, I presume, having ended the meeting.[1]

The account is more picturesque than most, and the procedures possibly more arbitrary than in other areas. But we can see here some of the old party abuses in action: the process was closed; the party veterans were hostile to party newcomers; the professionals were unwilling to allow for candidacies other than those they supported. To some degree this pattern occurred in most of the states.

The party's nominating process was closed in another sense also. In many states and localities, the process of selecting delegates to the national convention had begun well before the presidential election year. In 1968 a large number of the delegates were either party leaders or elected officials who supported the establishment Democrat, Humphrey, at the convention. Most of the delegates were chosen by their state and local parties because of their record of party service, and they were not officially committed to a specific candidate, even though most of them informally supported Humphrey. Here is one account of some of the problems with the preselection of 1968 delegates:

> The day Eugene McCarthy announced his candidacy [in November 1967], nearly one-third of the delegates had in effect already been selected. And, by the time Lyndon Johnson announced his intention not to seek another term [in March 1968], the formal delegate selection process had begun in all but 12 of the states. By the time the issues and candidates that characterized the politics of 1968 had clearly emerged ... it was impossible for rank-and-file Democrats to influence the selection of these delegates.[2]

The turbulence of the preconvention period in 1968 culminated in the disturbances of the convention itself, held in Chicago in August. The convention hall was the scene of dramatic confrontations, as supporters of McCarthy and Kennedy, who opposed the Vietnam War, challenged both the control of the convention by party regulars and the candidacy of Humphrey. Meanwhile, in the streets, Chicago police squared off with an assortment of antiwar and pro-civil rights demonstrators in a series of clashes that at times became quite violent and bloody. Predictably, the dominant feelings surrounding politics that year were confusion and bitterness, and the Democratic party was divided against itself.

The Reform Commissions and the Rules Changes

The events of 1968 proved so disruptive to the Democrats that they resolved to do what they could to see that the experience would not be repeated. Toward this end, the 1968 national convention authorized the creation of two reform commissions: the Commission on Party Structure and Delegate Selection (unofficially known as the McGovern-Fraser Commission) was established to evaluate and recommend changes in presidential nominating practices, and the Commission on Rules (the O'Hara Commission) was given a mandate to streamline and rationalize national convention procedures. The McGovern-Fraser Commission in particular was to prove to be the main instrument of change during the reform era; its work transformed the presidential nominating system in the United States. The commissions served as an arena for competing party factions to try to reshape the party and make it more responsive to the needs of particular interests. These intraparty power struggles have had profound effects on the operations of both parties.

During every four-year interval since 1964 the Democratic party has had in operation some sort of reform commission to study the party's rules, internal procedures, and convention processes. Table 2.1 provides an overview of those commissions and indicates the presidential election year in which their work was the most relevant.

Rather than review each of these party commissions, we will provide in the following subsections a conceptual grouping of the major areas of rules reform and how they originated with or were modified by each commission. Although our list is not intended to be all-inclusive, it does provide, in chronological order, the most important and most controversial changes. It also provides some explanation of the meaning of the technical rules and of how they affect party building and reform.

Rules Prohibiting Discrimination against Minorities and Promoting Inclusiveness for Previously Disadvantaged Groups. The Democratic National Committee's response to the 1964 MFDP challenge was to adopt, in January 1968, the "six basic elements," a set of rules that em-

Table 2.1 Major Democratic Party Reform Groups

Election year affected	Official name	Popular name	Chair
Presidential Nomination			
1968	Special Equal Rights Committee	Hughes Committee	Richard Hughes (N.J.)
	Commission on the Democratic Selection of Presidential Nominees	Hughes Commission	Harold Hughes (Iowa)
1972	Commission of Party Structure and Delegate Selection	McGovern-Fraser Commission	Sen. George McGovern (S.D.), then Rep. Donald Fraser (Minn.)
1976	Commission on Delegate Selection and Party Structure	Mikulski Commission	Rep. Barbara Mikulski (Md.)
1980	Commission on Presidential Nomination and Party Structure	Winograd Commission	Morley Winograd (Mich.)
1984	Commission on Presidential Nomination	Hunt Commission	James Hunt (N.C.)
	Commission on Low and Moderate Income Participation	Leland Commission	Rep. Mickey Leland (Texas)
1988	Commission on Democratic Participation	(To be appointed)	
National Party Processes			
1972-	Charter Commission	Sanford Commission	Terry Sanford (N.C.)

anated from the Hughes Committee (chaired by Gov. Richard Hughes of New Jersey). The rules stipulated that all public meetings of the party at all levels should be open to all members of the party, "regardless of race, color, creed, or national origin." [3] In addition, the six basic elements tried to outlaw racial discrimination in any form and promised to encourage voter registration without race discrimination. These rules and the additional recommendations of the Hughes Commission (chaired by Iowa governor Harold Hughes) became the foundation of the McGovern-Fraser Commission's work.

The most important, and most controversial, McGovern-Fraser Commission guideline addressed discrimination in the nominating process. Not only did the commission attempt to end discrimination on the basis of race, sex, and age, but it also required state parties to overcome the effects of past discrimination by taking affirmative steps to include minority groups in national convention delegations "in reasonable relationship to the group's presence in the population of the state." [4]

This requirement became the basis of the infamous quota system in operation for the 1972 Democratic National Convention. Quotas were controversial because they could be used to force change in the groups represented at national conventions, thus changing the balance of power within the party. Reaction to the quotas became so intense, both inside and outside of the party, that the next party commission, the Mikulski Commission, changed the rules for the 1976 national convention. The new delegate selection rules continued to require affirmative action for minority groups but explicitly abandoned the quotas.

The Winograd Commission reaffirmed the Democratic party's commitment to affirmative action requirements for the 1980 convention by requiring states to take demonstrable steps to achieve minority representation. In addition, the Winograd Commission mandated an equal division between female and male delegates for the first time in the 1980 convention; that requirement was reaffirmed by the Hunt Commission for the 1984 convention. In effect, the Democratic party rules now require that 50 percent of national convention delegates be female and that state parties employ affirmative action requirements in choosing minority delegates. The Leland Commission, also operating between 1980 and 1984, recommended, but did not require, the inclusion of low- and moderate-income groups at national conventions in its affirmative action guidelines. The Leland and Hunt commissions settled for a compromise statement that although these income groups would be included among the affirmative action target groups, they would not be given any other special status. [5] In summary, the Democratic party has adopted both quotas and affirmative action as devices designed to ensure a more open party in general and the access of previously left out groups to the presidential selection process in particular.

Rules Regarding the Inclusion of Party Leaders and Elected Officials. The McGovern-Fraser Commission regarded the domination of national convention proceedings and delegate selection procedures by party leaders and elected officials as a problem with which it had to deal, one manifestation of the closed nominating system. Accordingly, the commission proposed convention rules that required all delegates to be elected to serve at the national convention. This action effectively prohibited ex officio delegates, that is, anyone serving as a member of his state's delegation solely by virtue of his elected office or position in the party. The party subsequently adopted these rules for its 1972 national convention. The move was intended to ensure that all potential delegates run for convention seats either pledged to a particular presidential candidate or formally declared as uncommitted. All delegates were to be elected by party members. None were to receive free rides to the national convention.[6]

The Democratic party has subsequently modified these provisions substantially. Although the Mikulski Commission continued the prohibition against ex officio delegates for the 1976 national convention, it did provide convention privileges—that is, access to the floor but no voting rights—for major elected officials and party leaders who were not otherwise elected delegates. The Winograd Commission rules adopted for the 1980 convention were the first breakthrough on reversing the ex officio prohibition. In response to the complaints of party leaders and elected officials, whose numbers had indeed been reduced in both 1972 and 1976, the Winograd Commission and the Democratic National Committee approved an "add-on" provision for the 1980 delegate selection rules. This add-on awarded up to 10 percent in additional seats for party officials in each state's delegation and was intended to encourage the inclusion of party leaders and elected officials who were not otherwise selected in a state's delegation. It was, in effect, the provision of a safe seat for high-ranking officials who might need to use it.

The Hunt Commission took this provision a giant step forward for the 1984 convention. They provided for a total of 566 seats in the 1984 convention (or 14.4 percent of the total) to be designated for party leaders and elected officials. Furthermore, these delegates would be selected as technically uncommitted, thus providing them with maximum leverage in the prenomination maneuverings. They included 164 members of the House of Representatives chosen in January 1984 and 27 members of the Senate chosen in March.[7]

The provision guaranteeing seats to leading elected and party officials was immediately dubbed the "superdelegate" rule. Proponents of the superdelegate rule claimed that it would enhance and encourage the review of prospective presidential candidates by their party peers during the nomination process. This enhanced peer review would provide a built-in voice for those who presumably knew the candidates best and would have to work with the nominee should he be elected to the presidency. Proponents touted the rule as a way to improve the prospects for a Democratic candidate elected president to work effectively with the Congress. Critics saw the measure as backsliding toward an elite-dominated system which diluted the voice of the party membership. Nevertheless, the superdelegate rule was the top priority on the agenda of the Hunt Commission and was warmly supported by the Democratic National Committee as a reform of the reforms for the 1984 nomination season. In the June 1984 meeting of the rules committee prior to the Democratic National Convention, Hart's forces led a fight against the superdelegate status for public and party officials for 1988. The Mondale forces agreed to put this item on the agenda of a new reform commission to study the rules for 1988—the Commission on Democratic Participation—thereby ensuring that this controversy would continue.

Rules Regarding the Translation of Mass Preferences into Votes and Convention Seats. The McGovern-Fraser Commission was very concerned about the rights of minorities, whether racial minorities or delegates supporting other than the leading candidates. One of the earliest prohibitions the commission adopted was against the unit rule. The unit rule, which had been used by some state delegations for many years, allowed the choice of a majority of a delegation to a party convention (national- or lower-level) to bind the minority. The effect was to disallow any support for a candidate who attracted less than 50 percent of the delegation's vote, a practice that served to help the candidacies of front-runners and to limit both dissent and the alternatives available to delegates at the national convention. The rule was controversial. The unit rule was temporarily banned by the 1968 Democratic National Convention; the McGovern-Fraser guidelines made the ban permanent.[8]

The McGovern-Fraser Commission also sought to protect the rights of minorities by seeing to it that their preferences could be translated into votes at the convention; at the same time the commission outlawed a variety of other selection plans that had previously been used by some states.[9] Toward that end, the commission decided that two delegate selection methods were acceptable: the direct election of delegates through primaries and a system of caucuses and conventions open to everyone. The commission also encouraged state parties to adopt proportional representation to distribute delegates among various contenders for the nomination.

Proportional representation (PR) provides that each candidate's strength in a caucus or primary be directly reflected in the percentage of delegate seats received at each stage of selection. Thus, in theory, a candidate who receives 60 percent of the mass votes in a primary ought to get 60 percent of the final delegate seats. His opponent, in a two-person race, ought to get the 40 percent of the seats that would result from 40 percent of the mass vote.

In practice, however, PR almost never works out with such mechanical precision. The problems arise in the adoption of specific formulas designed to achieve the theoretical results. To avoid spreading delegate votes too thinly, candidates must exceed a set minimum threshold percentage of the vote to receive any delegates at all. The level at which that threshold is set will affect the distribution of delegates among the candidates. If the threshold is set low in a multicandidate race, the candidates running third, fourth, and so on, may well receive some delegates; but the number of delegates available to the top two candidates will in turn be reduced. On the other hand, if the emphasis in the assignment of delegates is on rewarding the front-runners, there are fewer seats left over to provide representation for the secondary candidates.

The McGovern-Fraser Commission set the initial threshold at 15 percent; thus each candidate who received more than the threshold 15 percent in a primary would be awarded a proportionate share of the delegate vote. The Winograd and Hunt commissions increased the threshold, allowing state delegations to choose for cut-off a point of up to 25 percent of the vote. This can cause problems. The Rev. Jesse Jackson's quarrel with the Democratic party's rules in 1984 was based on this point. Jackson received far fewer national convention delegates than his proportionate share of the primary vote would have indicated, while Mondale, the front-runner for the nomination, received a significantly greater share of the national convention delegates than his primary/caucus vote would have dictated. Specifically, Jackson received approximately 18 percent of the total primary votes cast nationwide; yet he got only 10 percent of the delegates. Mondale garnered 39 percent of the primary votes nationally, which translated into 52 percent of the delegates (see Appendix, Table A.4).[10]

Jackson repeatedly raised the issues of where the threshold should be set and how to translate minority votes into convention seats. The Hunt Commission had set the threshold at 20 percent of the popular vote for the 1984 campaign; in states or congressional districts where Jackson did not meet that threshold, he received no convention delegates. In states where Jackson did qualify for delegates, his supporters tended to be bunched in certain predominantly black congressional districts. In these areas, Jackson received large majorities of the vote (for example, 80 to 90 percent) when 50 percent would have been adequate to win all of the delegates from that district, thus "wasting" the excess 30 to 40 percent of the votes. Although Jackson received some delegate seats based on these districts, he often did not receive a share of the state's delegates that was proportionate to his statewide showing in the primaries. Mondale's more evenly spread vote got him proportionately more delegates. In addition, the Hunt Commission allowed states to adopt a "winner-take-more" plan that awarded a bonus delegate to the district or state winner as an extra reward for winning. This plan also worked to Mondale's advantage in 1984.[11]

Jackson's assumption that he should have received the same percentage of convention delegates as primary votes can only be realized by adopting PR at the statewide level for all states—and even then the translation of votes into delegates is likely to remain somewhat difficult. Although Jackson repeatedly complained that the rules put his candidacy at a disadvantage, they were adopted before his campaign began and were generally color blind in the sense that they disadvantaged any candidate other than a front-runner in the 1984 race. In practice, the PR system adopted by the Democrats for 1984 was intended to magnify the advantages of front-running candidates. It achieved this end.

The McGovern-Fraser Commission required the *direct election of delegates,* with 75 percent of the delegates to be elected at the congressional district level. This device was supposed to place power over nominations in the hands of the grass-roots party constituency and to allow all groups represented in any numbers at the congressional district level an opportunity to influence the nomination race. Changes in the rules at the congressional district level were later introduced to permit a winner-take-all primary. In any winner-take-all system, the votes of those who supported any candidate other than the winner naturally get lost. Thus, a winner-take-all system is directly opposed to a PR system.

The Mikulski Commission *required* state-level proportional representation for the 1976 convention. At the same time, however, that commission permitted primaries at the congressional district level, as long as the delegate contestants were voted on directly. As in 1972, the prospective delegates were required to state their presidential preferences (or list themselves as uncommitted) on the ballot. Thus, the voters could see what they were getting in each of the delegate slates offered to them on the ballot in the primaries. In 1976, 13 states took advantage of this loophole—thus *loophole primary*—and conducted delegate selection primaries at the congressional district level. In such a primary the presidential candidate strongest in a particular congressional district could have an entire slate of delegates pledged to his candidacy elected, effectively shutting out the other candidates in delegate returns and becoming winner-take-all at the congressional district level.[12]

Although the Winograd Commission refused to permit loophole primaries at the state level, two states—Illinois and West Virginia—received special dispensations from the Democratic party's Compliance Review Commission (CRC), which is in charge of monitoring state compliance with the national rules. These two states were allowed to continue to use their systems of direct election at the congressional district level during the 1980 elections, since the CRC did not want to extract the political price of finding them in noncompliance with the national party rules. The effect in Illinois was that the direct election at the congressional district level provided a solid 60:40 proportion in Carter's victory over Edward Kennedy in the presidential preference primary; however, Carter received 165 of the 179 delegates available in Illinois (approximately 91 percent). Under strict PR, Carter would have received 60 percent of the delegates, approximately 107 delegates. In general, winner-take-all systems favor the front-runners and help them achieve earlier majorities, while PR tends to make it worthwhile for the second- or third-place candidates to attempt to stay in the race until the convention.

The Hunt Commission made a significant reform of the reforms in this area for the 1984 convention, clearly stating that direct election primaries at the congressional district level were acceptable (and thus no longer to be regarded as a loophole). The rule change allowed for winner-take-all outcomes at the congressional district level in all states that chose to use that system. In 1984, 8 states (including Illinois and West Virginia) availed themselves of the new opportunity to use the direct election primaries. In contrast, the PR method is used in some form by 34 states in their Democratic primaries or caucuses. (For a complete listing of the selection plans utilized in each of the states see

Appendix Table A.5.) However, the Hunt Commission also required that all at-large delegates selected statewide in 1984 would continue to be apportioned by PR. Thus, in 1984 the state could choose from a variety of plans, provided that the state did not violate the national party's general guidelines. The mixture of plans was more varied in 1984 than it had been in either 1976 or 1980; however, it was still weighted toward PR.

One could easily argue that the various PR options in 1984 made it difficult for the original front-runner, Mondale, to pull together the winning coalition that he needed early. On the other hand, while Hart was able for a time to challenge Mondale, PR probably prevented Hart's victories from overwhelming Mondale by dividing up the seats between them. PR is part of the reason neither candidate could obtain the 1,967 delegates necessary to win the nomination before the June 5 primaries in California and New Jersey. From the experience of 1984 and other election years, we can see that in actual elections these rules do make a difference.[13]

Rules Providing for Candidate Right of Approval and Candidate Control of the Delegates. The McGovern-Fraser Commission was silent on the relationship between candidates and delegates and did not seem to regard it as a problem. The commission did try to discourage *slatemaking,* the practice whereby groups of prospective delegates run as the representative of either a candidate or an interest group. Any slates supporting the candidates should be "assembled with due consultation with the presidential candidate or his representative," according to the commission's guidelines.[14] In addition, slates were to be assembled only in meetings held with sufficient public notice and with guarantees of procedural rights for those who might challenge the slates. Many local and state parties resisted the commission's position; one of the most memorable battles in recent convention history broke out at the 1972 Chicago convention (see Chapter 3).[15]

The provisions of the McGovern-Fraser Commission proved inadequate to the immediate goal of ensuring that all prospective delegates actually supported the candidate they were pledged to support and that they were not just using a candidate's name to obtain a convention seat. In an effort to improve delegate loyalty, the Mikulski Commission greatly strengthened the requirement of candidate consultation for 1976. The commission's rule, known as the candidate right of approval rule, stipulated that a presidential candidate had the right to approve any slate of delegates or any individual delegates running pledged to him or her.

The Winograd Commission reaffirmed the candidate right of approval for the 1980 convention and took it a step further. In an extension little noted and little debated at the time, the commission provided that the delegates were bound to vote on the first convention ballot for the candidate they had represented in the primaries and caucuses (or until released by the candidate). In addition, a candidate had the right to remove from the convention floor and replace any delegate who contemplated switching to another candidate. This provision was the so-called bound delegate or loyal delegate rule, and it became the source of great contention between the Carter and Kennedy forces in 1980 (see Chapter 8). Carter's supporters, who ultimately prevailed, wanted the rule upheld, whereas the Kennedy forces wanted it removed. The Hunt Commission removed the bound delegate rule for 1984 but retained a provision confirming that candidates initially had the right to approve prospective delegates who used the candidate's name to get elected to a state delegation. Delegates were expected to vote for the presidential candidate on whose ticket they ran. The commission considered approval rights adequate to ensure reasonably loyal delegates.[16]

The commissions' changes in rules relating to candidate control and approval of delegates relate directly to a power shift in the delegate selection process. In the prereform era the state and local parties were virtually free to decide who the delegates would be. Convention seats were positions of honor, eagerly sought by the party faithful and used primarily as a reward for service rendered to the party. While elements of this picture remain intact today, the situation has changed considerably. Currently, state and local parties must seek the approval of the presidential candidates' national campaign organizations to run a committed slate of delegates. In addition, as we discussed previously, lower-level party organizations must balance delegate slates carefully in accordance with demographic and affirmative action requirements.

The national party and presidential candidate organizations have gained power in the delegate selection processes. The candidate organizations have become very active in recruiting state and local party leaders, and boosters of their candidate, to represent their organization on the primary ballots or in the caucuses. Although local leaders may be courted for the clout and respectability they can bring to the slate, their objectives now are tempered by the goals of the national campaign organization. The balance of power has shifted subtly away from the state and local party leaders.

There is a question implicit in the binding of delegates: How much control will voters have over the delegates to the conventions? Will the voters get delegates willing to obey the mandate of the primary vote or will they get delegates who are allowed to do what the delegates think best at the convention? The normative question is: How much independence should delegates have in their decision making at national conventions? Should the voters get delegates who will register their primary decision mechanically or ones who will exercise a certain amount of independent judgment? Who and what do the delegates represent?

The party must also consider the goals of the national convention. Should it directly reflect the party's mass will on nomination questions or should it attempt to be a deliberative body? If it is to be a truly deliberative body in choosing the presidential nominee, the delegates must have some ability to make up their own minds, regardless of the outcomes of the primaries or caucuses back home. In such a deliberative or brokered convention the nominating decision is made in the convention itself through a process of bargaining and compromise among the delegates. Brokered conventions were a hallmark of the old party system. Today, only if the primary and caucus season has not produced a clear-cut winner is a brokered convention likely to occur; in most years a candidate has obtained a majority of the delegates before the convention opened. While the primaries and caucuses were being contested, many observers believed that the 1984 Democratic convention might turn into a brokered convention, but Mondale obtained the necessary majority in the last wave of primaries (see Appendix, Table A.3).

On the other hand, if the results of the primaries and the caucuses/ conventions are to be the controlling factor in deciding the party's presidential nominee, then the delegates have to be bound by the rules—or at least they have to take the voters' wishes seriously when they go to the convention. Although legal sanctions may not be feasible, it would seem that there should be a degree of political accountability imposed on the delegate who chooses to ignore the wishes of the primary voters and caucus participants. This is probably all that can realistically be required in the effort to ensure the continued loyalty of the delegates in the period between the primaries and caucuses and the final roll-call vote on the convention floor. The exact role of the delegates in relation to the voters and the candidates is likely to remain uncertain. Both total freedom and total lack of freedom for the delegates have drawbacks, and the dilemma is how best to satisfy fairly the needs of all concerned.

Rules Regarding the Timing of Primaries and Caucuses. Many critics have argued that the primary and caucus season is much too long and that there ought to be rules controlling the length and timing of the nomination season (see Chapter 3). The first concern of the McGovern-Fraser Commission was with the "timeliness" of the selection process. By that term the commission meant that the delegate selection process should not begin too far in advance of the presidential election (which, as we saw, happened in the 1968 contest), and it adopted a rule requiring that the entire delegate selection process begin in the same calendar year as the presidential election. That rule has been maintained by each successive commission and is no longer controversial.

Party commissions have also addressed the concept of a limited period of time (a *window*) for the primaries and caucuses. The Winograd Commission, for 1980, was the first to adopt a window for primaries and caucuses. This window was defined as the period from the second Tuesday in March through the second Tuesday in June. Both the Winograd Commission and its successor, the Hunt Commission, tried to enforce that window; however they agreed to let Iowa and New Hampshire violate the rule by up to two weeks to maintain their traditional first-in-the-nation caucus and primary. The commissions were simply unwilling to bear the political costs that would have resulted from forcing the two states into compliance with national party law.

Another aspect involving the timing of primaries and caucuses is *front loading,* the practice of scheduling primaries and caucuses as early as possible, when they will have the greatest impact and will obtain the most media and candidate attention. The front-loading phenomenon, which can have a profound impact on the way in which presidential candidates conduct their campaigns, will be discussed in greater detail in Chapter 3.

Rules Regarding Closed versus Open Primaries. Of the many points on which state primaries differ, one of the most crucial is who may vote in the primary. If some test of party loyalty is required, the primary is *closed.* If no test of party loyalty is required, the primary is *open.* Party organizations understandably do not like open primaries because they do not promote party loyalty and they make it more difficult for presidential nominations to remain under party control. The most reliable way to close a primary is to require party membership: a person must declare identification with one of the parties when registering to vote. A weaker test of party affiliation is to ask voters to declare a party on the day of the election and choose either the Democratic or the Republican ballot. Many variations on open and closed primaries exist, so primaries are rather difficult to classify.[17]

The Democratic party in recent years has been trying to close all of its presidential primaries, in hopes of allowing only party members to choose the party's presidential nominee.[18] Their well-founded concern is that if independents and Republicans can participate in the nominating processes, a candidate other than the one preferred by the party faithful may emerge victorious. In 1984, for example, exit polls showed that Hart had done well among those who considered themselves usually independent or Republican and Mondale had been supported by Democrats. Mondale's organization could argue that their candidate, the traditional Democrat, would best represent the party in November, whereas Hart's campaign maintained that their man would be a stronger vote-getter against Reagan in the general election.

The party commissions have favored closed primaries. The Mikulski Commission for 1976 adopted language encouraging the states to eliminate open primaries, but that hortatory language apparently had little effect. The Winograd Commission then took a hard line against open primaries, declaring them to be unacceptable for 1980. That provision brought the national party into direct conflict with some states, most notably Wisconsin and Michigan, that prized their open primaries. Michigan acquiesced in 1980, adopting a caucus/convention method for the selection of its delegates. Wisconsin defied the national party and held its open primary anyway. The national party fought Wisconsin all the way to the Supreme Court (see the discussion of *Democratic Party of the United States v. La Follette* in Chapter 3), and in 1981 the Court upheld the national party's primacy in establishing the nominating system. Wisconsin's solution in 1984 was to hold an open presidential preference primary (a beauty contest, which Hart won) and closed caucuses for delegate selection (which Mondale won). No doubt this split decision will intensify the controversy in Wisconsin. More important, the Wisconsin results give some credence to the argument that the two processes can produce different results, even in the same state.

The debate over open versus closed primaries does not yet appear to be settled in the Democratic party. This controversial issue has important implications for party building and party loyalty.

Rules Requiring Public Notice and Other Due Process Procedures. During the prereform period, party leaders, in an effort to retain control of the nominating system, sometimes refused to provide basic information about the process to rank-and-file party members wishing to participate. As we showed earlier in this chapter, one of the charges leveled at the party during the 1968 convention was that

McCarthy supporters and other antiwar insurgents never had an opportunity to learn what the nomination rules were or where caucus meetings were to be held. The McGovern-Fraser Commission determined that such practices violated fundamental concepts of fairness or due process and discriminated against those who were not a part of the party establishment:

> Therefore, the Commission requires State Parties to adopt and make available readily accessible statewide Party rules and statutes which prescribe the State's delegate selection process with sufficient details and clarity.... Among other things, these rules should provide for dates, times, and public places which would be most likely to encourage interested Democrats to attend all meetings involved in the delegate selection process.[19]

These elementary due process requirements have become a core of the party's law. Several similar rules also originated with the McGovern-Fraser Commission. These included rules regarding proxy voting (the presentation at a party meeting of votes on behalf of absent members), quorum requirements (that a minimum number of people be present to conduct party business), filing fees, and the selection of alternate delegates. Each succeeding reform commission has reaffirmed these rules; they have rarely been the subject of debate since their initial adoption. In fact, the adoption of these rules may represent one of the most significant legacies of the reform era.

Although such rules have not been controversial, they represented a procedural revolution when they were instituted. The national party was presuming to tell the state parties how to conduct the business of presidential selection, and they were making those requirements stick by threatening not to seat the state's national convention delegation. Today there is a very well developed body of national party law in the Democratic party, and it is backed by potent sanctions. The changes in favor of the national party organizations are a major element of what is often referred to as the *nationalization* of the parties; that nationalization is a crucial feature of the transformation that marked the reform era.[20]

Republican Party Reform

For many years there has been little desire among Republicans for basic change in the party. Party members have generally appeared to be pleased with what the party has represented and with its electoral and policy successes. After all, despite its minority status the party has controlled the presidency for over 60 percent of the period from 1952 to 1984; in 1980 Republicans won command of the U.S. Senate, and that majority is likely to remain intact at least through 1986. Nonetheless, the Republicans did establish two reform commissions of their own. Why?

Problems in the Party

In spite of the general contentment within the party, the party had (and continues to have) serious problems. The party's electoral base has been in a steady decline for five decades, to where it now hovers at around one-fifth of the electorate. In terms of allegiance, both Democrats and independents do significantly better than Republicans. The Republican leadership has just cause to be concerned about the stability of the party's foundation. The base of Republican support has been getting older; young people and newcomers to the electorate have been unwilling to affiliate in large numbers with either party, at least up to the Reagan era. Demographic changes in the general population, such as the increase in the number of black and Hispanic voters (who tend to identify with the Democratic party) and the intensified political activity of women, have not yet changed the base of the Republican party. The party has suffered from the decline of the 1950s model of family life and the comfortable assumptions about society and government that accompanied that era. As the more homogeneous of the two parties, the Republicans have perhaps suffered more from a decline of their traditional base with the increased fragmentation of the American society. On the other hand, tradition, habitual voting patterns, the chronic disarray of the opposition Democrats, and the functional pressures of a two-party system act to counter some of these trends and to ensure a place for the party.

In part, concerns for the continued vitality of the party have been acknowledged by a succession of Republican leaders (for example, in varying contexts, Eisenhower, Rockefeller, Nixon, and Reagan) and by the party elite. President Richard Nixon's policy was to promote the party as being the "party of the open door," and to a limited degree the means of expanding the party's base were explored, though, as we will see, not implemented.

In spite of the leadership's awareness of the party's declining base, it took the actions of the Democratic party, augmented by the general proreform leanings of public opinion and the media, to draw the Republican party into the reform era. The aspects of the Democratic reforms that most influenced the Republican approach to presidential nomination were the emphasis on open, grass-roots-oriented prenomination campaigns and the increase in rank-and-file participation in decision making. (Indeed, Reagan's within-party challenge to an incumbent Republican president in 1976 (Ford) might not have come about without increased grass-roots involvement in the prenomination campaigns.) In addition, many of the Democratic reforms that we have outlined—especially those affecting primaries—required changes in state law. Such changes affected both parties, as did Supreme Court decisions that potentially strengthened the hand of the Republican National Committee (see Chapter 3). With proreform pressures on the outside and some responsiveness within, the party did begin the process of formal self-examination.

Republican Reform Groups

The Republican party's reform groups were far less numerous and markedly less influential than their Democratic counterparts.[21] The groups did not attack the entire nominating system through rules reform; their motivation and their approach were much more cautious and their results much more difficult to pin down than those of the Democrats. Nonetheless, the Republican party did experience some degree of change, and the events are worth examining.

The first Republican reform commission was the DO (Delegates and Organizations) Committee, which operated from 1969 to 1972.[22] The 16-member committee was composed entirely of Republican National Committee (RNC) members, a group unlikely to find serious flaws in nominating procedures that they had played a prominent role in designing and perpetuating and that had served them well over the years. Such was the case. The DO Committee made a series of mild recommendations, roughly parallel to the concerns of the Democratic McGovern-Fraser Commission but—unlike those of McGovern-Fraser—not required of the state parties.[23] Included among these recommendations were the following:

> Convention delegate selection meetings at local and state levels should be open to party members.
> No unreasonable fees should be demanded of candidates for delegate positions.
> The national party should assist state parties with delegate selection problems.
> No proxy voting and no automatic (ex officio) delegates should be allowed.
> Each state should strive for an equal number of men and women in its convention delegation.

> Each state should include its delegation to the national convention persons under 25 years old in proportion to their voting strength within the state.

The recommendations did not have the force of party law; the state parties could adopt or discard the broad suggestions as they saw fit. In keeping with the party's emphasis on the dominant role of the state parties over the national party, there were no penalties tied to noncompliance. In fact, as we have mentioned, the recommendations were not intended to have much impact, since reform was not a major party issue within the Republican leadership ranks.

The second, and more aggressive, Republican reform body was the Rule 29 Committee (named after the party by-law under which it was established), which was created after the 1972 national convention to explore the issue of minority representation within the party ranks. Unlike the DO Committee, the Rule 29 Committee, with 57 members, was a large committee and was composed of a variety of party representatives, though the national convention members and party conservatives still held the balance of power. The committee, under the leadership of Wisconsin Rep. William A. Steiger, did make a conscientious effort to address some of the more vexing problems confronting the Republicans, particularly those of concern to the moderate wing of the party. The Rule 29 Committee recommended, in effect, an affirmative action program that encouraged each state party to broaden its base. Its ultimate success, however, was no greater than that of the DO Committee. To implement the measures to broaden the party's base, the committee would have had to develop ways to make the party more attractive to minorities, blue-collar workers, and politically active women and force the states to comply by threatening to refuse to seat their national convention delegates. But the strongest proposals for expanding the party's base and developing outreach programs to increase the role of minorities in party deliberations were systematically diluted or voided by the balance of the committee's membership, led by some of its more conservative members. In any event, the party was not willing to institutionalize the participation of any group in the process. The RNC in 1975 refused to accept the Rule 29 Committee's recommendations. It adopted instead a weaker proposal that urged the states to take "positive action" to become more inclusive of minorities; however, no compliance mechanisms were attached to the proposal.

Since 1976 any questions of party reform have been the province of the RNC and its Rules Committee. This group has mainly been concerned with modest technical improvements in convention operations and party rules and has made no effort to impose national party standards, comparable to those of the Democrats, on Republican state parties.

Republican party reforms did not change the party's internal decision-making mechanisms, the rules governing nominations, the participation of the party elite in the convention, or the dominant role of the state parties in the process—even though the national party's presence could have been greatly strengthened during the 1970s. There was, however, subtle but significant change in the party's approach to selecting a presidential candidate, as expressed in the use of the primary by more states; the resulting emphasis on state-level rank-and-file dominance in the selection process; and the candidates' willingness to compete openly in primaries and caucuses for the presidential nomination.

The lack of large-scale change is not surprising, since, as we have mentioned, the party's leadership seemed content with the status quo and the party's grass roots did not agitate for change. The two Republican commissions tended to be dominated by factions that had vested interests in maintaining the status quo and that had a philosophical stance opposing any change in the party's balance of power. Party regulars were generally satisfied with the procedures as they stood; party conservatives feared that any change of consequence would weaken their influence on the choice of a party nominee, which they had controlled since 1964. Yet the views of the majority of reform commission members were not out of line with those of the party activists more generally. There was virtually no discontent within party ranks with the party's nominating practices or national convention operations. While the processes were not as open as the postreform Democratic party's, they were clearly understood, well articulated, and broadly accepted.

In addition, the party's middle- and upper-middle-class base has generally been satisfied with Republican economic and social philosophies and has not been inclined to change the nature of the party or its procedures. Party members have tended to accept outsiders who want to go along with Republican policies and procedures as they are but have not been willing to change the party to attract a broader base. In fact, such an approach has worked frequently enough (as was seen in the party's appeal to blue-collar workers in 1968 and 1972 by Nixon and in 1980 by Reagan) to assure party activists of its viability. Unless its electoral losses increase dramatically or its victories significantly expand the party's base, the Republican party is not likely to face the intense internal demands for reform with which the more heterogeneous Democrats have wrestled for decades.

What the Republicans have done quite successfully is to build a very strong national organization in the RNC. This organization is very well financed and equipped to help recruit and support Republican candidates. They have a very effective mass mailing facility, a mass media facility, and polling capabilities, all of which can be made available to state and local candidates at the RNC's discretion. Thus, through electoral support, rather than the development of national party rules, the Republican party has also significantly increased its national strength.

The Consequences of the Reform Era

For more than 50 years, from the apex of the Progressive movement in 1916 to the mid-1960s, the U.S. presidential nominating system remained essentially unchanged. It was dominated by party organizations and major interest group leaders; caucuses and conventions were the main nominating processes, and primaries played a less important role. The reform era that began in the mid-1960s set off a period of dramatic change, especially in the Democratic party, that quickly transformed the nominating system. With the conventions of 1976 the quieter postreform era, which is dominated by a mixed nominating system that is driven by the primaries, began. What have the Democratic and Republican reforms meant in practice? We have seen that there has been increased emphasis in both parties on formal written rules to govern presidential delegate selection and to ensure fair, open (to party members), and impartial regulations governing all aspects of party decision making. We have looked in some detail at the nature of the rules; we will turn now to the larger issue of what the reforms have accomplished.

The new order has been characterized by several large-scale differences. First, there has been a centralization of power over delegate selection procedures in the national party, rather than in the states. Second, decision making in presidential nominations has shifted to the party's rank and file, as represented by those who participate in state and local party primaries and caucuses. Third, the parties have made an effort to obtain both wider participation in party decision making and greater representativeness and coherence in party policy formulation through the inclusion of previously underrepresented groups.

In connection with these changes, and as a result of the same reforms, the nation witnessed until 1980 an accelerated move toward a great reliance on presidential primaries in national convention delegate selection, to the point that some began to feel they would completely replace caucus/convention nominating structures at the state level. This was not to happen: 1984 saw some modest movement back toward the caucus/convention approach. Nonetheless, primaries did become significantly more important in the presidential nominating process during the postreform era. In contrast to the case of Humphrey's nomination in 1968, no candidate can now seriously expect to become his party's nominee without contesting at least some of the primaries.

A secondary consequence of the greater reliance on primaries was the increased influence of the media, particularly television, in the nominating process. Television has emerged as the chief conduit of information between candidates and the electorate. Some observers of the postreform nominating process felt that the media threatened to replace the party as the most significant factor in deciding presidential nominations; others believed it already had. (For a more extensive discussion of the role of the media in the current nominating process, see Chapter 3.)

Participation in presidential candidate selection has increased enormously since the introduction of the reform rules. Between two and three times the number of party members participate in the process today, compared with the prereform era—perhaps 20 percent of the adult population, according to Thomas R. Marshall.[24] The representation of women, minorities, and, to a lesser extent, youth—groups favored by the reforms—in presidential nomination decision making has advanced rapidly. For example, women, the group that has gained the most from the reform changes, are now guaranteed a 50 percent representation in Democratic national conventions, as we have mentioned. On the other hand, some groups that had previously been influential in the nominating process have seen their influence diminished. Through 1980 the Democratic party in particular witnessed an overall decrease in the participation and influence of elective office holders at national conventions—a situation that the Hunt Commission addressed for 1984 by adding reserved seats for leading public officials and party leaders. The issue is a sensitive one and a continuing source of controversy within the party.

The changes adopted since 1968 have created a substantially new system of presidential selection, one that is more open to challenge by a variety of contenders for the nomination. The postreform nominating system is generally less respectful of party leaders and elected officials than that of the prereform era, though recent developments may indicate another change in this aspect of this system in 1988. At present, decision-making power is centered in the parties' grass roots, reflecting the reform-era trend toward a presidential nominating system more inclusive of all party members.

Conclusion

This chapter has covered the period 1964-1984, 20 turbulent years of American history. The period began with a challenge to the established order raised by civil rights groups in 1964; witnessed the era of the Vietnam war, the civil rights movement, and the women's movement in the reform era of 1968-1972; and continues with the incremental changes of the postreform era. The transformation of the presidential nominating system has been widely accepted and institutionalized during this period.

The United States now has a *mixed system* for presidential nominations. The mixed system includes all of the nominating institutions developed over the years: caucuses, conventions, and primaries; but the primaries command center stage and the lion's share of media attention and candidate effort. Both the party leaders and those who identify with the party at the grass-roots level are important actors, though the party identifiers, by voting in the primaries and participating in the caucuses, probably play the dominant role. The current system is highly permeable: new groups and new candidates can make their presence felt quickly and easily, as Hart and Jackson did in 1984. But the newcomers must still compete with the more established centers of power and the candidates who represent them (for example, Mondale in 1984). Although the system is relatively stable, it is subject to continual adjustment through rules changes, especially in the Democratic party, which can subtly alter the balance of elements. Figure 2.1 depicts the processes of the mixed system and their development.

Party government in the postreform era is perhaps best depicted as a federal system, in which both the national parties and the state and local parties play an important role. Before 1968 the state and local parties were nearly autonomous and formed a loose confederation. The changes wrought during the reform era, however, resulted in a greater centralizaton of authority in the national party. The Democrats have moved further in the direction of concentrating power in the hands of the national party than have the Republicans, although the Republicans have initiated some centralizing changes as well. The national parties demand a certain level of uniformity while allowing for a wide variety of state-to-state variation, especially in the Republican party. Federalism

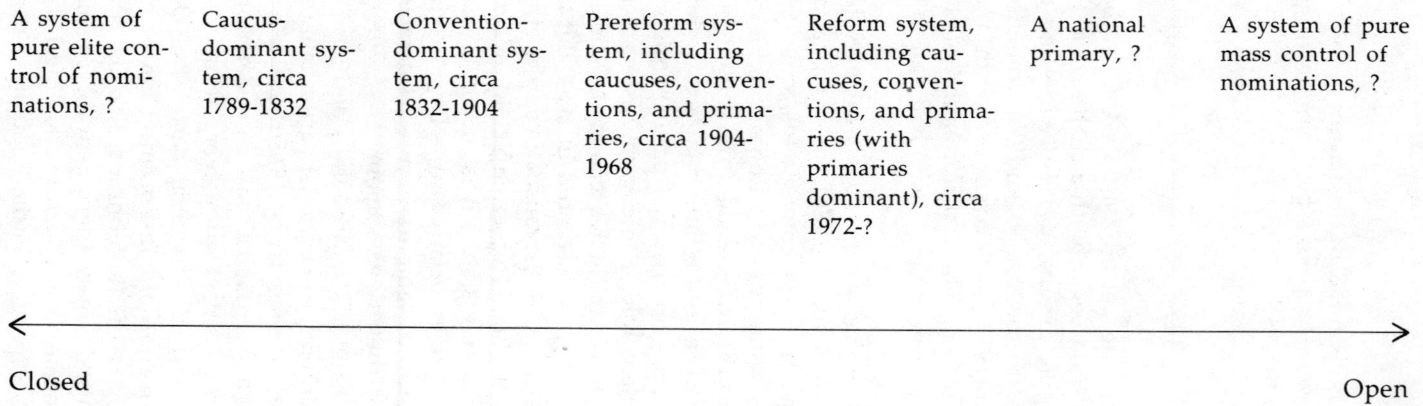

A system of pure elite control of nominations, ?

Caucus-dominant system, circa 1789-1832

Convention-dominant system, circa 1832-1904

Prereform system, including caucuses, conventions, and primaries, circa 1904-1968

Reform system, including caucuses, conventions, and primaries (with primaries dominant), circa 1972-?

A national primary, ?

A system of pure mass control of nominations, ?

Closed ←————————————————→ Open

Figure 2.1 Presidential Nominating Systems

in the party system is analogous to federalism in the national political system; the pendulum of dominance continues alternately to favor the national government and the states, though the arc of the swing is narrower than it used to be.

Change, so far incremental, continues to affect the nominating system, which is unlikely to reach any final "perfect" state. The Democratic party's Hunt Commission, for example, made several adjustments in rules regarding primaries and conventions. The Democrats' reform commission for 1988 may revise those adjustments. Republicans continue to face the problem of broadening the party's base. The parties do not operate in a vacuum, isolated from the rest of the political and social system. They feel the effects of social and political change and try often to respond, occasionally even to lead. The system can never return to the prereform status quo; instead, we go forward to a new mixture, retaining the basic structures of the old system while reforming some aspects of the system and counterreforming others. This pattern of continunity and change is likely to prevail as the two parties try to negotiate the remaining years of the twentieth century.

NOTES

1. Quoted in William Crotty, *Decision for the Democrats: Reforming the Party Structure* (Baltimore: Johns Hopkins University Press, 1978), 47.
2. Commission on Party Structure and Delegate Selection (McGovern-Fraser Commission), *Mandate for Reform* (Washington, D.C.: Democratic National Committee, 1970), 30. This report is cited hereafter as *Mandate for Reform*.
3. *Mandate for Reform*, 39.
4. *Mandate for Reform*, 40. See William Crotty, *Party Reform* (New York: Longman, 1983) and *Decision for the Democrats* for more detailed discussion of this and other issues discussed in this chapter.
5. David E. Price, *Bringing Back the Parties* (Washington, D.C.: CQ Press, 1984), 165-166.
6. *Mandate for Reform*, 46.
7. "Mondale Wins Big among House Delegates," *Congressional Quarterly Weekly Report*, January 28, 1984, 132.
8. *Mandate for Reform*, 44.
9. Byron Shafer, *Quiet Revolution: The Struggle for the Democratic Party and the Shaping of Post-Reform Politics* (New York: Russell Sage Foundation, 1975), 117, 155. See also Byron Shafer, *The Party Reformed* (New York: Basic Books, 1984).
10. "1984 Democratic Party Rules Pad Mondale Delegate Lead," *Congressional Quarterly Weekly Report*, June 23, 1984, 1504-1505.

11. Ibid.
12. Price, *Bringing Back the Parties,* 218-222, discusses in detail rules regarding primaries.
13. "Democratic Rules Help Pad Mondale Lead," *Congressional Quarterly Weekly Report,* April 21, 1984, 910.
14. *Mandate for Reform,* 48.
15. See also Crotty, *Party Reform,* 155-202, on the unseating of Mayor Richard Daley's Chicago delegation in the 1972 national convention.
16. Price, *Bringing Back the Parties,* 214-217.
17. See Malcolm E. Jewell and David M. Olson, *American State Parties and Elections,* rev. ed. (Homewood, Ill.: Dorsey, 1982), 110, for a classification of the state primaries.
18. See Gary Wekkin, *Democrat versus Democrat: The National Committee's Campaign to End the Wisconsin Open Primary* (Columbia: University of Missouri Press, 1984).
19. *Mandate for Reform,* 42.
20. Crotty, *Decision for the Democrats,* 254-273.
21. See Crotty, *Party Reform,* 205-232.
22. Ibid.
23. Delegates and Organizations Committee (DO Committee), *The GOP and Reform Report* (Washington, D.C.: Republican National Committee, 1971).
24. See Thomas R. Marshall, *Presidential Nominations in a Reform Age* (New York: Praeger, 1981).

Presidential Nomination in the 1980s | 3

We have looked briefly at the development of the presidential nominating system, and we have outlined the progress of party reforms in that context. Examining the current nominating system, we will turn to several characteristics of particular importance to this study: the centralization of party power in the national party, the operation of the nomination rules in the parties, the impact of changes increasing the importance of primaries, social change from 1960 to 1980, and the influence of the media.

The Centralization of Party Processes

The nationalization of ultimate power over presidential nominations has been a major consequence of the reform movement. Related to this has been the movement to centralize at the national level the resources needed to support party activity.[1] In the Democratic party the movement originated in party divisions as well as being a natural outgrowth of events and forces external to the party. But the trend has continued far enough to cause concern among party leaders. Some fear that recent events—especially several court decisions, as we will discuss—may have put the national parties into a position that is not fully understood and for which the parties are not prepared. Ultimately, the legal redefinition of the parties' powers and the reshaping of their role—in relation to the state and local parties, as well as to the state governments and to the courts—has implications well beyond the parties' concern with internal housekeeping matters.

Centralization and Reform

In the prereform, old party system the national party, whether Democratic or Republican, was very weak as a party organization.[2] Parties were decentralized; state and local parties enjoyed a good deal of autonomy. In his classic textbook, published in 1958, V. O. Key said that the national parties had little power vested in them and possessed no real authority over state and local party organizations or elected officials: "There are no national parties, only state and local parties."[3] Key's was a typical account of the locus of party organizational power in the prereform era. In presidential selection, as well as in other party affairs, the states and state parties in that era were largely free to set their own rules and establish their own procedures.

The reform era has changed the role of the national party in presidential delegate selection and has brought about to some degree the nationalization of many aspects of party operations: campaign matters, party organization and administration, and policy.[4] Charles Longley, writing about the transformation in the Democratic party that took place during the reform period, concludes:

> The party-reform effort initiated at the 1968 Democratic national convention led to the emergence of a more authoritative national Democratic Party organization. Most notably, the adoption of uniform delegate-selection standards, which in turn sparked a series of court tests, [has] *clearly established the supremacy of national party rules over state party practices and state law.* Additionally, the Democratic Party charter both codified and symbolized the preeminent role of the national party charter (while still allowing, of course, state and local parties considerable autonomy and discretion.[5] [Emphasis added.]

Centralization and the Supreme Court

The accumulation at the national level of power over presidential nomination has been codified through the actions of the courts. Most significant has been the Supreme Court's assertion that the parties' national law (as set forth in the parties' charters) and procedures take precedence over a state's control of its prenomination delegate selection machinery in presidential contests. The courts have lent unanticipated support to the reform movement and have hastened the transformation of the parties' roles in the American political system.

The two major cases, both eventually decided by the Supreme Court, that dealt with this matter of the state law versus national party procedures are *Cousins v. Wigoda* (1975) and *Democratic Party of the United States of America v. La Follette* (1981). Because these cases have profoundly affected the current nominating system, we will look at them in some detail.

The Case of the Daley Delegation. The more important of the two cases is *Cousins v. Wigoda.* Prior to the *Cousins* decision, states had largely been free to regulate their own elections, including prenomination delegate selection practices, although the national parties had established guidelines regarding the certification of delegates at the conventions, as we have seen in Chapter 2.

The case arose in the prenomination events of 1972. In the Illinois primary 59 Chicago delegates (including Chicago Mayor Richard J. Daley) had been elected as delegates to the Democratic National Convention in accordance with state party rules and state election statutes.[6] In the aftermath of the primary election, an alternative and largely self-selected delegation, led by Alderman William Singer and the Rev. Jesse Jackson, charged that the 59 Chicago regular delegates had deliberately and willfully violated the national party's McGovern-Fraser guidelines, particularly those requiring proportional representation of minorities and women and those regarding slatemaking.[7] After an emotional and complicated set of hearings, the 1972 Democratic National Convention agreed that the selection of the Chicago delegates had violated the national party's delegate selection rules; the convention denied the Chicago delegation seating and replaced them with the Singer-Jackson insurgent delegation. The Chicago regulars instituted a series of court proceedings at the state and then the federal level in an effort to reverse the national party's stand.

In their argument before the Court, which was backed by extensive legal documentation, Mayor Daley and his delegation attempted to demonstrate the primacy of the state in choosing its delegates. Some of their points were the following:[8]

1. A state has a compelling interest in protecting the integrity of its electoral processes and the right of its citizens to effective suffrage under the state and federal constitutions. In developing this point, the Chicago delegates contended that if their ejection from the national convention were allowed to stand, roughly 700,000 voters (those who participated in the original delegate selection primary) would be disenfranchised.

2. The states have long had the power and authority to provide for citizen participation in the affairs of political parties through regulated primary elections for party officers and candidates. The

Chicago delegates argued that nomination had become a statutory right, granted by the legislature.[9]

3. Political parties and national conventions cannot constitutionally supersede a valid state primary law providing for the popular election of convention delegates. This position was the crux of the dispute.

In addition, the lawyers for the ousted delegates contended that "the choice as to who shall be the 'representatives of the people' in national conventions has traditionally been left to the state parties and legislatures," which was correct.[10] They also argued that a historic review of the deliberations of the national convention's credentials committee did not reveal the existence of a compelling national party interest to overturn the results of free and open primary elections, or, for that matter, any national convention interest "of sufficient importance to overcome the compelling interest of the state in maintaining the integrity of its primary election laws."[11] All in all, it is a powerful argument, grounded in legal precedent and in the traditional academic perceptions of how the parties operated. But the Supreme Court did not concur.

Citing its own legal precedents, the Court ruled, "The National Democratic Party and its adherents enjoy a ... right of political association 'that is protected from both federal and state encroachment by the First and Fourteenth Amendments to the Constitution.' "[12] As to the argument that Illinois had a compelling interest in protecting the integrity of its electoral processes and the right to effective suffrage of its citizens, the Court first distinguished between primary and general elections and then made the point that this primary election was intended to elect delegates to the national convention. From here it went on to the crux of the decision:

> Delegates perform a task of supreme importance to every citizen of the Nation regardless of their state of residence.... *The States themselves have no constitutionally mandated role in the great task of the selection of Presidential and Vice-Presidential candidates.* If the qualifications and eligibility of delegates to National Political Party Conventions were left to state law ... "each of the 50 states could establish the qualifications of its delegates to the various party conventions without regard to party policy, an obviously intolerable result." ... *The Convention serves the pervasive national interest in the selection of candidates for national office, and this national interest is greater than any interest of an individual State.*[13] [Emphasis added.]

This ruling constituted the lodging of enormous discretionary power over the presidential nominating process in the national party. The Republican party chose not to exploit that power, as we will discuss later in this section; however, the Republicans have experienced intraparty court challenges to their national convention delegate apportionment formula. The national party's right to affix the formula has been upheld by the courts.[14]

A number of states contested the implications of *Cousins*, mostly by attempting to refine and delimit its impact through a succession of cases in the state courts. For example, a Massachusetts court interpreted the ruling as follows:

> Although the Legislature may not select delegates to a national political convention, it has the right to prescribe procedures to be followed on the selection of delegates . . . provided that it does not intrude unconstitutionally on the rights of association of the political parties.[15]

This is a narrow reading of the Supreme Court's original ruling. Cases like this set the stage for a renewed test of a political party's authority in delegate selection.

The Matter of Open Primaries. The specific case that led to the Court's second ruling on the question involved the state of Wisconsin, in *Democratic Party of the United States of America v. La Follette* (1981). Wisconsin has historically held open primaries, a tradition the state is proud of and one that reaches back to the origins of the presidential primary in the Progressive era of the early 1900s. The state did not want to abandon its tradition when the national Democratic party decreed closed primaries and fought the party with every means at its disposal. The controversy eventually ended up in court, with the Wisconsin Supreme Court holding for the state. In 1981 the U.S. Supreme Court reviewed the *La Follette* case. In its decision the Court emphatically reaffirmed its commitment to the doctrine, enunciated in *Cousins*, that the national parties' concern with presidential nomination takes precedence over the interests of the individual states:

> A State, or court, may not constitutionally substitute its own judgment for that of [a] Party. A political party's choice among the various ways of determining the makeup of a State's delegation to the party's national convention is protected by the Constitution. And, as is true of all expressions of First Amendment freedoms, the courts may not interfere on the ground that they view a particular expression as unwise or irrational.[16]

In 1984 Wisconsin held both a caucus to select national convention delegates (to comply with party law) and an open presidential preference primary (reflecting the state's desire to retain its favored process), as we discussed in Chapter 2.

(The Republicans have declined to follow the Democrats into the thicket of controversy over the open primary and have never fought the states on this issue. Republican party rules require closed primaries *unless* prohibited by state law.)

As a result of these cases, the national party has the authority in presidential delegate selection to exercise a great deal of autonomy, subject only to the U.S. Constitution, and its powers are now codified in party law. The party can now determine its membership for the purpose of nominations, place restrictions on states' delegate selection processes, and certify delegates to the conventions.[17]

Party Differences in Centralization

Within party circles the national party's power over presidential delegate selection is unassailable. The Democrats exercise this power; the Republicans—retaining a more traditional conception of the American party—do not. In fact, the degree of centralization within the parties is a major manifestation of their most fundamental differences.

The Democrats have instituted a highly centralized system since 1968: the national party—usually through party committees established after each presidential election to review the rules for the next nomination contest—formulates and interprets the regulations covering nominating processes and compels state parties to comply with them. Each state party must adapt to the nationally promulgated rules, and most now do so with little question. If there is debate over the substantive meaning of provisions or the degree to which various alternative solutions or applications meet national party criteria, the national party resolves the issue. The Democratic party's Compliance Review Commission operates in the two years preceding the nominating race to handle disputes over state compliance with and interpretations of the rules. The commission also oversees the implementation of regulations established by other party bodies. The commission membership, selected by either the national chair or the president (if he is a Democrat), ultimately answers to the party leadership. Commission deliberations are closely monitored by the national party and by the few presidential contenders aware of the practical implications of commission decisions. The commission enjoys a wide degree of latitude in defining acceptable state party practices, and its decisions are virtually unappealable. In these regards, the centralization of authority has devolved upon a relatively few people at the national level.

In terms of enforcement, the national party can refuse to certify or accept national convention delegates elected under rules or selection plans it finds objectionable. Although the final decisions are made by the national convention and its credentials committee, the threat of sanctions has normally been sufficient to keep states in line with national party rules.

The Republican party travels a quite different road. Its directives to the state parties are essentially recommendations or statements of broad principle it hopes the state parties will honor. The party makes neither explicit nor implicit threat of retribution. Republicans continue to view the national party as a coalition of state parties in which the real authority, power, and control over presidential nominations resides at the state level. The national party concentrates on planning and managing orderly national conventions. The current Republican approach is basically a states' rights approach, long familiar to both parties.

The difference in outlook is a result of the reform era and the Democrats' specific concern with ensuring safeguards and adequate representation to minorities (particularly blacks) and women. From this initial thrust in the Democratic party, a formidable superstructure of national party rules, commissions, mandates, and the like has emerged. The unintended consequence of the changes has been to reduce the state parties to a position of subservience to the national Democratic party in regard to presidential nominations. This centralization, however, has not carried over into all other areas of party activity; in recruiting and supporting state and local candidates, for example, the state and local party organizations show signs of considerable vigor in carrying out the functions that remain under their control.

In a few short years the presidential selection process has changed from one of anarchic diversity to one that could potentially be totally controlled by the national party. Has the process of centralization gone too far? In the case of the Democratic party at least, some critics would answer yes and would contend that more state autonomy and flexibility would be advisable. In our own view, the parties should attempt to balance national party guarantees of equity and fairness to all those who participate in the process with the states' legitimate need for flexibility in adapting the system to their own situations. State and local parties are essential to the strength of the party system, and any other steps that can be taken to further strengthen the state and local parties, as organizations, and to modernize their operations would be welcomed by all who value the role parties play in a mass democracy. But national parties have shown themselves to be essential as well. It seems only logical to allow the national parties to exercise power over a matter of compelling national importance, the choosing of party nominees for the only national office.

The Dominance
of the Primaries

As we outlined in Chapter 2, primaries were introduced during the Progressive era and enjoyed a brief heyday before returning to very limited usage. During the New Deal, or old party, period, an average of about 15 states employed presidential primaries and selected between 33 and 45 percent of the national convention delegates using this method. But since 1968, both the number of presidential primaries and the proportion of committed delegates selected in these primaries have increased (Figure 3.1, Table 3.1). By 1980 over 70 percent of the delegates to the national convention were selected through primaries. (The trend seems to have reversed slightly since then: by 1984 this percentage had declined to just over 60 percent for the Democrats and 71 percent for the Republicans.) Just as important, the number and percentage of delegates committed through the primaries to vote for a specific candidate, at least on the first ballot, has increased dramatically since the reform era began, thus reducing the decision-making flexibility of the national conven-

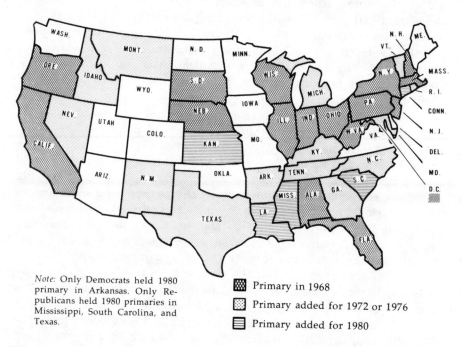

Note: Only Democrats held 1980 primary in Arkansas. Only Republicans held 1980 primaries in Mississippi, South Carolina, and Texas.

▨ Primary in 1968

▦ Primary added for 1972 or 1976

▤ Primary added for 1980

Figure 3.1 Growth of Presidential Primaries, 1968-1980. (From *Congressional Quarterly Weekly Report*, February 2, 1980, 283.)

Table 3.1 Influence of Presidential Primaries in Convention Votes, 1968-1984

	Democrats			Republicans		
Year	No. of primaries	No. of delegate votes	Percent of all votes	No. of primaries	No. of delegate votes	Percent of all votes
1968	17	983	37.5%	16	458	34.3%
1972	23	1,862	60.5	22	710	52.7
1976	29	2,183	72.6	28[a]	1,533	67.9
1980	35	2,378	71.8	34[b]	1,516	76.0
1984	25[c]	2,431	62.1	30[c]	1,551	71.0

[a] Does not include Vermont, which held a nonbinding preference primary but chose delegates by caucus/convention.

[b] Includes Puerto Rico and D.C. Does not include Vermont.

[c] Includes Puerto Rico and D.C. Does not include five states that held nonbinding primaries but chose delegates by caucus/convention.

Source: Congressional Quarterly Weekly Report, January 31, 1976, 225-242; July 5, 1980, 1870-1873; February 11, 1984, 252; June 16, 1984, 1443. Comparable data have been compiled by James W. Davis, *Presidential Primaries* (Westport, Conn.: Greenwood Press, 1980), 7, and Austin Ranney, *Participation in American Presidential Nominations, 1976* (Washington, D.C.: American Enterprise Institute, 1977), 6.

tions. The effect has been to give primaries the dominant role in presidential candidate selection (see Chapter 1). But the dominance of primaries is not looked upon favorably by some students of the nominating system and by many party leaders.

Reforms never make everyone happy, as the evidence of history shows, and there have frequently been counterreforms. Especially in regard to such elusive goals as electing better presidents and ensuring the accountability of public office holders, structural change may in the end be of limited use in addressing the larger political problems toward which the criticisms are really directed. With that caveat in mind, let us review some of the frustrations expressed in the postreform era.

Many critics contend that primaries have hastened the decline of the parties. Primaries have become rather like general elections. Citizens who merely identify themselves as party members can vote; they need not be informed about their party. Open primaries even allow members of the opposition party to choose state and local candidates, indicate presidential preferences, or choose delegates for the nominating convention. However, as newspaper columnist David S. Broder points out, the destructive effects of the primaries on party structure may not have been unintentional in the context of the late 1960s:

> The proliferation of primaries reflected the instinct for self-expression dominant in the culture of the 1960s and also the Vietnam period's hostility to political institutions and leaders. The belief was that "the people," not the politicians, should choose the presidential candidates, even though "the people" often turned out to be mainly political activists.[18]

What happens to the nominating process in the absence of strong party organizations? Many charge that the process becomes a race in which candidates compete for votes through the mass media. In the opinion of political scientist James L. Sundquist:

> There is no screening mechanism. A party nominee for president now is someone who has been able to devote enough time to shaking hands in the early primary and caucus states and to forming an effective get-out-the-vote organization there, who has raised enough money to put himself on television throughout the primary season, and who has proved to have popular appeal.[19]

Similarly, Michael Walzer notes:

> The candidate makes his appeal not through an articulated structure but through the mass media. He doesn't negotiate with local leaders, speak to caucuses, form alliances with established interest groups. Instead, he solicits votes, as it were, one by one ... among all the registered voters, without regard to their attachment to the party.... In turn, the voters encounter the candidate only in their living rooms, on the television screen, without political mediation.[20]

Clearly there are consequences in terms of the kinds of candidates that emerge victorious in such a process, candidates who represent the parties without being sufficiently accountable to them. Here is Sundquist's profile of such a candidate:

> He may be an outsider to the national political process. He may have no experience in the federal government he seeks to head. He may be a neophyte in dealing with complex issues of foreign relations and the domestic economy. He may be in no sense the natural leader of large and crucial elements of his own party.[21]

Broder has an even more disheartened view of the process and the candidates it produces:

> In the present nominating system, the determinants of success are the size of the candidate's ambitions, the extent of his leisure time, and the tolerance of his family, his budget and his job for almost unlimited travel.
>
> These characteristics have almost nothing to do with the qualities that make an effective president—as the results show. It is a recklessly haphazard way to choose the candidates for that demanding office.[22]

Sundquist and Walzer agree with Broder that the nominating system causes problems in the presidency. Sundquist's concern is that the nominee without close ties to a party organization

> may be a stranger to the people in Congress with whom he has to work, and he may have little sense of how to get along with them. He may have little idea of the kind of talent he needs to help run the executive branch, and no network of experienced advisers to help him find the way.[23]

Walzer's concern is more with the issue of accountability:

> We have no firm expectations as to how he will behave once in office. We have no way of enforcing whatever expectation—pious hopes, leaps of faith—we allow ourselves. For it is not his party loyalty, his stand on issues, his ties to other politicians ... that count, but only his "personality"—the image he projects, the mask he wears.[24]

The other side of the argument is that primaries help ensure that the most popular presidential candidate—and therefore the one with the greatest likelihood of representing the broadest coalition of party voters and with the best chance of winning the general election—will be nominated. That has yet to be shown; but as we mentioned in Chapter 1 the winner of a group of primaries does show an ability to command votes.

Some of the critics' worst fears, of a virtually complete takeover of the nominating process by primaries, seem to be modestly allayed at this point, since the number of primaries declined slightly in 1984. Still, primaries retain a dominant position in the mixed nominating system of the 1980s; they are clearly still the driving force behind a successful campaign for the nomination.

One of the quotes by James Sundquist in this section refers to the early primaries and caucuses as having special significance. Others have also noted that the early processes seem to carry great weight. In the following paragraphs we look more systematically at the influence of the timing of these processes, particularly primaries, on the nominating system.

In the period before 1972 approximately one-third of the national convention delegates were selected through the earliest primaries of the season. That figure has risen steadily in recent elections, until it reached 60 percent by 1980. The phenomenon of increasingly earlier primaries in increasingly more states, *front loading,* has become a serious matter. More and more states have moved—or are considering moving—the dates of their primaries forward in hopes of attracting candidate and media attention and in an effort to maximize their influence on the outcome of the nomination processes. In turn, it is possible for presidential contenders who do well in the earliest of the delegate selection contests, as both Jimmy Carter and Ronald Reagan did in 1980, to grab the spotlight and the momentum for their campaigns, thus effectively neutralizing their opposition. For all practical purposes, these candidates would have the nomination won by late March or early April, rendering the later contests irrelevant.

The front-loading phenomenon is apparently gathering momentum. The attention attracted by these early and generally unrepresentative contests, such as Iowa and New Hampshire, and the influence wielded by them on the nominating process have prompted some of the larger states to begin moving their own delegate selection processes up as early as possible in the nominating season. These larger states elect far more delegates to the parties' national conventions and wish to exercise the influence in the nominating process that they feel their size and political importance justify. For example, in the early 1980s California—which traditionally held its primary on the last day of the nominating season (in early June)—and New York, two states that together account for between one-fifth (in the Republican party) and one-quarter (in the Democratic party) of the total national convention vote, were threatening to move their primaries forward into the late winter months. The national Democratic party, in particular, has resisted such moves, fearful of accelerating the front-loading tendencies. In the process the national party has put forward its own proposals in hopes of stabilizing or reversing the trend.

The emphasis on front loading is a reversal of the pattern evident in the years preceding the reform era, when the "Super Bowl" primaries—those held during the last days of the primary season—were often the most significant. In 1968, for example, the major industrial states of California, Illinois, and New Jersey held their primaries on the same day in early June. The primaries held on this one day accounted for 38 percent of both parties' national convention delegates and, more often than not, were considered crucial to a candidate's chances for the nomination.

In 1968 the New Hampshire primary was held in mid-March, and the Iowa caucus results received virtually no attention and had no national significance in influencing opinions about a presidential nominee. Seventy percent of the national convention delegates were chosen after May 1. As the earliest primaries got earlier, the nominating season got longer, eventually lasting as long as six months. In 1980 the Iowa caucuses were held in January and the New Hampshire (Democratic and Republican) and Puerto Rico (Republican) primaries took place in late February. The problems of front loading and a creeping expansion of the time frame for selecting national convention delegates have become associated in many minds.

In regard to the influence of the early states, many believe that in the nomination process it is unfair to the other states, especially the large, industrial states, to pay such close attention to Iowa and New Hampshire; these are especially unrepresentative in regard to minority groups and urbanization and in their general election vote (normally solid Republican). But others argue that the parties in the early states have been built up a good deal as a result of the attention and that these states represent groups toward which the Democratic party should direct its attention. Everyone agrees that success in the early states improves the chances that a relatively unknown candidate or one with less support from the party organization will obtain his party's nomination, as we noted in Chapter 1. Supporters of a strong party structure condemn that consequence of front loading, and those who favor the most open and direct participation welcome it.

Critics stress disadvantages to the candidates and the public of the long season: the current process, they say, exhausts the candidates physically and financially and bores the public; a long campaign also favors the person who does not hold another job and can campaign full time. On the other hand, some observers defend the current long season, pointing out that it tests the mettle of the candidates and their organizations in some ways analogous to the presidency itself. In addition, the parties benefit from the lead time to the convention built into a long nominating season and the candidates have more time to conduct their fund-raising efforts.[25] States might also incur great expense and suffer the loss of prestige and media attention in rescheduling their systems. Besides, defenders argue, it is impossible to control the media and the candidates' desire to start early, and attempts to do so will probably prove futile.

The Democratic party's Winograd and Hunt commissions have championed a shorter and more compact delegate selection period with restrictions placed on front loading (Chapter 2); the season has in fact been shortened, but front loading is as prevalent as before. One effect of an abbreviated prenomination campaign period is to make challenges by little-known candidates more difficult. The outsider strategy, employed most notably by Jimmy Carter in 1976, involves concentrating on and winning the early delegate selection tests and then depending on media publicity and public appeal to build the financial and organizational resources necessary to compete in each successive wave of delegate selection contests over the long nominating season. It is a strategy that has become considerably more difficult to pursue.

It has already become more difficult for new candidates to successfully compete with the winner of the early contests in the later primaries. If the parties were to institute a three-month preconvention nominating period, with filing deadlines ranging anywhere from 30 to 90 days before the primary date, an early front-runner who appeared to stumble would still be relatively secure; it would be difficult for a latecomer to qualify to enter the remaining primaries and even more unlikely, in light of front loading, that he or she could win the necessary bloc of national convention delegates needed to seriously contest the nomination.

Observers with a more national perspective continue to worry about front loading and to make efforts to attack it through the national party rules. Those with a state perspective or with a particular candidate's interest in mind continue to resist efforts to reduce their maximum freedom of action in scheduling delegate selection contests. Behavior that is directed at advancing the interests of the candidates or the parochial interests of the states has proved to be very difficult for the national parties to regulate. Nevertheless, the national Democratic party has, at least until recently, continued to try to exercise such regulation and accept the attendant political flak.

The campaign of 1984 illustrates these observations. Walter Mondale clearly had more support than any other candidate among party leaders and elected officials. He was also heavily supported by the most important interest group affiliated with the Democratic party, the labor unions. While Gary Hart was perhaps not a real outsider, he also was not the first choice of most party and elected officials. Yet Hart scored early victories in the New Hampshire primary and other New England delegate selection contests. Mondale's campaign began to falter in the face of Hart's rapidly building momentum, but a respectable showing in a round of primaries and caucuses held March 13, dubbed "Super Tuesday," paved the way for a Mondale comeback on the East Coast and in the Midwest. Although Mondale stumbled again in May, losing contests in Ohio and Indiana, his delegate count was growing inexorably based on his superior organization and party organization support. The Mondale campaign had also filed delegate slates for each delegate selection contest, another factor that worked to increase Mondale's delegate lead over Hart. Ultimately, Mondale won the most caucus states, won the states with winner-take-all plans, and won on superior organizational strength. His campaign was better designed for the long haul through the entire nominating season than either the Hart or Jackson campaigns. This is why Mondale became the 1984 Democratic presidential nominee.

Social Instability and
the Nominating System

The interrelationship of the political parties, the presidential campaigns, and the American society is in transition. The parties, as intermediaries between their members and the political leadership, have been forced to try to respond to changes in society through organizational reform. The changing social composition of the electorate and the restructuring of the nation's economic base have put pressure on the parties and their nominating system. The emergence of television as the dominant medium of communications has had a profound impact on political processes, particularly on the conduct of presidential nominations. It may well be that the ability of the parties to meet these external challenges could determine whether political parties continue to be relevant to American society.

A full discussion of these external challenges would be beyond the scope of this book. But some familiarity with the nature of social change in the past few decades is essential to our evaluation of this period of ferment and experimentation within the parties.

In a very short period of time the social order in the United States has undergone profound changes. By looking more closely at certain aspects of social change and comparing census data from recent decades, we can begin to gain a sense of the nature of these changes and an appreciation of the external forces at work on our political parties. The balance of power among the parties' constituencies has changed and the old means of appealing to them have lost their relevance.

Population Changes

The United States is growing, not only in population, but also in income and education levels (Table 3.2). In just the 20 years from 1960 through 1980 the U.S. population increased about 25 percent, to 226.5 million. We are far beyond the time when a legislator could expect to know most of his voters; but even in contemporary terms a larger population is more difficult to involve in the political process. The nation is also better educated; the proportion of high school graduates has increased 2.7 times since 1940, and there has been a threefold increase in college graduates in the same period. A better informed and more literate population is more demanding of political parties, particularly in relation to political issues. It becomes more important to the parties to take a stand and offer a relevant policy choice to the electorate. The better educated also tend to be fairly independent of party labels, in

Table 3.2 Changes in U.S. Demographic Characteristics

A. Population, 1790-1980

Year	Population	Percent increase	Year	Population	Percent increase
1980	226,504,825	11.5%	1880	50,155,783	26.0%
1970	203,211,926	13.3	1870	39,818,449	26.6
1960	179,323,175	19.0	1860	31,443,321	35.6
1950	150,697,361	14.5	1850	23,191,876	35.9
1940	131,669,275	7.2	1840	17,069,453	32.7
1930	122,775,040	16.1	1830	12,866,020	33.5
1920	105,710,620	14.9	1820	9,638,453	33.1
1910	91,972,266	21.0	1810	7,239,881	36.4
1900	75,994,575	20.7	1800	5,308,483	35.1
1890	62,947,714	25.5	1790	3,929,214	—

B. Income, 1960-1980

	1960	1970	1980
Over $50,000		5.5%	6.7%
$25,000-$50,000	18.9%	32.0	32.6
$20,000-$25,000	10.6	11.3	13.7
$15,000-$20,000	22.8	19.7	14.0
$10,000-$15,000	20.2	13.6	14.2
$5,000-$10,000	16.1	11.7	12.7
Under $5,000	11.4	6.1	6.2
	100.0	100.0	100.0
Median income	$15,637	$20,926	$21,023

C. Education, 1940-1980

	High school only	Four or more years of college
1940	24.5%	4.6%
1950	34.3	6.2
1960	41.1	7.7
1970	55.2	11.0
1980	66.3	16.3

Source: Andrew Hacker, ed., *U/S: A Statistical Portrait of the American People* (New York: Viking, 1983), 14, 143, 251. Hacker used U.S. Census data. Reprinted by permission.

effect more likely to shop between the parties and the nominees. They are less guided by party loyalties.

The combination of a lower birth rate and longer life expectancy means that the population is rapidly getting older; in the United States between 1960 and 1980 the number of children under 5 decreased by 20 percent while the number of people over 65 increased 54 percent. Andrew Hacker dramatically restated these statistics: "In 1960, for every 100 children under 5 there were only 81 persons of age 65 or older. By 1980, for every 100 children there were 156 senior citizens." [26] Older people often have different concerns: for example, they no longer have children in school; they are usually no longer in the work force; they are directly involved with the Social Security system. Clearly, their self-interest—particularly in regard to what they want for themselves and how they want the government to operate—tends to be very different from that of younger segments of the population. The shift of interests with age is not a new phenomenon, but the large numbers of older people and their consequent political power make today's situation quite different from that of just a few decades ago.

Family size is declining, and the participation of women in the work force has increased. Women are making more forceful demands on the political system and the parties for recognition; they have drawn attention to their economic needs as well (especially the differential between their wages and men's) and to their restricted job and educational opportunities. The parties must respond to such social concerns, and to an extent both have in recent elections. Before the 1984 convention, in fact, Mondale named Rep. Geraldine A. Ferraro of New York as his running mate.

Another population shift has been geographical. Recently many areas of the South and West—the Sunbelt—have rapidly gained population and jobs (Table 3.3). At the same time parts of the North and East have lost population and jobs (Detroit, one of the most dramatically affected cities, lost one-fifth of its population in 10 years). Political power has followed this shift. Aside from intrinsic regional differences of history, terrain, and climate, it is clear that the political concerns of newer, booming cities and states are different from those of older, economically more troubled regions. The poor, blacks, ethnic minorities, Eastern city dwellers—in other words, those who formed the basis of the predominantly Democratic New Deal coalition—will find their influence in national politics declining. The political power of the more conservative Mountain, Southwestern, and Southern states—with economies based on energy and computer technology and with a population dominated by the upwardly mobile, young middle class (the "Yuppies"

Table 3.3 Geographical Distribution of U.S. Population, 1970-1980

A. Fifteen States with the Largest Absolute and Percentage Population Gains

	Absolute gain			Percentage gain	
Rank	State	Number	Rank	State	Percentage change
1	California	3,697,493	1	Nevada	63.5%
2	Texas	3,029,728	2	Arizona	53.1
3	Florida	2,948,574	3	Florida	43.4
4	Arizona	942,467	4	Wyoming	41.6
5	Georgia	876,335	5	Utah	37.9
6	North Carolina	790,018	6	Alaska	32.4
7	Washington	716,919	7	Idaho	32.4
8	Virginia	694,831	8	Colorado	30.7
9	Colorado	679,238	9	New Mexico	27.8
10	Tennessee	664,732	10	Texas	27.1
11	Louisiana	559,335	11	Oregon	25.9
12	Oregon	541,130	12	Hawaii	25.3
13	South Carolina	528,495	13	New Hampshire	24.8
14	Oklahoma	465,803	14	Washington	21.0
15	Alabama	445,707	15	South Carolina	20.4

B. Population Changes in the Nation's 15 Largest Cities

1980 rank	City	1980 population	Percentage change since 1970
1	New York	7,071,639	−10.4%
2	Chicago	3,005,072	−10.7
3	Los Angeles	2,966,850	+ 5.4
4	Philadelphia	1,688,210	−13.4
5	Houston	1,595,138	+29.4
6	Detroit	1,203,339	−20.4
7	Dallas	904,078	+ 7.1
8	San Diego	875,538	+25.7
9	Phoenix	789,704	+35.9
10	Baltimore	786,775	−13.1
11	San Antonio	785,880	+20.1
12	Indianapolis	700,807	− 5.9
13	San Francisco	678,974	− 5.1
14	Memphis	646,356	+ 3.7
15	Washington, D.C.	638,333	−15.6

Source: Andrew Hacker, ed., *U/S: A Statistical Portrait of the American People* (New York: Viking, 1983), 16, 18-19. Hacker used U.S. Census data. Reprinted by permission.

who provided the basis of Hart's challenge to Mondale)—will continue to increase.

Economic Changes

In conjunction with the geographical population shift there has been a relocation of many companies from the Frostbelt to the Sunbelt. But even more important has been the fundamental restructuring of the nation's economic base. Factory employment fell 24.8 percent from 1970 to 1980, and many workers in older industrial areas have been displaced. (For the Democrats this has meant an erosion of one of its major constituencies, union labor). Meanwhile, professional, technical, managerial, and administrative occupations gained workers, rising from 11.0 percent of the workforce in 1970 to 38.3 percent in 1980. Poorly paid custodial and fast-food jobs were available, but well-paid factory jobs were not; and the well-educated industrial manager could not become a systems analyst or electronic engineer overnight.

Although real income increased over 130 percent from 1960 to 1980, many Americans saw their own condition worsen as unemployment climbed from a low of 3.5 percent in the base year of 1969 to a high of 10.7 percent in December 1982, at the height of the recession. To compound the problem, inflation shrank the value of the dollar by two-thirds between 1967 and 1980. Basic items such as fuel, housing, and medical costs went up as much as 700 percent. Although inflation and unemployment have eased somewhat since 1982, many fears remain among the population. As a consequence, voters have become more concerned with how much of their money goes to the government and how it is spent.

Attitude Changes

The past few decades have also seen radical changes in attitude among the citizenry: there has been a real decline in the level of trust and support accorded the political institutions of the United States. The changes in population and economy that we have outlined contributed to some extent to this loss of faith. But there have also been many crises to undermine the public trust and change the American view of government: the sixties saw the Bay of Pigs incident, urban race riots, and Vietnam War protests; the seventies saw widespread disillusionment with the Vietnam War, the Arab oil embargo and resulting energy crisis, Watergate, and increased fears of nuclear proliferation. The list could go on. The result has been an erosion of belief in the government's ability to master the challenging domestic and international problems of the day. Many observers have noted this tendency.[27] As Alex Inkeles writes:

> Whatever interpretation is put on it, there seems no denying the fact. The Americans' previously exceptional pride in their governmental institutions and their vibrant confidence in their personal political efficacy have vastly declined. What was previously a great, almost deadening, "hurrah" has now shrunk to a barely audible whisper.[28]

These shifts in population, the economy, and the attitudes of Americans toward their government have combined with another element, the increased importance of the mass media, particularly television, to continue to apply pressure on the presidential nominating process. In the next section we will examine in detail the role of the media in the nominating system.

The Influence of the Media

Many have observed that the media, especially television, have become a powerful factor in helping decide the outcome of presidential nomination battles in recent election years. In fact, considering that the era is marked by disaffected voters, by a deterioration in each of the parties' coalitions, by the parties' loss of control over their own nominating methods, and by the reliance placed on television by the average citizen, some conclude that the media now constitute the single most dominant influence in presidential nomination decisions. Richard L. Rubin, in his study of the interaction between parties, the media, and the presidency, has written:

> Television journalism has vastly increased the influence of the press as a whole in the nomination process by becoming the most important connecting link between a variety of competing candidates and an unsettled party electorate.... Whether by setting criteria for media coverage of candidates or issues, or by establishing benchmarks for candidates' success or failure in actual primary elections, the press has assumed much of the recruitment and evaluative role that was once reserved for practicing politicians.[29]

The role assumed by the media has disturbed many political observers. But the contenders for the presidential nomination are not likely to quarrel openly with the press. Consider the following testimonials to the prevalence of the press's role in nominating campaigns. Here is what Ronald Reagan's 1976 campaign press secretary, Lyn Nofziger, had to say:

> You go into a place like New Hampshire and you've got two things in mind. Primarily is winning New Hampshire. Secondly is getting out the stories about your candidate and where he stands and all that to the rest of the country.... The more we have Ronald Reagan's name with the proper things in the papers, the better off we are, because it looks like he's moving around and it looks like he's active and it looks like he's campaigning.[30]

Jimmy Carter's media adviser, Barry Jagoda, made a more general statement:

> The television news organizations in this country are an enormously dominant force in primary elections. They're [there] every Tuesday night, not only counting the votes, but, in some cases, setting the tone and, in almost all cases, reinforcing the tone of what the issues are that week.[31]

Although these comments were made in relation to the 1976 prenomination campaigns, they apply as well to any recent presidential campaign.

It has been argued that primary elections are particularly suited to the needs of television for entertainment, pictorial quality, action, scenic footage, and brief (30- to 90-second), superficial information. As a consequence, as the absolute number of primaries has increased in the postreform era and as their influence in the nominating process has become greater (through rank-and-file democratization), television's influence has been disproportionately magnified. As Rubin points out:

> The new [post-1968] pattern of primaries does not ... merely repeat the old Progressive pattern.... It is rather a major change suited to, and shaped by, a new era of mass communications—with durable effects on present and future party structures.[32]

The information transmitted by television in particular tends to be superficial, based on image more than substance. Politics is a game, say the media, a contest among individuals, and the only thing of relevance is winning. This approach plays to a certain streak within the American character. The emphasis is on the horse race aspects of primary contests: who's ahead, who's behind, what the polls show, upsets, unexpected successes and failures. The media and other observers set well-publicized but arbitrary and artificial standards regarding expected strength and momentum, which may be illusory but are nonetheless influential in determining a candidate's relative success in a primary contest. Considered less newsworthy, and certainly less attractive for the brief treatment that can be given them on the evening news, are a candidate's policy evaluations, in-depth analyses of the relative differences among contenders in issue areas, and the type of background and personality profiles some believe might help to weed out those with the least desirable personal and motivational qualities for high office.[33] Without doubt, the media perspective emphasizes fun, excitement, drama, and competition, and it is easily understood by the average television viewer. Whether the dominant approach should be the only aspect of reporting on prenomination contests is, of course, another matter.

One especially distorting effect of media coverage correlates with the front-loading phenomenon. Unusually heavy media attention is given to the earliest of the primary and caucus state outcomes to the neglect of later, and potentially more representative, state outcomes. The pattern is easily detected. Based on his extensive analysis of the media's coverage and relative priorities early in the 1976 prenomination campaign (specifically, November 24, 1975 through February 27, 1976), Michael J. Robinson reached the following conclusions about network news coverage and newspaper stories:

1. All 50 state primaries combined received 616 news stories; New Hampshire's alone received 250 news stories (41 percent of the total).

2. The second most closely covered state primary, that of Massachusetts, received 71 stories, 28 percent of the New Hampshire total.

3. All 10 non-primary state caucuses which began *before* the New Hampshire election received a total of 77 news stories; New Hampshire, alone, received more than three times as many, despite the fact that these 10 non-primary states represented more than 500 delegates to the nominating conventions (more than 12 times as many as New Hampshire).

4. The Iowa [caucus], which by all rights was the first delegate selection [contest], received a total of 40 news stories. New Hampshire got more than six times as many.[34]

Robinson's analyses also demonstrated a different emphasis between electronic and print journalism:

1. Although 34 percent of all campaign stories in print were about New Hampshire, 54 percent of all campaign stories on television were about New Hampshire.

2. Although 42 percent of all the campaign news space in print was devoted to New Hampshire, a full 60 percent of the news time on TV was devoted to New Hampshire.

3. Although the two most populous states, California and New York, received one-third the attention given to New Hampshire in print (a notable statistic in its own right!), those same two states received only one-twentieth the attention given to New Hampshire on television.[35]

The conclusion is inescapable that the media, especially television, overemphasize the early delegate selection contests—New Hampshire's most of all.

For the political parties, the implications of media influence on presidential nominations are very serious. Many observers believe that as the media's influence increases, the parties' control decreases. They see the media as taking over functions previously in the domain of the party organizations (such as informing the voters about policy issues), hastening the devitalization of the parties that has long been under way.

All in all, few applaud the quality of coverage or the aftereffects of the media's significant position in relaying information to the voter, in structuring the decisions of voters and conventions, and in determining both the nature and the limits of the nominating contest.

Yet the problem is not easily resolved. As F. Christopher Arterton writes, summarizing his own research on the relationship between the media and the presidential prenomination campaigns:

> There are unique characteristics of the presidential nomination system which frequently make the perceptual environment in which candidates compete more important than the political realities. Since much of the perceptual environment is created/communicated by the news media, campaigners come to look upon the community of journalists as an alternative electorate in which they must conduct a persuasive campaign. The dominance of perception over concrete political support is particularly marked during the preprimary and early primary periods. The latitude of journalistic interpretation is also greatest at this time, when the indicators of growing or declining political support are at their poorest in predictive validity.[36]

The relationship between politics and the media has always been a sensitive one. There is little the political parties can do legally to restructure the interaction, given the First Amendment freedom the press enjoys, and there is probably little that they would want to do along these lines. Indeed, it is hard to know whether the press would behave much differently if the parties were suddenly to shift entirely to the less dramatic, smaller, and harder to cover party caucuses. The media have their own internal drives of competition, celebrity, and profit, and they are likely to mold the story line to fit those needs regardless of the preferences of the party organizations or the candidates.

The response of the parties and the presidential contenders is to cultivate the reporters, draw attention to the candidates' evaluations of events, supply information favorable to the campaign, and restrict or minimize developments that might hurt a candidacy.[37] The parties and the candidates have come to depend on the media to disseminate their information to the voters. Through the media the parties and candidates educate the voters and mobilize them at election time. In a way, primary and general election campaigns are made to order for television.

By now, too much is invested in the status quo for much change to occur in the near future. Nevertheless, concerned individuals must continue to raise and document the shortcomings of media coverage of the nominations. We can and must continue to ask for more hard information, more analysis, and more assessment of the policy implications of the campaigns, in short, for a sharper focus on the issues of the nominating season than the media have delivered in the past. If the American voters are one day even to approximate the informed electorate called for by classical democratic theory, then the candidates, the media, and the parties must take seriously their obligations to educate, not bamboozle, the American people.

NOTES

1. Charles Longley, "Party Reform and Party Nationalization: The Case of the Democrats," in *The Party Symbol*, ed. William Crotty (San Francisco: W. H. Freeman, 1980), 359-378; Longley, "Party Nationalization in America," in *Paths to Political Reform*, ed. William Crotty (Lexington, Mass.: Lexington Books/D. C. Heath, 1980), 167-205; John F. Bibby, "Party Renewal in the National Republican Party," in *Party Renewal in America*, ed. Gerald M. Pomper (New York: Praeger, 1980), 102-115; Robert Harmel and Kenneth Janda, *Parties and Their Environments: Limits to Reform?* (New York: Longman, 1982), 95-120.
2. See Cornelius Coter and Bernard Hennessy, *Politics without Power* (New York: Atherton, 1964) for a major study of the national committees.
3. V. O. Key, *Politics, Parties and Pressure Groups*, 4th ed. (New York: Thomas Y. Crowell, 1958), 361. Key was elaborating on a statement Eisenhower made to this effect.
4. William Crotty, "Philosophies of Party Reform," in *Party Renewal in America*, 31-50. See also William Crotty, *Party Reform* (New York: Longman, 1983) for a more detailed discussion of this and other matters treated here.
5. Longley, "Party Reform and Party Nationalization in America," 374-375.
6. Crotty, *Party Reform*, 153-202, contains an in-depth analysis of this case.
7. See Crotty, *Party Reform*, on unseating the Daley delegation.
8. Respondent's Brief, *Cousins v. Wigoda* (1973).
9. Joseph Starr, "The Legal Status of American Political Parties," *American Political Science Review* 34 (December 1940): 439.
10. Respondent's Brief at 50.
11. Ibid., 55.
12. *Cousins v. Wigoda*, 419 U.S. 477 (1975) at 487.
13. Ibid., 489-490.
14. *Ripon Society v. National Republican Party*, 525 F.2d 565 (1975); cert. denied 424 U.S. 933 (1976).
15. Albert J. Beveridge, "*Democratic Party of the United States of America v. La Follette* (49 U.S.L.W. 4178 February 24, 1981)," Memo, Files of the Democratic National Committee, Washington, D.C., n.d. The case in question is *Sears v. Secretary of the Commonwealth*.
16. Ibid., 7.

17. Ibid., 7-8.
18. David S. Broder, "Endless Primaries Net Endless Candidacy," *Washington Post*, June 9, 1980, 5.
19. James L. Sundquist, "The Crisis of Competence in Our National Government," *Political Science Quarterly* 95 (Summer 1980): 193.
20. Michael Walzer, "Democracy vs. Election," *New Republic*, January 3, 1981, 18.
21. Sundquist, "Crises of Competence," 193.
22. Broder, "Endless Primaries," 5.
23. Sundquist, "Crises of Competence," 193.
24. Walzer, "Democracy vs. Election," 18.
25. "Timing of the Delegate Selection Process," Option Paper no. 3, Winograd Commission, Democratic National Committee (Washington, D.C., n.d.), 3.
26. Andrew Hacker, ed., *U/S: A Statistical Portrait of the American People* (New York: Viking, 1983), 29. Most of the U.S. census data cited here are taken from Hacker's compilation.
27. See Jack Dennis, "Changing Public Support for the American Party System," in *Paths to Political Reform*, for a discussion of this point. See also S. M. Lipset and William Schneider, *The Confidence Gap* (New York: Free Press, 1983); and William Crotty, *American Parties in Decline*, 2d ed. (Boston: Little, Brown, 1984).
28. Alex Inkeles, "The American National Character," in *The Third Century*, ed. S. M. Lipset (Stanford, Calif.: Hoover Institution Press, 1979), 413-414.
29. Richard L. Rubin, *Press, Party, and Presidency* (New York: W. W. Norton, 1981), 209.
30. F. Christopher Arterton, "Campaign Organizations Confront the Media Environment," in *Race for the Presidency*, ed. James David Barber (Englewood Cliffs, N.J.: Prentice-Hall, 1978), 5.
31. Ibid.
32. Rubin, *Press, Party, and Presidency*, 202.
33. Erwin C. Hargrove, "What Manner of Man?," in *Choosing the President*, ed. James David Barber (Englewood Cliffs, N.J.: Prentice-Hall, 1974), 7-33. See also James David Barber, *The Presidential Character*, (New York: Prentice-Hall, 1972).
34. Michael J. Robinson, "Media Coverage in the Primary Campaign of 1976: Implications for Voters, Candidates, and Parties," in *The Party Symbol*, 183.
35. Ibid.
36. Arterton, "Campaign Organizations Confront the Media Environment," 4.
37. See Robert E. Di Clerico and Eric M. Uslaner, *Few Are Chosen: Problems in Presidential Selection* (New York: McGraw-Hill, 1984), 43-75, for a related discussion.

Part II

Studies of the Nominating System

The Voters: Participation and Representativeness

4

Because the primaries have increased both in number and in influence in the nominating system, it is important to examine what we know about them and about who participates in them. Who are the voters in the primaries and how do they differ from the nonvoters? How do primaries compare with caucuses? This chapter begins with a review of the empirical studies of other scholars who have done research on the primaries. Since much of this work began at the start of the reform era in 1968, we have a basis for examining in the remainder of the chapter new empirical data on the 1980 primaries. In all of this enterprise, our major concerns are with the issues of participation and representativeness in the nominating process.

Participation is simply a measure of how many voters choose to take part in an electoral process, such as a primary or a caucus. In evaluating participation, we can compare primaries to caucuses to determine whether more people in fact take part in the primaries, as was intended by the Progressives and successive primary supporters. We can also look at how prenomination participation compares with general election participation. These questions are fairly easy to answer; however, the implications of participation are rooted in deeper issues of democracy. Reformers pushed for more inclusive processes and got them; party supporters have fought the weakening of the parties, which they believe results from the move to primaries.

Without question, participation in presidential nomination has increased significantly in the postreform era: between 1968 and 1980 the number of people who took part in the parties' presidential nomination processes rose from 13 to 32 million. Over 90 percent of the increase is accounted for by primary participation, which indicates that—as expected—when more states have presidential primaries, more people do participate. The primaries outdraw the caucuses by ratios between 10 to 1 and 18 to 1. Actual figures are sketchy, but it has been estimated that primaries on the average draw roughly one-half of a party's eligible electorate, whereas caucuses tend to draw about one-twentieth.[1] Primary turnout is smaller in relation to either the *voting age population* or the *general election turnout*. Austin Ranney, a leading student of the primaries, examined 11 competitive primary states in the period from 1948 to 1968. Ranney found that turnout in those primaries averaged 39 percent of the voting age population, compared to 69 percent in the ensuing general elections in those states.[2] For 1976 Ranney found that in the competitive primary states primary turnout was 28.9 percent of the voting age population and general election turnout was 53.3 percent of the voting age population.[3] The figures and relative proportions may differ from year to year and from state to state, but the general trend is clear: a smaller proportion of the population participates in the primaries than in the general election. The rule of thumb is that primary turnout tends to be about half of general election turnout for the same office.

Representativeness, how well the participants reflect the rest of the population, is a more complex issue. We need to identify the important characteristics for comparison, and we need to choose segments of the population to evaluate. Once the comparisons have been made and representativeness analyzed, the problem of evaluation remains: how important is representativeness to the parties, to governance, and to democracy?

Primary representativeness is an evaluation of how well the primaries are capable of living up to their promise. It is one thing to offer all voters the right to help choose the nominees of the major parties; it is quite another for all to take advantage of that opportunity. If the participants in the primaries are systematically biased, then the effective primary electorate is likely to support positions that are distortions of what voters in the mass public, or even in the parties' bases, would prefer. If certain groups or strata of society are likely to participate more, then they may be able to help select presidential candidates more to their liking and more sympathetic to their own policy preferences, while others may feel left out or may in fact *be* left out in wielding political influence.

In theory, no one should be left out. American political thought holds that politics is supposed to be the great equalizer. People who demonstrably are not economically or socially equal are supposed to be able to attain some measure of equality before the law and in the political system because of their ability to exercise political influence, especially at the ballot box.[4] The voting booth is supposed to be the one place where the patent inequalities in social standing and economic resources can be counterbalanced. On the other hand, perhaps the promise of mass democracy is a false one, and inequalities in social and economic resources will inevitably be translated into inequalities in political resources as well. We are dealing here with some of the fundamental questions of democratic theory: What are the best means of linking the mass public and the political decision makers? What should the role of the political elites be? What is the effect of changing participation and representativeness on the American political process?

Representativeness of Primary Voters

Representativeness must be determined in the context of populations to be compared. Should the primary voters be representative of the party's mass base or of all Americans of voting age? Since those who are voting in a primary are choosing the nominees for a political party, a strong philosophical case can be made for the proposition that the primary voters should represent the party's mass base rather than all potential voters. This is the argument made by party professionals and the supporters of strong party organizations. In fact, the strongest supporters of the party organizations would prefer that if primaries must be used at all, they should be *closed*, that is, restricted to party members. If the party cannot control its most crucial function, then it has little reason to exist, say the proponents of closed primaries. Thus, the advocates of party control through closed primaries judge the representativeness of the primary voters in terms of how closely they resemble those who identify with the party.

On the other hand, advocates of the broadest possible participation, through open primaries, see the primaries as important devices for narrowing the field to the two candidates who have the greatest likelihood of victory in the general election. According to this view, any voter should be allowed access to the primary of either party. Advocates of open primaries judge the representativeness of primary voters in terms of how the primary voters compare with the population at large.

For both schools of thought we are interested in examining representativeness in relation to three key questions about voters in the primaries:

1. How representative demographically are they?
2. How representative in party identification are they?
3. How representative are they in terms of ideology and issues?

These questions define three dimensions: demographic, partisan, and ideological. Conventional wisdom in political science holds that the primary voters are unrepresentative of party identifiers and of the mass public on all three major dimensions. Specifically, compared to those who do not vote in primaries, primary voters are usually expected to be somewhat higher in socioeconomic status and stronger in their attachment to the parties, and they tend toward the extremes of the political continuum in ideological commitment. This position is most often identified with the work of V. O. Key, the political scientist who in 1956 observed that primary voters tended to be different from both the general electorate and the party identifiers:

> The effective primary constituency of the state as a whole may come to consist predominantly of the people of certain sections of a state, of persons chiefly of specified national origin or religious affiliation, or people especially responsive to certain styles of political leadership or shades of ideology, or of other groups markedly unrepresentative in one way or another of the party following.[5]

Since Key wrote those words numerous studies have been designed to test the representativeness of the primary electorate. Some of these studies have examined presidential primaries in a single state, several states, or nationwide. Others, although focused on gubernatorial primaries in a single state, have produced results relevant to our interests. In this chapter we review in more detail some of the most recent research focused on the presidential primaries of 1968 through 1980.

Research through the 1976 Primaries

The most important early research on the representativeness of the primaries was done by Austin Ranney, by himself and with Leon Epstein.[6] For 1964 through 1968 Ranney studied gubernatorial and presidential primaries in Wisconsin and other states. In general he found that the primary electorate did reflect an upper-middle-class composition bias and a bias in favor of the strong party sympathizers. However, Ranney found only limited support for Key's proposition that primary voters showed significant issue or ideological differences in comparison with those who did not vote in primaries. On this dimension Ranney concluded that those who voted in primary elections were not much different from those who voted in the general elections.

James I. Lengle, concentrating on the California primaries in 1968 and 1972, has done one of the most extensive analyses of presidential primary turnout and its political repercussions.[7] Lengle takes Key's premise about the unrepresentative character of the primaries as his fundamental point of departure. His theses are that turnout is always lower in the primaries than in general elections and that turnout is crucial to the representativeness of the primaries. His data show that turnout in the primaries suffers from an upper-middle-class bias, a tendency that has been well documented by other researchers as well. Race is another area of bias: blacks and other minority groups do not participate in primaries at nearly the level of whites. His argument is that the core groups who comprise the backbone of the Democratic party in the general election are significantly underrepresented in the primaries. In these regards Lengle's findings coincide with Ranney's.

Lengle's major contribution was to link turnout bias first to systematic biases in the ideological and issue-based composition of the primary electorate and then to biases in support for certain candidates and certain types of candidates. Specifically, in 1972 socioeconomic class was strongly related to ideological self-identification in the Democratic party: as socioeconomic status increased, liberalism increased among Democrats. In addition, in 1972 the more highly educated were much more strongly committed to ending the war in Vietnam, and they were more supportive of action on environmental issues. The less well educated Democrats were more concerned about social issues, such as drugs, crime, and taxes. About welfare spending there was a coalition of support at the top and bottom of the class scale, whereas the middle class was less supportive.

All of this ideological and issue-position distortion in the primary electorate leads inevitably to distortion in candidate support. Lengle shows that the upper socioeconomic status groups strongly supported George McGovern in the 1972 California primary, whereas the lower status groups overwhelmingly supported Hubert Humphrey. The skewed nature of participation that year was enough to enable McGovern to edge out Humphrey. In 1968 the same demographic bias worked in favor of Eugene McCarthy and against Robert Kennedy—although Kennedy overcame the bias and won in California anyway. The effects of the unrepresentativeness of the voters can be quite dramatic, as these cases show.

When he examined the data from the primaries in Wisconsin, Florida, Michigan, and Pennsylvania, Lengle found the same biases in turnout at work, and he concluded that the pattern of bias is related to the party's nominating behavior in the reform era. Lengle divides the

Democratic party into three major factions: the New Deal, the New Politics (represented by, for example, McGovern-McCarthy activists), and the southern factions. He contends that the rules and the nominating system of the prereform era tended to favor the party regulars, the New Deal faction. After 1968 Lengle sees a decided shift toward the New Politics and, to a lesser extent, the southern factions. This shift has been led by the increasing importance of the primaries. Lengle summarizes the permanent bias in the representation of the primaries and its association with various factions within the Democratic party as follows:

> In today's nomination system . . . the New Politics faction, its candidates, and its issue-concerns are advantaged, since the constituency to which these kinds of candidates and issues appeal is over-represented in presidential primary electorates. This over-representation . . . will be translated into an over-representation of delegates which, even if tied to several different New Politics candidacies, will magnify New Politics sentiment at the convention, in its credentials, rules, and platform committees and on the floor itself.[8]

If Lengle's rather serious charge is accurate, the unrepresentative factions in control of the Democratic party's nomination will tend to select candidates who are likely to be weak in the general election.

Another scholar, Herbert Kritzer, thoroughly examined the issue of the representativeness of the voters in the 1972 Democratic presidential primaries.[9] In general, Kritzer found very few ways in which the 1972 Democratic primary voters were different from party identifiers and general election voters. The primary voters did tend to be somewhat more likely to be union members and to identify themselves as liberals. He looked at positions on eight issues and found that primary voters were more liberal on only one of these, busing. Where there *were* differences the major variable was party identification: Kritzer found that the more strongly the person identified with the party, the more likely he or she was to vote in the Democratic presidential primary. Kritzer concluded that the Democratic primaries well represented the party rank and file on most issue positions and on party loyalty in 1972.

Needless to say, proponents of the presidential primaries have been pleased with the results of Kritzer's study and with his conclusion. Those who are more critical of the primaries rest their criticism partly on Lengle's work.[10] As in any scientific enterprise, different methods are likely to yield different results, and each new primary season is the occasion for a new study. Richard L. Rubin looked at the 1976 presidential primaries for both parties and at primary voting turnout over the period from 1912 to 1976.[11]

In essence, Rubin's 1976 findings for both parties tended to support Kritzer's 1972 findings for the Democrats. Rubin generally found few systematic differences between primary voters and general election voters. He did find that Democratic union members tended to vote in very high proportion in the Democratic primaries compared to non-union Democrats and to Republican or independent union members. These researchers have unearthed several findings relevant to our discussion. Rubin's summary about the increased importance of the primaries in presidential nominations is worth quoting at some length:

> Although the primaries themselves are in part responsible for weakening the parties, the primaries are not only a "cause" but also an "effect," produced in part by a powerful demand by the American people for more influence on the choice of the presidential nominee. As a result, the role of party leaders in shaping the two major choices presented to the American people has been greatly diminished in favor of rank-and-file influence through primary politics. It is still unclear whether the new combination of mass partisan participation and media influence will serve better or worse than the old combination of a few "proving ground" primaries coupled with "brokerage" by party elites.[12]

Before turning to our own consideration of the 1980 primaries, we will summarize the work of the other researchers here:

1. Most studies agree that the primary voters are likely to be unrepresentative in demographic characteristics, compared to the total electorate.[13] Specifically, the voters in the primaries are likely to be somewhat higher on the socioeconomic ladder than are party identifiers or the electorate as a whole.

2. There is some evidence that those who are strong partisans turn out for the primary vote at higher rates than the weak partisans or the independents.[14] This would constitute a partisan bias in favor of the most dedicated, loyal, and active elements of each party, and against the lukewarm partisans and independents.

3. There is mixed support for the proposition that those who turn out in the primaries are ideologically more extreme and take issue positions that are unrepresentative of the parties' mass bases and of the electorate as a whole.[15] In practice this means that the Democratic primary electorate can be expected to be more liberal and the Republican primary electorate more conservative than the general electorate.

New Research on the 1980 Primaries

In an effort to further develop our knowledge of the representativeness of primaries, a study of the 1980 primaries was done for this book. The proliferation of primaries peaked that year, with 33 states, the District of Columbia, and Puerto Rico holding them. Meanwhile, reaction was setting in. As we mentioned in Chapter 2, in the Democratic party at least, many felt that the party elites needed to be brought back into the nominating process in greater numbers—and that was done in 1984. In our research we were concerned with tracking the impact of the primaries and evaluating their role in the nominating system.

Our study is a secondary analysis of the national surveys done by the Center for Political Studies at the University of Michigan. In this section we examine only those respondents living in sampled states that held primaries in 1980. In those states we will look at those who voted in the primaries compared to those who did not vote in the primaries (whether or not they voted in the general election). Thus, the comparison is with the total voting age population in those sampled primary states.

Demographics. In the first analysis we examined the representativeness of those who voted in the primaries with regard to demographic characteristics and partisanship. On demographic characteristics we expected to find an upper-middle-class skewness to the primary electorate, as the earlier researchers had; our data confirmed the bias. For class characteristics we examined data on class identification, occupational prestige, income, and education. The trends demonstrated in the education-level data are typical (Table 4.1).

The table shows that there is a strong positive relationship between educational level and primary turnout. For example, only 32 percent of those without a high school diploma and only 31 percent of those with a high school diploma voted in the 1980 presidential primaries. Conversely, 55 percent of those with graduate and professional degrees and 55 percent of those with college degrees voted in the primaries. Clearly, the less well educated did not vote in the same proportion as the well

Table 4.1   Turnout in 1980 Primaries, by Education Level

Voted in primary?	12th grade or less	High school grad	Some college	College grad	Advanced degree
Yes	32%	31%	38%	55%	55%
No	68	69	62	45	45
N	(367)	(468)	(273)	(130)	(69)

$\chi^2 = 38.23$ $p < 0.001$

educated, which means that the primary voters were not representative on this variable.

In general the remainder of our data, which will not be reproduced here, show that as socioeconomic class increased, the propensity to vote in the primaries increased. This finding has become one of the most consistent generalizations in all of political science, and our study supports the results of other scholars, most notably Lengle and Key.

We looked next at the relationship between race and voting in the 1980 presidential primaries. If Lengle and Key are correct in their assumptions, we should find that minorities have lower rates of participation than non-Hispanic whites. It is obvious from Table 4.2 that our expectations were borne out. Of the sampled individuals 38 percent of those who were classified as white voted in the primaries compared to 30 percent of those who were black and none of those few sampled who were of Hispanic, native American, and other minority extraction. Whites voted out of proportion to their numbers, which adds a racial dimension to the demographic bias.

Party support. With regard to partisanship, our expectation was that those who had voted in the primaries would be more partisan than those who had not. As Table 4.3 shows, our expectations were handsomely supported. Fifty-one percent of those who claimed to be party supporters voted in the primaries, whereas only 28 percent of the nonsupporters said they voted in the primaries. On this indicator of partisanship, then, it is clear that primary voters are somewhat atypical of the total population.

Results are similar when several other indicators of partisanship are employed. For instance, the respondents were asked, using a seven-point scale, *how strongly* they supported their party—regardless of which party they supported. We found that 56 percent of those who claimed to support their party "very strongly" voted in the presidential primaries,

Table 4.2 Turnout in 1980 Primaries, by Race

Voted in primary?	White	Black	Hispanic, native American, other
Yes	38%	30%	0%
No	62	70	100
N	(1,134)	(166)	(9)

$\chi^2 = 9.24$ $p < 0.01$

Table 4.3 Turnout in 1980 Primaries, by Party Support

Voted in primary?	Party supporters	Party nonsupporters
Yes	51%	28%
No	49	72
N	(502)	(775)

$\chi^2 = 66.97$ $p < 0.001$

whereas only 22 percent of those who rated their party support as "not very strong" voted. Indeed, there is a clear progression from weak to strong partisanship: the stronger the support, the more likely a person was to vote in the primaries.

A similar progression was evident when the respondents were asked on a seven-point scale *how close* they felt either to the Republican or to the Democratic party. Sixty-six percent of those who said they felt "very close " to the Republican party also reported having voted in the 1980 presidential primaries; 56 percent of those who felt very close to the Democratic party were primary voters. These results provide some support for the idea that there were some interparty differences in 1980, with the Democrats being somewhat less likely to vote in the primaries than the Republicans. In a related vein, we found that of those who were independents in 1980 only 36 percent voted in the presidential primaries, leaving 64 percent who did not.

The data on partisanship add considerable support for the proposition that the 1980 presidential primary voters were unrepresentative of the general voting age population. As we had expected, they were considerably more likely to be the stronger partisans—a finding that reinforces Key's original work on this subject.

Ideology. The next important question about the representativeness of the primaries concerns the political values of those who participate in them. As we explained earlier in this chapter, Key's original premise was that those who were more ideologically committed were more likely to vote in the primaries. Lengle built much of his work around this thesis. However, other scholars, such as Ranney, Kritzer, and Rubin, have found only mixed support for the proposition. Accordingly, it is worth reexamining the matter using 1980 data.

Table 4.4 documents the relationship between the self-identified ideology of the respondents and their tendency to vote in presidential

Table 4.4 Turnout in the 1980 Primaries, by Ideological Self-Identification

Voted in primary?	Extremely liberal	Liberal	Slightly liberal	Moderate	Slightly conservative	Conservative	Extremely conservative
Yes	58%	53%	31%	41%	39%	45%	52%
No	42	47	69	59	61	55	48
N	(19)	(73)	(106)	(235)	(169)	(166)	(25)

$\chi^2 = 37.49$ $p < 0.001$

Note: The question was worded as follows: "We hear a lot of talk these days about liberals and conservatives. Here is a seven-point scale on which the political views that people might hold are arranged from extremely liberal to extremely conservative. Where would you place yourself on this scale, or haven't you thought much about this?"
Source: Data from Inter-University Consortium for Political and Social Research, American National Election Study, vol. 1: *Pre- and Post-Election Surveys,* 2d ed. (Ann Arbor, Mich., 1982), 150.

primaries. Our data show the highest likelihood of voting at the extreme ends of the ideological continuum. Fifty-eight percent of the "extreme liberals" said they voted in the primaries, followed by the "liberals" (53 percent). The next most likely group of voters were the "extreme conservatives" (52 percent), followed by the "conservatives" (45 percent). The three middle categories had the lowest proportion of primary voters. Consequently, we can conclude that there is clearly some association between ideology and turnout in the primaries.

Following this trail, we then looked at the issue stances of those who voted in the primaries as opposed to those who did not. Several major national issues were examined, including respondents' stances on (a) increasing or decreasing defense spending, (b) reducing government services in order to reduce spending, (c) reducing inflation versus reducing unemployment, (d) allowing or banning abortion, (e) approving Reagan's 30 percent tax cut, and (f) approving Carter's energy program. Out of this array of issues, only item (b) showed any systematic differences. In this case those who took the most conservative stance— those who were highly in favor of reducing government services in order to reduce spending—were the most likely to vote in the primaries.

Compared to our findings on ideology, our findings on the issue positions may seem somewhat anomalous. After all, the self-identified ideologues were more likely to vote than those who were not; however, these differences followed little pattern when specific issues were examined. Actually, scholars have recognized for some time now that the great mass of the American people do locate themselves somewhere on the ideological continuum without having a deeply held set of systematic political beliefs about specific issues. Some scholars have said the American people are "symbolic conservatives and operational liberals." [16] Perhaps it is not too surprising, then, to find a lack of systematic differences on issue positions.

From our study of the data presented here it appears that the 1980 primary voters were different from the general electorate in some important respects. They were more likely to be the party loyalists; they were more likely to fit themselves on the extreme ends of the ideological continuum; and they were not likely to be much different from nonvoters on the specific issues.

Implications of the Research

The empirical evidence gathered to date is rather strong on the demographic unrepresentativeness of the primary electorate. There is widespread agreement that the effective primary electorate is biased in favor of those from the upper and upper-middle socioeconomic classes. Thus groups with more economic resources are also likely to exert more political influence through the ballot box than groups without advantages. Although the evidence on ideological and issue-oriented unrepresentativeness has not been unambiguous, there does appear to be a bias toward the extreme ends of the ideological continuum. If the fervent ideologues can have more than their share of impact on the outcomes of the primaries, then the candidates who are likely to appeal to such voters (the conservatives among the Republicans and the liberals among the Democrats) are more likely to win disproportionately in the primaries. We would therefore posit an interaction of ideological candidates, delegate contestants (party activists, usually) who are attracted to them, and voters who select both in the primaries. This mixture, of course, would be expected to disadvantage the more moderate candidates, party activists, and voters.

From the findings of the research outlined in this chapter, we could project that the primary candidates who are most likely to be successful in appealing to the primary electorate would apply the following strategy:

Stress themes that will appeal to the most active and loyal partisans. (The evidence points to themes of shared party history and values for a Republican and various themes from the liberal tradition for a Democrat.)

Identify the candidate's image in terms of the ideological continuum (generally liberal for a Democrat and conservative for a
Republican).

Do not emphasize specific issue appeals. (Some specific issues may
work for some candidates in particular primaries. But issues are
the handmaidens of candidate image and position on the ideological spectrum.)[17]

These are some of the implications of the primaries for candidacies. Do
caucuses actually favor a different sort of candidate, as is widely
assumed?

Caucuses versus Primaries

In this section we examine the implications of using caucuses instead of
primaries as the method of delegate selection. Although the number of
caucuses declined between 1968 and 1980, they are still the means for selecting approximately 25 to 40 percent of the delegates to the national
conventions.

To begin with, we will assume that the delegates selected in the
caucuses are likely to support candidates different from those the
delegates selected in primaries will support. The differences stem from
the fact that caucus-selected delegates are more likely to be insiders in
terms of party history and service and delegates selected through
primaries are more likely to be toward the extremes of the political
contiuum. We will examine this assumption in light of the evidence on
the representativeness of caucus participants.

Thomas R. Marshall is a scholar who has devoted particular
attention to the matter of representativeness in the caucus states.[18] In
line with our earlier findings for the primaries, his study found that in
Minnesota in 1972 the upper socioeconomic classes tended to be
overrepresented among the caucus participants. We witness this result
consistently; apparently it is a characteristic of all forms of voluntary
political participation.

On the matter of ideological and issue representativeness, Marshall
found only very small differences between those who participated in
caucuses and party supporters in general who did not attend the
caucuses. The few differences were in the predicted direction—for
example, the Democratic caucus participants were somewhat more
liberal that the party supporters. How does the ideology relate to
candidate support?

Several of the critics of the 1972 reforms suggested that the McGovern forces had unfairly loaded the Minnesota caucuses with their supporters, a possibility that Marshall tested. His study showed only very modest differences between the caucus participants and party supporters in general, with the caucus participants slightly more inclined toward George McGovern than toward the state's favorite son, Hubert Humphrey. The differences, however, were not statistically significant. The study concluded that the caucuses were a fairly faithful representation of the party's mass base in the state, with the exception of the demographic differences. Countering the assumptions of supporters of primaries, Marshall contends that the caucuses are no less representative than the primaries demographically and ideologically. In addition, he feels caucuses have the edge because they can conduct other important matters of party business, such as debating the issues, identifying and encouraging potential new activists, and fostering relationships within the party.[19]

In all discussions of primaries versus caucuses, the most important question is whether the candidates favored by primaries are different from those favored by caucuses. Which system is most likely to support the choice of the party organization?

The *Congressional Quarterly Weekly Report* provided extensive data on the differences between delegates produced by the caucuses and those produced by the primaries in 1980.[20] In the Democratic race Carter was the incumbent, the choice of the party organization, and he won a far larger percentage of the delegates selected by the caucuses than Kennedy did (64 percent versus 25 percent). The challenger, Kennedy, did somewhat better in the primary states than he did in the caucus states. This result, of course, tends to confirm the premise that those in control of the reins of power at any one time are more likely to be favored by the caucus/convention method than by the primary method.

If there was a party establishment favorite in the Democratic nominations for 1984, it was Walter Mondale. He, for example, obtained far more endorsements from superdelegates who were members of Congress than did any other candidate. Gary Hart in 1984 played the role of challenger. The *Congressional Quarterly Weekly Report* found in 1984 that Mondale did much better in the caucus states than Hart did. Mondale also won more primary votes than Hart did, but here the margin was closer and Hart's strategy clearly depended on primary victories in states where large numbers of delegates were at stake.[21] That strategy ultimately failed, as did Hart's candidacy.

The story is more complicated for the Republicans in both 1976 and 1980. In 1976 Ronald Reagan, the challenger, got 55 percent of the caucus states' delegates in his nomination battle against Gerald Ford. Ford, however, did better than Reagan in the primaries and eventually won the nomination. Although Reagan lost the nomination in 1976, he did have the support of the powerful conservatives in the Republican party establishment; these inside connections would prove useful during Reagan's 1980 campaign. Reagan won heavily in both the primaries *and* the caucuses in 1980. He got 60 percent of the Republican primary vote, which translated into 78 percent of the primary states' delegates. He fared even better in the caucus states, capturing 83 percent of the caucus states' delegates and leaving George Bush far behind with only 8 percent. Thus, Reagan's appeal to the Republicans in 1980 cut across all segments of the party. Both the 1976 and the 1980 outcomes indicate that Reagan had long been very popular among those hard-core Republican party activists who attended the caucuses and conventions.[22] In 1980 Reagan was also very popular among the Republican rank and file who voted in primaries. (In 1984 there was, of course, no real contest for the Republican nomination; Reagan, being very popular within his party, was not challenged for renomination.)

There is not much doubt that the primaries are now the dominant arena of the presidential selection process, although the caucuses made some comeback in 1984. What is more problematic is the quality of the choices the parties have been offering to the American people in the presidential elections. Considerable controversy rages over the issue of whether caucuses do a better job of nomination as compared to the primaries.

Conclusion

We have begun to understand some of the patterns of participation and representativeness in the presidential nomination processes. As we have seen, different systems emphasize the participation, and presumably the influence, of different groups. But the issue remains of what types of participants are needed to ensure the most effective conduct of the democratic system.

As a result of the increased use of the primaries during the postreform era, there are now two rather distinct schools of thought on the number and significance of the primaries. We will call these the proreform school and the restoration school. The proreform school values the primaries as intrinsically important because of their ability to increase the participation levels of the rank-and-file voters while decreasing the power of the party leaders.[23] A leader of the turn-of-the-century primary movement, Sen. Robert La Follette, put the case for the primaries in the following words:

> No longer will there stand between the voter and the official a political machine with a complicated system of caucuses and conventions, by the manipulation of which it thwarts the will of the voter and rules of official conduct.[24]

According to this school, increased participation is an advantage to the political system: the mass voters are the best repository of the wisdom and good judgment needed to make the crucial collective choice of the major parties' nominees. In addition, the outcomes of the electoral processes and the government they produce are more legitimate because of the opportunity for participation offered to the mass public.

There are advantages to the voters as well. Reform proponents believe the voter learns, grows as an individual, and becomes a better citizen and member of society through the process of participation.[25] And the movement to open up the parties and the nomination process and to let more grass-roots voters participate is seen as a salutary response to the mass alienation and dissatisfaction with the political system endemic to the late 1960s and early 1970s. However alienated and distrustful the mass public is today, the situation could have been much worse if the political parties had not opened up their processes somewhat after the turmoil of 1968, and the pressures for significant changes are now much reduced compared to that earlier era, according to this view. This faith in the primaries generally reflects the faith in mass democracy that characterized the Progressive movement.

The restoration school of thought, the antireform view, is much more critical of the primaries, their use, their impact on the party organizations, and their impact on presidential politics since the reform era began.[26] This school would like to restore things as nearly as possible to the situation that existed during the prereform era. According to their view, a primary-dominant system, because primaries are more inclusive, is indiscriminate about who participates and careless about the consequences of the choices being made for the party and the nation. Caucus nominating systems, predominant throughout most of the old party period, include fewer people and magnify the importance of those closest to the parties—who, presumably, are more concerned with the party's long-run well-being. Without question, the postreform era has witnessed a dramatic increase in the participation of blacks and women and a corresponding decline in the influence of party officials and officeholders.

The antireformers argue that there has been a shift in power over nominations, particularly among the Democratic party electorate, and that the changes are detrimental to the nation. Jeane Kirkpatrick has been perhaps the most outspoken proponent of this point of view. Her argument is that the party reforms have been forced by a new group of antiparty activists and are therefore ineffective:

> The persistence of the American party system through the last century of rapid, unprecedented social, cultural, and economic transformation testifies to the parties' strength. In the past decade ... they have also had to conform to new rules whose goal is to make parties reflect the desired balance of power, not the actual strength of actual social groups.... The effort to make institutions conform to abstract principles is the very essence of the "rationalist" approach to politics ... [which] assumes that institutions and people are more malleable than they are, and that the reformers are more prescient than they are.[27]

Kirkpatrick feels that a dangerous new class has come to be the dominant force in nominations: issue-oriented, personally involved, active, middle-class citizens. Along the same lines, Austin Ranney has charged that the Democratic selection rules "were consciously designed to maximize participation by persons who are enthusiasts for a particular aspirant *in the year of the convention*." [28]

These new political elites have replaced the party regulars, labor leaders, and others who were conscious of their responsibility to represent broader constituencies and who had to be accountable to their organizations. In contrast to those they have replaced, Kirkpatrick charges, the new breed has no interest in the health of the parties: they do not rely on party support for their motivation; they do not wish to preserve the party organization; they are more committed to an ideology than to a party; they do not represent the traditional geographical constituencies; and they are "symbol specialists" who place ideological goals over traditional values.

The restoration school would like to restrengthen the hand of the political party organizational elites and to bolster the role played by the professional politicians in the nomination process. The restorationists believe that the party elites, who dominate caucuses and conventions, can make the most rational calculations of both party and public interest, balance the competing group demands, and pick the nominees who are likely to have the greatest potential for successful leadership. In contrast, such mass participation devices as the direct primaries are considered unwise because they are likely to be dominated by issue-oriented, candidate-oriented, and ideological extremists who want to win their positions at all costs. Worse still, these essentially unrepresentative people are likely to choose nominees who are bad for the political parties, who prove to be unattractive to the mass public in the general election, and who cannot govern if they do happen to get elected.

According to this view, the best of mass democracy is likely to result from spirited competition between the two major parties and not necessarily from the intrusion of greater mass participation into the internal business of the political parties. Thus, what strengthens the political parties ultimately strengthens democracy.

There are no definitive answers to these controversies. Trade-offs must be made in adopting either position. There are some advantages to mass participation and there are some advantages to elite-dominant decision making in the nominating process. The American solution is often to compromise, in this matter by trying to capture the best of both processes to create the mixed nominating system we have today.

NOTES

1. William Crotty, "Two Cheers for the Presidential Primaries," in *Rethinking the Presidency,* ed. Thomas E. Cronin (Boston: Little, Brown, 1982), 67-68.
2. Austin Ranney, *Participation in American Presidential Nominations, 1976* (Washington, D.C.: American Enterprise Institute, 1977), 24.
3. Ibid., 25.
4. For other discussions of the various stages in the evolution of the nominating system see: James W. Ceaser, *Presidential Selection: Theory and Development* (Princeton, N.J.: Princeton University Press, 1979); Austin Ranney, *Curing the Mischiefs of Faction: Party Reform in America* (Berkeley: University of California Press, 1975); and Thomas R. Marshall, *Presidential Nominations in a Reform Age* (New York: Praeger, 1981). Marshall refers to the nominating system produced by the reforms as "the system of popular appeal."
5. V. O. Key, Jr., *American State Politics: An Introduction* (New York: Knopf, 1956), 153.
6. Ranney, *Participation in American Presidential Nominations;* Austin Ranney and Leon D. Epstein, "The Two Electorates: Voters and Nonvoters in a Wisconsin Primary," *Journal of Politics* 28 (August 1966): 598-617; Austin Ranney, "The Representativeness of Primary Electorates," *Midwest Journal of Political Science* 12 (May 1968): 224-238; Austin Ranney, "Turnout and Representation in Presidential Primary Elections," *American Political Science Review* 66 (March 1972): 21-37.
7. See James I. Lengle, *Representation and Presidential Primaries: The Democratic Party in the Post Reform Era* (Westport, Conn.: Greenwood Press, 1981). Lengle compared primary voters to the pool of party identifiers, whereas other studies have compared primary voters to primary nonvoters. His major data set was provided by the respected Field Poll in California. This was supplemented by *New York Times-Time* magazine poll data for 1972 on the primaries in Wisconsin, Florida, Michigan, and Pennsylvania for confirmation of the California results. Thus his data may not be applicable to the

nation as a whole and may also be limited by the particular election years studied; however, his basic thesis is an important one.

8. Lengle, *Representation and Presidential Primaries*, 78.

9. Herbert Kritzer, "Representativeness of the 1972 Presidential Primaries," in *The Party Symbol: Readings on Political Parties*, ed. William Crotty (San Francisco: W. H. Freeman, 1980), 148-154. Kritzer used data drawn from the 1972 national survey of the Center for Political Studies. (Since Kritzer used a national sample, we would not expect him to produce the same findings as Lengle, who used a more restricted data base.)

10. For example, see Nelson W. Polsby, *The Consequences of Party Reform* (New York: Oxford University Press, 1983), 159-160.

11. Richard L. Rubin, "Presidential Primaries: Continuities, Dimensions of Change, and Political Implications," in *The Party Symbol*, ed. William Crotty (San Francisco: W. H. Freeman, 1980), 126-147.

12. Ibid., 143.

13. This finding is supported by Ranney and Epstein for the Wisconsin gubernatorial primary of 1964 ("The Two Electorates"); Ranney for the Wisconsin gubernatorial primary of 1966 ("The Representativeness of Primary Electorates); Ranney on the Wisconsin and New Hampshire presidential primaries of 1968 ("Turnout and Representation in Primary Elections"); and Lengle on the California primaries of 1968 and 1972 (*Representation and Presidential Primaries*).

14. Ranney and Epstein found mixed support for this proposition in the Wisconsin gubernatorial primary of 1964; Ranney again found mixed support for the 1968 Wisconsin and New Hampshire presidential primaries. Lengle, on the other hand, found that "traditional Democratic party support groups, i.e., blacks, lower education and income groups, etc. were disproportionately unrepresented in the 1968 and 1972 California primaries," although he was answering a slightly different question (*Representation and Presidential Primaries*).

15. Ranney and Epstein rejected this proposition for the 1964 Wisconsin gubernatorial primary. Ranney reported weak issue differences for the 1966 Wisconsin gubernatorial voters and nonvoters. Ranney's study on the Wisconsin and New Hampshire presidential primaries of 1968 found mixed support for this proposition. Kritzer found the Democratic presidential primary voter of 1972 to be slightly more liberal than the nonvoter. Again, Lengle, using a slightly different methodology, found strong support for the proposition in the 1968 and 1972 California primaries and in the 1972 primaries in the other four states he studied. Rubin found only limited support for this proposition for the 1976 primaries.

16. See Everett Carll Ladd, *Where Have All the Voters Gone? The Fracturing of America's Political Parties*, 2d ed. (New York: W. W. Norton, 1982).

17. For discussions of campaign strategies see: Nelson W. Polsby and Aaron Wildavsky, *Presidential Elections: Strategies of American Electoral Politics*, 5th ed. (New York: Charles Scribner's Sons, 1980); John Kessel, *Presidential Campaign Politics: Coalition Strategies and Citizen Response* (Homewood, Ill.: Dorsey Press, 1980); Benjamin I. Page, *Choices and Echoes in Presidential Elections: Rational Man and Electoral Democracy* (Chicago: University of Chicago Press, 1978); Herbert Asher, *Presidential Elections and American Politics* (Homewood, Ill.: Dorsey Press, 1980).

18. Thomas R. Marshall, "Turnout and Representation: Caucuses versus Primaries," *American Journal of Political Science* 22 (February 1978): 169-182; Thomas R. Marshall, "Delegate Selection in Nonprimary States: The Question of Representation," *National Civic Review* 65 (September 1976): 390-393; Marshall, *Presidential Nominations in a Reform Age*, 118-120.
19. Marshall, "Delegate Selection in Nonprimary States," 393.
20. "Carter, Reagan Exhibit Similar Assets in Preference Primaries," *Congressional Quarterly Weekly Report*, July 5, 1980, 1870-1875.
21. For the details on the 1984 primaries see *Congressional Quarterly Weekly Report*, especially the following articles: "Mondale Wins Big among House Delegates," January 28, 1984, 132; "Democratic Rules Help Pad Mondale Lead," April 21, 1984, 910-911; "Ohio, Indiana Wins Revive Hart Candidacy," May 12, 1984, 1083-1085; "Hart Cuts Mondale Lead in Total Primary Vote," May 19, 1984, 1179-1182.
22. John S. Jackson III, Barbara L. Brown, and David Bositis, "Herbert McClosky and Friends Revisited," *American Politics Quarterly* 10 (April 1982): 158-180.
23. For discussions by authors who have been supportive of the reforms see: William Crotty, *Decision for the Democrats: Reforming the Party Structure* (Baltimore: Johns Hopkins University Press, 1978); William Crotty, *Political Reform and the American Experiment* (New York: Thomas Y. Crowell, 1977); William Crotty, *Party Reform* (New York: Longman, 1983); Kenneth A. Bode and Carol F. Casey, "Party Reform: Revisionism Revisited," in *Political Parties in the Eighties*, ed. Robert A. Goldwin (Washington, D.C.: American Enterprise Institute, 1980), 3-19. Fred Harris, who is now a professor of political science at the University of New Mexico, and who, as former chairman of the Democratic National Committee, appointed the original McGovern-Fraser Commission, has also supported the reforms.
24. Austin Ranney, *Curing the Mischiefs of Faction*, 124.
25. See Carole Pateman, *Participation and Democratic Theory* (Cambridge: Cambridge University Press, 1970).
26. We would include the following works under the restoration school as samples of the more notable criticisms of the reform era and its consequences: Polsby, *The Consequences of Party Reform*; Lengle, *Representation and Presidential Primaries*; Jeane J. Kirkpatrick, *Dismantling the Parties: Reflections on Party Reform and Party Decomposition* (Washington, D.C.: American Enterprise Institute, 1978); Ceaser, *Presidential Selection*; James W. Ceaser, *Reforming the Reforms: A Critical Analysis of the Presidential Selection Process* (Cambridge, Mass.: Ballinger, 1982).
27. Jeane J. Kirkpatrick, *The New Presidential Elite* (New York: Russell Sage Foundation, 1976), 241.
28. Ranney, *Curing the Mischiefs of Faction*, 153.

A Profile of the National Convention Delegates

5

The delegates to the national conventions are the major products of the primary and caucus season; they nominate the candidates and engage in all convention deliberations. We will now focus on these national convention delegates, their personal characteristics, political backgrounds, and motives for this high-level party service. In addition, we will examine their political attitudes, policy views, and ideological positions. Our profile covers delegates from 1968 through 1984, from the prereform era through the reform and postreform eras, so that we can assess how the characteristics of national convention delegates changed during that important period in presidential politics. The goal of this inquiry is to understand the relationship between the types of delegates at the conventions and the very important decision they make in choosing the Democratic and Republican presidential nominees.

Because the national conventions are in a sense legislative bodies, as we will show in more detail in Chapter 8, we are concerned here with issues of *representation* as well as with *representativeness*. That is, whom do the delegates represent and in what manner? The issue goes to the heart of the party debate we have been referring to throughout the book. Three basic perspectives on the possible constituencies emerge from the literature on the subject.

1. Convention delegates should represent the leadership and most active elements of the parties. Proponents of this perspective include those who believe in a strong party organization that rewards party loyalty, as did the party regulars who dominated the prereform or old party system before 1968. Others in this

camp include many of the academics we identified in Chapter 2 as advocates of the restoration movement. Strong supporters of the caucus selection system tend to hold this view as well.

2. Convention delegates should represent those who identify themselves as party members, that is, the parties' rank and file. Those who are willing to have primaries play a significant role in the nominating system but who prefer closed primaries would adopt this view on the question of representation.

3. Convention delegates should represent the U.S. mass public. Reformers have often held this view, and certain factions in the parties and the general public continue to express it. Those who are the strongest supporters of primaries in general and of open primaries in particular espouse this view.

Party rules can be changed to favor one of these constituencies at the expense of others. As we saw in Chapter 4, different selection systems attract somewhat different kinds of voters and favor somewhat different kinds of candidates; likewise, different types of delegates may result from primaries as compared with caucuses.

To understand who best represents each of the three groups, we must consider the nature of the representation. Do delegates cast their votes as individuals, according to their own beliefs and characteristics? Or do they put aside their own personalities and interests in favor of their constituents? Quite apart from what the delegates do is the question of what they *should* do to represent their constituencies, that is, there are both empirical and normative arguments here.

The Theory of Representation

Hanna F. Pitkin is the leading theoretician on representation. She has analyzed in great detail the various definitions and dimensions of representation employed by political observers over several centuries.[1] We will adopt Pitkin's terminology to capture two important components of representation.

Pitkin calls her first theory of representation *descriptive,* or *Standing For.* According to this theory, a legislative body should mirror the composition of the constituency. Descriptive representation has an objective dimension and a subjective dimension, which need not coincide.

In its plainest form, the objective dimension of descriptive representation is a reflection of demographic characteristics of the constituency.

For example, some believe that blacks best represent blacks, women best represent women, and so on. Many people feel that this objective form of descriptive representation is important to those groups, both symbolically and substantively, as a necessary step in their drive to attain recognition of their political claims and to gain political power. This theory is behind affirmative action and racial and sexual quotas. And Democratic party reform has been based in part on the same notion.

The subjective dimension of descriptive representation relates to the political attitudes and values of the representative. Under this concept liberals would be represented by liberal legislators, conservatives by conservatives, and so on. Of course, this kind of Standing For is much more difficult to arrange through formal rules. Color, sex, or age are easy to identify and correlate, whereas attitudes and values are not. Nevertheless, although among its proponents the goal may remain implicit, the subjective dimension is an important aspect of representation.

The second major theory of representation Pitkin refers to as the *Acting For* theory. The emphasis here is on what the representative *does* in the decision-making context, not on who the legislator is or on what characteristics are shared with the constituents. The representative acts on behalf of or as the agent of the constituency. The representative is also to be held accountable for his or her actions. Pitkin says, "Accordingly only this concept supplies us with standards for judging the representative's action, for deciding whether he has represented well or ill (as distinct from whether he is a good likeness, a typical man)." [2]

In the context of presidential nominating conventions, the two theories of representation have practical implications. Those who favor Standing For representation believe that the conventions should function as faithful reflections of their constituencies (which they would define as either the party identifiers or the public as a whole). Presumably the delegates, who would be demographically representative, would ratify the vote of the primaries (the primary being the most appropriate process in this view). The success of the convention itself is judged by what the delegates are like demographically. Candidates—usually Democrats—who are outsiders in some sense often argue along these lines, as did Jesse Jackson in 1984.

Most of those who favor a strong party organization are proponents of Acting For representation in the conventions. In this view delegates should be free to exercise independent judgment; the conventions should be bargaining and decision-making bodies. No matter what the delegates are like, the success of a convention is evaluated by its actions and outcomes. Proponents of this sort of convention see the constituency as party members—either the entire base or the most active elements—and the caucuses as the most effective delegate selection process. Party insiders tend to favor this view.

The current nominating system strikes a balance between the Standing For and Acting For approaches that is typical of the mixed nominating system described earlier. Party rules and processes can be made to favor one sort of representation or the other, but there is no general agreement on which approach works best in terms of preparation for the general election. Since there is no consensus, we find elements of all three approaches to the role of delegates to the conventions in the party rules and in the delegations themselves.

The focus of this chapter is for the most part on the demographic and attitudinal characteristics of the delegates, with a view toward evaluating how *representative* they are. We are not now evaluating the actions of the convention as a decision-making body, a subject we will return to in Chapter 8. We can, however, offer empirical data describing the delegates and evaluate how well they represent their constituencies, including their party's mass base, their party's elected leadership, and the American public.

The Representativeness of the Delegates

Demographic Representativeness

Convention delegates are not just a slice of Americana. They are not like the respondents to a Gallup Poll or Harris Survey, chosen in a random process designed to provide a representative cross section of the American public. They are chosen in political processes that recognize political clout or resources and that reward party service and fidelity to a candidate. Not surprisingly, then, the convention delegates are political elites and share many of the characteristics of other political elites. Nevertheless, some selection systems may lead to more elitism than others and some eras have been marked by more elitism than others.

The original, landmark study of national convention delegates was conducted by Paul T. David and his associates. Published in 1960, the study concentrated on the era between 1948 and 1956.[3] Relying on their data, Frank Sorauf later provided the following description of a typical group of delegates:

> They are as a group overwhelmingly white and male—about 90 percent male and 98 percent white in the 1952 conventions. They are Protestant, although less dominantly so within the Democratic Party. They are, furthermore, well-educated and well-off. A large percentage are

lawyers (over 35 percent in 1948) and either public officials or high ranking party officials. As a group they appear to be representative of activists in the two parties.[4]

This is a thumbnail sketch of the convention delegates in the prereform era, a sketch that would probably be accurate all the way back to the first national conventions, in 1831-1832. Clearly, the delegates were not representative of the parties' bases, much less of the general public. But until the 1964 Democratic National Convention there was little questioning of the demographic makeup of conventions. By 1968 enough political pressure had come to bear on the problem of the unrepresentativeness of the national convention delegates to force the party to take action.

At the 1968 convention the Democratic party established the McGovern-Fraser Commission (Chapter 2). After conducting its study of the delegate selection process, the McGovern-Fraser Commission found much to deplore about the operation and consequences of that process. One of the commission's major complaints was with the unrepresentativeness of the national convention delegates. The commission established new rules and guidelines, which were in part designed to increase the representativeness of the delegates, most notably in a demographic sense. Successive commissions have continued to address the demographic issue, with varying results, as we will see.

Sex, Race, and Age. Party procedures have dealt most readily with the most visible aspects of demographics: sex, race, and age. Table 5.1 gives the composition of the convention delegations in both parties with regard to these characteristics. We will refer to this table throughout the following paragraphs.

The history of the Democrats' rules regarding women is particularly instructive. The McGovern-Fraser rules required only that women (along with blacks and young people) should receive delegate status "in reasonable relationship to their presence in the population of the state," that is, in comparison to the mass public (as opposed to the party base).[5] Although the language is ambiguous, this requirement was widely interpreted as mandating quotas for 1972, and the data do show a significant shift—from 13 percent female in 1968 to 40 percent female in 1972.

As reaction against the McGovern-Fraser guidelines set in after 1972, the Mikulski Commission changed the rules for 1976. The Mikulski rules continued to provide for affirmative action for minority groups and women in the delegate selection process, but did away with quotas. There were indeed some reductions in the percentages of female (and

Table 5.1 Sex, Race, and Age Composition of National Conventions, 1968-1984

	1968		1972		1976		1980		1984	
	D	R	D	R	D	R	D	R	D	R
Female	13%	16%	40%	29%	33%	31%	49%	29%	50%	44%
Black	5	2	15	4	11	3	15	3	18	3
Under 30	3	4	22	8	15	7	11	5	8	*
Median age (in years)	(49)	(49)	(42)	*	(43)	(48)	(44)	(49)	*	*

* Data not available.

Source: CBS News-*New York Times* poll data. See Warren J. Mitofsky and Martin Plissner, "The Making of the Delegates, 1968-1980," *Public Opinion* (October/November 1980): 43, for 1968-1980 data. Data for 1984 Democratic delegates taken from CBS News-*New York Times* survey of 1,561 of the 3,944 delegates; see *New York Times*, July 15, 1984, 26. Data on the 1984 Republican delegates supplied by the Republican National Committee; see *New York Times*, August 21, 1984, 1.

black) delegates at the 1976 convention. Then in the 1976 to 1980 interim, the Winograd Commission reinstated a quota, specifically, 50 percent for female delegates to the national convention. (Actually, the new rule was first incorporated into the procedures for the 1978 Democratic Mid-Term Conference in Memphis.) In 1980 the Democrats nearly realized their demographic objective with respect to women, reaching 49 percent at the convention (women make up 52 percent of the U.S. population). By the 1984 convention the 50 percent mark for women delegates was precisely achieved through the demands of the national party rules.

The matter of black delegate percentages also illustrates a larger point about representation. Black delegates comprised approximately 5 percent of the total delegate population in 1968. With the McGovern-Fraser guidelines, blacks gained a good many more convention delegates, achieving 15 percent of the delegate slots in 1972. Black percentages continued to parallel women's in 1976 and 1980, even though the Democratic party's rules have stood by affirmative action, not quotas, for minorities. The year 1984 was a particularly strong one for black representation because of the candidacy of Jesse Jackson. At the end of the primary season Jackson's delegate count stood at 375, or almost 10 percent of the total, and a large percentage of Jackson's delegates were black. Mondale had a sizable contingent of black delegates in at the 1984 convention as well. Overall, 1984 represented a high-water mark for black convention delegates: 18 percent of the delegates were black. In fact, black representation at the Democratic convention has exceeded the goal of matching the population as a whole, which is now about 12 percent black. However, since that party claims the loyalty of the vast majority of black voters, many black groups have argued that the proportion of black delegates should reflect the party's demographics rather than the nation's.[6] So far, the Democratic party has not definitively answered the crucial question of who should be represented.

Young people (under 30) were also one of the original target populations of the McGovern-Fraser rules. This concern for adequate representation for young people grew out of the 1968 Democratic convention experience and the Vietnam War protests. It may also have reflected a recognition of the need to ensure the future of the party in the loyalties of the young. Youth were not well represented at the 1968 national convention (Table 5.1) in comparison to their position in the national electorate, roughly 30 percent. Under the impetus of the Democrats' rules, the convention participation of young people increased dramatically in 1972. After 1972, however, both concern over representation for young people and the number of younger delegates at the national convention declined. In spite of some modest action by the youth caucus at the 1972 convention, young people in general are not a coherent group with shared long-term interests. In comparison to either blacks or women, young people have simply failed to develop any lasting organizational bases for sustained political action. Of course, each election year finds a new group of young people, since no one remains under 30 forever (as many former youth activists have discovered). By contrast, the membership of the black and women's caucuses is not constantly changing, and these groups can develop more durable organizations.

Several lessons can be drawn from these data. First, within the Democratic party, the percentage of black and female delegates has changed dramatically over the last four conventions; the radical change from 1968 to 1972 was apparently a direct result of party reform. Second, it has now become evident that a national party can adopt national rules that will realize some limited objectives rather efficiently; the rules can be set up to direct substantial changes in the delegate selection process, as we see in comparing the data for the 1972 and 1980 conventions, when strict guidelines were employed, with the data for 1976, when looser rules were used.

The book on demographic representation among the Republicans is somewhat different. As the data in Table 5.1 indicate, the face, if not the color, of the Republican convention changed over the 16 years between

1968 and 1984. Female delegates comprised 16 percent of the 1968 Republican convention, and their numbers ranged from 29 to 31 percent until the 1984 convention. In that year the Reagan campaign, in an effort to narrow the "gender gap," put pressure on the states to voluntarily send more women to the national convention. The strategy worked, and 44 percent of the 1984 delegates were women. In contrast, black delegates comprised only 2 percent of the 1968 GOP gathering, and the range in years since has been 3 to 4 percent. (The low figure of black representation should be viewed in light of the facts that only 5 to 10 percent of black voters have supported the Republican presidential nominee in recent years and that only a very small percentage of registered Republicans are black.)

The Republicans have never worried much about providing representation for young people at the party conventions, except in the most theoretical sense of being concerned about the party's long-term prospects for survival. The Republicans have provided a fairly consistent level of youth representation, generally in the range of 4 to 8 percent (Table 5.1). As in the Democratic party, there is simply no organized constituency supporting a special emphasis on youth within the GOP.

Not coincidentally, the debate over demographic representation within the Republican party has not approached the intensity of the debate among the Democrats. Nevertheless, questions of demographic representation have arisen, particularly in the form of attempts to broaden the party's base, which we discussed in Chapter 2. Because of their view of the role of the national party, the Republicans have not emphasized the substantive rules changes nearly so markedly as have the Democrats. The Republican rules commissions (Chapter 2) issued reports that were only advisory. Although these reports sometimes used language reminiscent of the Democrats' McGovern-Fraser Commission with respect to achieving female and minority representation, the Republicans have not developed a body of national party law that would even remotely suggest quotas. It would seem that such change as the GOP has achieved in this regard is partly the result of internal party pressures and partly the result of a spillover effect from the Democrats.

In fairness to the Republican party, we should point out that it may well be foolish to tamper with success. After all, the 1968-1980 era has produced three Republican presidential victories and one narrow loss. And with a Republican victory in 1984, the party will have controlled the White House for 16 out of the 20 years between 1968 and 1988. Ironically, either marked success or marked failure could upset the GOP's satisfaction with the status quo. Marked Republican success could cause the party to expand and become attractive as a home for more heterogeneous groups. If the party were to become a majority or near-majority party, its size and diversity alone would undoubtedly breed intensified pressures for more heterogeneous representation among the party's elite groups.

By the same token, failure breeds soul-searching and the quest for alternatives, for broadening the base and for new formulas to lead the party out of the political wilderness. Such failure might also lead the Republicans to be more mindful of the Democrats' model and to be more sympathetic to adopting the opposition's methods.

Meanwhile, although expanded representation could pay symbolic as well as substantive dividends in the long run, for the GOP the symbolic gains to be achieved by increased demographic representation have just not been worth the risk of some substantive trade-offs that they feared could be the purchase price.

Class. Whatever the racial and sexual heterogeneity achieved among the Democrats, and to a lesser extent among the Republicans, in the 1968-1984 era, the socioeconomic makeup of the conventions remained pretty well unchanged. Delegates have continued to come predominantly from the upper socioeconomic classes, as Table 5.2 demonstrates in regard to education and occupation among the Democratic delegates. (While exactly comparable GOP data are not available, other studies clearly show that the Republican delegates are even more of an elite group than are the Democrats.) Warren J. Mitofsky and Martin Plissner report that the average Republican delegate's income in 1980 was $47,000 a year, well above the Democrats' average of $37,000 per year in 1980.[7] Compared to the party's mass base or to the population as a whole, the delegates fit into higher socioeconomic categories.

The perpetuation of class bias among the convention delegates is not difficult to understand. Becoming a delegate takes time, money, and political connections. Delegate status is a much sought-after political prize; for many delegates it is a high point in their political careers. Delegates must campaign on behalf of a candidate and be endorsed by the candidates. They must have enough understanding of the party and state rules to make their way through a complex nomination process. Usually they must pay their own way to the convention. Members of lower socioeconomic status groups ordinarily do not have sufficient personal and political resources to pursue a seat at the national convention.[8]

The inequality has not gone unnoticed. In spite of some early concern with the matter, Democratic party reform commissions found themselves unable to agree on how to structure the rules to favor groups

Table 5.2 Occupational and Educational Characteristics of Democratic National Convention Delegates, 1968-1980

	1968	1972	1976	1980
Occupation				
Technical, professional, managerial	—	64%	62%	74%
Clerk and sales	—	11	15	6
Craftsmen and operatives	—	4	1	3
Service	—	1	1	2
Laborer	—	0	4	0
Farm	—	1	1	2
Retired	—	0	2	4
Housewife	—	13	9	5
Student/unemployed	—	7	5	4
N		(2,623)	(499)	(497)
Education				
High school graduate or less	18%	17%	10%	12%
Some college	19	27	19	22
College graduate or study beyond college	19	27	30	31
Professional or graduate degree	44	29	41	45
N	(2,359)	(2,641)	(511)	(497)

Note: Occupational data for 1968 not available.

Source: Educational data for 1968 based on CBS News, *Campaign '68: Democratic National Convention,* 143-144. Data for 1972 based on Jeane J. Kirkpatrick, *The New Presidential Elite* (New York: Russell Sage Foundation, 1976). Data for 1976 and 1980 based on surveys by John S. Jackson III.

with lower socioeconomic status. By 1980 the Democrats had became acutely conscious of the class bias among their delegations and very concerned over the inability of the party rules to resolve this bias. Under pressure from the Association of Community Organizations for Reform Now (ACORN) the convention that year created a new study commission charged with exploring ways to diversify the party's socioeconomic composition for the 1984 national convention and throughout the party. In introducing the report from the rules committee, Peter Kelly of California said, "Since the founding of this great political party, it has been the poor people, the working poor, and the low and moderate income Americans who have been the backbone of this party and without whom the Democratic Party does not win elections." [9] In this succinct quote we find both the idealism and the pragmatism involved in trying to achieve adequate representation for powerless groups. Resource deficits, beyond cost alone, suffered by the poor and working classes are long-term, structural obstacles to their joining political elite groups in achieving fair representation in party affairs.

The data for 1984 indicate that the Democrats did not succeed in creating more economic diversity in the convention that year. A *Washington Post*-ABC News survey disclosed that only 11 percent of the 1984 delegates had annual incomes under $20,000, whereas 42 percent had annual incomes above $50,000. Indeed, the 1984 delegates were more affluent and better educated than the 1980 delegates had been.[10] The goal of creating economic diversity in the Democratic conventions has proved to be an elusive one not easily addressed by the national rules.

We can generalize to some extent about demographic changes as a result of party reform: to some extent white, male, upper-middle-class political elites were replaced with black or female upper-middle-class political elites. The parties are aware of the demographic realities, and they have made decisions on the basis of their most important political goals for representativeness.

The Representation of Party and Public Officials

Being selected to run as a delegate has traditionally been considered a reward for party service. In the prereform system, the old party system, professional politicians at all levels dominated the delegate slates. And as we have just discussed, virtually all convention delegates are political elites, a condition that has not changed with reform. But recent conventions have witnessed a steady decline in the participation of party and elective officials, as Table 5.3 shows for the years 1972-1980. In both parties the proportion of public office holders declined over 12 years by about 15 percent, to 25 percent of the delegates. Even more dramatic, the proportion of party officials declined by almost 20 percent in the Democratic party and over 30 percent in the Republican party. Without question the party and elective officials as a group have lost representation at the conventions of both parties. This change is in part a result of rules adopted during that period banning ex officio delegates.

Reform commissions were aware of the domination of party officials at the conventions, and the rules reforms were instrumental in changing the makeup of the conventions. By 1980 the question of upper-level party representation had come to the fore as an issue of contro-

Table 5.3 Public and Party Officials at National Conventions, 1972-
1980

	1972		1976		1980	
	D	R	D	R	D	R
Public office holders	39%	40%	33%	*	25%	25%
Party office holders	72	92	63	*	50	60

* Data not available.

Source: Data for 1972 from Jeane J. Kirkpatrick, *The New Presidential Elite* (New York: Russell Sage Foundation, 1976), 6, 10-11. Data for 1976 and 1980 assembled from CBS News-*New York Times* polls and the surveys of John S. Jackson III. See Warren J. Mitofsky and Martin Plissner, "The Making of the Delegates, 1968-1980," *Public Opinion* (October/November 1980): 42-43.

versy, as the party organizations worried about their loss of influence in the nomination process. The most intense debate centered on the role of high-level elected officials in the conventions. Table 5.4, which includes governors and members of Congress in both parties, shows the changes from 1968 to 1980. The data change to some extent from election year to election year, but a few long-range trends have emerged. Among Republicans the number of governors attending conventions showed a sharp decline between 1968 and 1976. The number of senators attending the Republican party's national convention has remained about constant and actually increased in 1980, while the number of House members increased in 1976 and 1980. Among Democrats the number of members of Congress who were delegates fell drastically. The most substantial change occurred from 1968 to 1972, which correlates with the influence of party reform in other areas we have examined.

What has discouraged these officeholders from participating in the conventions? The system has changed with the reforms. First, all delegates in the Democratic party had to be elected, most often directly by party members participating in the caucuses. Many elected officials chose not to present themselves to the party electorates for fear of a rejection that could do little to help their political careers. Second, the reforms forced more delegates to be committed to and approved by a presidential candidate when they announced themselves for a state's primary or caucus. Being publicly committed to a candidate could cause problems at the local and national levels for a member of Congress or governor. Then at the convention most delegates were obligated to vote for the candidate they were pledged to; public and party officials lost the brokering role they played in the old party system.

Table 5.4 High-Level Elected Officials at National Conventions, 1968-1980

	1968		1972		1976		1980	
	D	R	D	R	D	R	D	R
Governors *(N)*	(23)	(24)	(17)	(16)	(16)	(9)	(23)	(13)
Senators *(N)*	(39)	(21)	(15)	(22)	(11)	(22)	(8)	(26)
Representatives *(N)*	(78)	(58)	(31)	(33)	(41)	(52)	(37)	(64)
Total	(140)	(103)	(63)	(71)	(88)	(83)	(68)	(103)

Source: Data assembled from CBS News-*New York Times* surveys.

The Democratic party's Hunt Commission, established at the 1980 convention, recommended the provision of automatic delegate status for a significant number of high-level party and public officials. Some 14 percent of the delegate slots at the 1984 Democratic convention were set aside for governors, members of Congress, and state party chairs—in a sense, this rule established a quota like the quota for women. These have been dubbed the "superdelegates." Critics have complained about the granting of automatic status to a large number of public and party officials who also have the added advantage of remaining uncommitted during the primary season.

Supporters, which included most of the members of the Hunt Commission and the Democratic National Committee, contended that this infusion of political experience would allow for more peer review of potential presidential candidates. In this view, the superdelegates would be in a position to judge the candidates according to their governing experience in Washington and the states; they would have a more realistic view of the candidate's leadership potential. The supporters also argued that the inclusion of these officials in the conventions, with a large role in the decision making, would pay dividends in the nominee's ability to govern should he or she be elected president. According to this view, if members of Congress are consulted by the party through the nominating and platform-writing processes, they can be a moderating influence on the results of the convention and they can be expected to support the president and his program. Of course, whether future Democratic administrations actually will benefit from the involvement of these high-level party and elected officials remains to be seen.

The experience of the 1984 national convention indicates that the superdelegates were a moderating and pragmatic influence in general. And members of Congress chaired two of the most crucial committees of the convention: Rep. Geraldine Ferraro of New York chaired the platform committee, and Rep. Julian Dixon of California chaired the rules committee. Both were credited with producing realistic compromises that helped ensure the unity of the convention.[11] In this sense, the superdelegate plan worked as it was intended to.

In each of the demographic and participation issues we have examined so far in this chapter, a constant theme has been the Democrats' faith in the efficacy of party rules for bringing about important change and reform in the party and in the government. Indeed, as we have seen, the rules can be written in such a way as to deliberately change the composition of the national conventions on straightforward demographic characteristics such as sex and race, and they can ensure a certain level of political experience through reserved delegate positions for public and party officials.

All of the specific concerns we have addressed so far in this chapter are easily identified and measured; these are objective components of Standing For representation. We turn next to the subjective aspects of Standing For representation, political attitudes as expressed in the delegates' ideology and issue stances.

Ideology

Attitudes must be inferred from the responses people make to questionnaires or from the actions they take, and for analysis people must be classified on the basis of these rather imprecise methods. A delegate says that he or she is liberal or conservative, favors Medicare or private health insurance, supports Mondale or Reagan; we take the attitude set as a reliable and valid indicator of some deeper beliefs. The accumulated evidence of years of survey research and public opinion polling indicates that there *is* a relationship, although an imperfect one, between what people believe and what they do, between attitudes and behavior. And in evaluating delegates, we are dealing with long-term personal and political commitments made by people who are, for the most part, highly aware of and sophisticated about the political world and their place in it. Attitudes are the basis of the subjective form of Pitkin's Standing For representation, and are therefore intrinsically important in the study of representation. Further, because delegates' issue and ideological positions are the keys to how they act at the conventions, attitudes are also important in understanding Acting For representation. Here is a link between the two theories of representation.

Ideology and issue positions, particularly in the form of single-issue politics, have received a good deal of attention in recent years. Many feel that ideology plays a disproportionate role in the current nominating system. Through our survey of studies of the political attitudes of national convention delegates we will examine to what extent the delegates have become ideological and issue-oriented, whether the delegates are representative in this respect, and how markedly the national elites of the two parties differ.

Self-Identification

Political ideology is usually considered to be a coherent pattern of political beliefs and values.[12] In the research under consideration here it is the most straightforward component of political attitudes: How conservative or liberal does a person identify him- or herself as being? To understand ideology in the context of representation, we also need to determine how representative the convention delegates are in relation to the mass public and to the parties' bases. When asked about their ideological positions, each of these constituencies might be expected to respond with differing degrees of awareness: the mass public is widely held to have a vague sense of ideology; most delegates are politically sophisticated and self-aware; party identifiers probably fall in between.

The data confirm common empirical observations about the delegates to the parties' conventions from 1972 through 1980 (Table 5.5). Not surprisingly, far more Republican delegates than Democratic delegates identified themselves as conservative. Nearly 50 percent of the 1976 Republican delegates and nearly 60 percent of the 1972 and 1980 Republican delegates said they were conservative, whereas consistently under 10 percent of the Democratic delegates identified themselves that way. Conversely, far more Democrats than Republicans called themselves liberal; the high point was in 1972, when 79 percent of the Democratic delegates labeled themselves liberal. As Kirkpatrick has pointed out, the delegations that year were taken over by liberal activists, elected at the grass-roots level, who were committed to George McGovern.[13]

A greater percentage of Democrats than of Republicans called themselves moderates; self-identified moderates outnumbered the other ideological groups at the 1976 and 1980 conventions. In relation to those who identified themselves as Democrats—the party's mass base—many more of the party's convention delegates have been liberal and many fewer conservative, while self-identified moderates were present in similar proportions both in the party's mass base and at the conventions

Table 5.5 Self-Identified Ideology of National Convention Delegates, Party Members, and Mass Public, 1972-1980

Self-identified ideology	1972		1976		1980		Party members (1980)		Mass public (1980)
	D	R	D	R	D	R	D	R	
Liberal	79%	10%	40%	3%	46%	2%	21%	13%	19%
Moderate	13	35	47	45	42	36	44	40	49
Conservative	8	57	8	48	6	58	26	41	31

Source: Data for 1972 from Jeane J. Kirkpatrick, *The New Presidential Elite* (New York: Russell Sage Foundation, 1976), 169. Data for 1976 and 1980 based on CBS News delegate surveys; data for party identifiers based on CBS News-*New York Times* polls; both sets reported in Warren J. Mitofsky and Martin Plissner, "The Making of the Delegates, 1968-1980," *Public Opinion* (October/November 1980): 43. Mass public data from Gallup Poll for September 1980, published in *Public Opinion* (February/March 1981).

(except in 1972, of course). In other words, the liberal Democrats have been vastly overrepresented at the conventions and the conservative Democrats vastly underrepresented. Compared to the population as a whole, the situation is even more extreme, with somewhat fewer liberals and somewhat more conservatives in the mass public than in the Democratic base. A similar pattern holds in reverse for the Republicans. In 1980 the Republican delegates were almost as far out of ideological step with their mass base and with the American public to the right as the Democratic elites were to the left.

Clearly, the 13 percent of Republicans who called themselves liberal and the 26 percent of Democrats who said they were conservative were virtually left out of their respective parties' convention delegations and, therefore, of the final stages of the nominating process. Political scientists have long been expecting an election era that would bring about an ideological realignment, in effect purifying the two parties of their *misidentifiers* (the conservatives in the Democratic party and the liberals in the Republican party).[14] The data presented here indicate that at the party elite level a gradual realignment has indeed occurred.[15] One current view is that the movement to the right of the Republican party elite has encouraged the perception of a conservative majority nationally.[16] Whether the mass base of the two political parties will witness a realignment remains to be seen. As Table 5.5 shows, the mass base of both parties is currently made up of more self-identified conservatives than liberals. A realignment would mean that all or most conservatives would identify themselves as Republican, at least at the polls. So if future elections produce a lasting Republican majority in the Senate and a new Republican majority in the House, it will be time to start announcing the realignment. Otherwise, and more likely, 1980 will come to be viewed as an aberration caused by the specific candidates and the public's reactions to them.

It is clear that the ideologically committed do have an advantage over their fellow party activists in seeking the delegate slots. Considering the rigors involved in becoming a delegate in the postreform era, it follows that a prospective delegate must believe strongly in an issue, a cause, or a candidate to mount such a determined bid. Perhaps it is not too surprising, then, to find that the ideologues of the left and the right in the Democratic and Republican parties, respectively, meet this challenge somewhat more successfully than do others.

The Professional-Amateur Dichotomy

One of the most important concepts in the study of the political attitudes and orientations of delegates was formulated by political scientist James Q. Wilson. In a book published in 1962 he delineated the concept of a dichotomy of amateur and professional politicians.[17] This typology expresses differences in the delegates' personal backgrounds, their orientations toward the parties and the issues, their political activities, and their role in the national conventions.

According to Wilson, the amateurs were upper-middle-class reformers who were interested in politics as a means of bringing about change by force of argument, by appeal to issues, ideologies, and principles that were, they believed, inherently the definition of the common good or the public interest. They were likely to be lawyers, professors, or housewives, and they pursued politics as a part-time interest. For the amateur the political party was important as a vehicle for the larger ends of issue and program pursuits; in addition, democracy within the party was thought to be important in itself.

The professionals, by contrast, were supposed to be the lower-middle-class politicians who were attracted to politics by materialistic motives, by the desire for a job for themselves or their friends, for example. The professionals were described as being pragmatic, results-oriented people. They were the "ward-heelers," the precinct leaders, the foot soldiers of the well-oiled urban political machines of yesteryear. They were not supposed to be much interested in issues, and even less in ideologies. And they were likely to pursue politics as a full-time occupation. For the professional the party was inherently important and satisfying; democracy within the party could be sacrificed to the need for competition between the parties. Clearly, for Wilson there were significant differences between amateurs and professionals in party politics.

Aaron Wildavsky took essentially the same concepts and applied them to delegates to the 1964 conventions, which nominated Goldwater and Johnson.[18] Wildavsky described the ideologically and issue-oriented delegates of the Goldwater camp as *purists*—corresponding roughly to Wilson's amateurs—and the more pragmatic delegates in the other camps as *politicians*—corresponding to the professionals. He also left little doubt that he thought the purists had taken over the Goldwater-conservative movement and that they would create serious problems for the future of presidential politics in this country.

John W. Soule and James W. Clarke, in studying delegates to the 1968 conventions, were the first to structure the terms in such a way as to apply them to convention delegates.[19] They developed a 10-item scale that included (a) attitudes supportive of intraparty democracy (amateurs score high); (b) preoccupation with winning (professionals score high); (c) willingness to compromise (professionals score high); (d) support of programmatic parties, the development of policy programs by the parties and the willingness to enact these programs once in office (amateurs score high); and (e) active role in party by citizen-volunteers (amateurs score high). Their results indicated that, by their definition, 46 percent of the 1968 Democratic delegates were professionals; 23 percent were amateurs; and 29 percent were semiprofessionals, that is, they fell between the other two groups. Obviously, then, the professionals dominated this prereform convention that nominated Humphrey. Soule and Clarke's conclusion coincides with the popular and common-sense interpretations of what happened in 1968 in Chicago.

Soule and Wilma McGrath applied the same concepts in their study of the 1972 Democratic National Convention.[20] Their research indicates that 1972 was probably the high-water mark for convention attendance by the amateurs in the Democratic party. Both the rules changes and the McGovern candidacy were undoubtedly responsible for the large number of amateurs attending the 1972 convention. Popular, and some academic, interpretations of that convention have held that the amateurs took advantage of the new McGovern-Fraser rules and rode the antiwar and proreform fervor of the day into delegate seats. Political scientist Austin Ranney, a critic of the reforms who himself served on the McGovern-Fraser Commission, has written, "The reforms were intended to maximize the representation of the 'purists' not of 'professionals.' "[21] This view holds that the reformers left the professionals from the traditional party and labor union centers of power behind in their wake as the Humphrey, Muskie, and Jackson supporters were soundly defeated. Soule and McGrath's data indicate that there is some empirical support for these stereotypes from 1972. In addition, Jeane Kirkpatrick's voluminous 1972 study provides further empirical evidence that the amateurs disproportionately favored McGovern that year.[22]

Research on the mid-term conference of 1974 indicates that the period between the national convention of 1972 and the mid-term conference of 1974 may have been a crucial turning point for the Democrats.[23] It was an era when the professionals reasserted themselves and when those who were formerly amateurs had been around long enough to have gained power.

Studies of the 1976 and 1980 Democratic convention delegates indicate that the professional outlook continued to dominate in both of those meetings. In 1976, 61 percent of the Democratic delegates responded as professionals by characterizing themselves as someone who "works for the party year after year, win or lose, and whether or not you like the candidates or issues."[24] In addition, 68 percent of the 1976 delegates said they considered themselves party regulars, which roughly corresponds to the percentage of professionals. Even more Democrats in 1980 could be characterized as professionals: 82 percent said they worked for the party year after year regardless of the candidates or the issues, and 86 percent said they considered themselves party regulars.

Thomas Roback's studies of the Republican delegations in 1972 and 1976 have produced results that are consistent with the findings for the Democrats. Roback adopted the classic concept of organizational incentives, originally formulated by Peter B. Clark and James Q. Wilson, to help unravel the mystery behind what gets people interested in politics and what keeps them active in the parties.[25] These incentives include: *purposive* incentives, which relate to public interest oriented motivation, such as issues and ideology; *solidary* incentives, such as friendship and social contact; and *material* incentives, such as money or business advancement. Clark and Wilson point out that the motives for *initial* entry into an organization may be different from the motives for *sustained* activity in the organization. In other words, a party leader may be attracted initially by purposive incentives, only to remain active years later because of solidary rewards. Roback made the observation that the purposive incentives are usually associated with the amateur type of activists, while the material and solidary incentives are associated with the professional outlook.

Roback's research did indicate that there were some differences in the initial and the sustaining incentives of the delegates. He also found that these incentives tended to vary among the supporters of different candidates. The Reagan supporters in 1976, for example, were more likely to claim purposive motives for their actions than were the Nixon delegates in 1972 or the Ford delegates in 1976. Roback writes, "Thus the Reagan Republican seems to sustain his activism by his belief in issues and his ideological commitment to his candidate, and less by personal friendships, family, group excitement or other material rewards." [26] The three concepts are not mutually exclusive, a point that Roback emphasizes. Many people are motivated by a complex mixture of purposive, solidary, and material incentives. The characterizations express predominant tendencies rather than pure types; nevertheless, these remain our most viable conceptual explanations of why people initially become involved and remain active in political party organizations.

Within both parties particular political environments have favored the recruitment of first-time participants. These neophytes were probably very issue oriented and ideological, and they were attracted to specific candidates. Among the Democrats this group included the McCarthyites of 1968 and the McGovernites of 1972; a small-scale version of the phenomenon was seen in the support for Edward Kennedy at the 1980 convention. On the Republican side this group of amateurs was made up of the rock-ribbed conservatives first attracted into the party by Goldwater in 1964. Some of those dedicated conservatives remained active and became the party establishment. They were then joined by a whole new wave of Reagan enthusiasts in 1976 and 1980. By 1980 the once-minority conservatives had become the mainstream of the Republican party.

The dichotomy between amateurs and professionals in politics has blurred considerably since Wilson first introduced the concept. In fact, the former amateurs may have become the establishment within both parties. Many who entered the Republican party on the wave of the Goldwater movement in 1964 or the Democratic party with the McGovern movement of 1972 now occupy official positions of leadership and power in their parties. These issue and ideological enthusiasts tend to be devoted to specific candidates; when those candidates prosper, these groups prosper. At the very least, we must conclude that the former amateurs now share power with the professionals and have taken on many of the characteristics of the professionals; we might call these people the "new professionals."

In contrast to Wilson's professionals, the new professionals are likely to be college graduates working in a service profession. They are familiar with all the paraphenalia of modern campaigning. The new professionals also are likely to care deeply about at least some issues:

they have a firm grasp on where they fit on the ideological continuum, and they are discerning enough to latch onto a candidate who can articulate and advance their favorite causes. They also care, sometimes passionately, about their party. The new professionals derive personal satisfaction from being actively involved in their party, and they see the parties as the best vehicles for advancing both their concept of the public interest and their own political careers. Both generational change and socialization into the norms of the organization have helped produce these new professionals.

In general, the old dichotomy between the professionals and the amateurs probably has less meaning today than at any time since Wilson introduced it in the early 1960s. But as we proceed to examine the policy stances and ideology of the delegates, we will continue to find the categories useful in untangling the complexities of the delegates' attitudes.

Issues and Issue-Based Ideology

People can think of themselves as liberals or conservatives and have positions on issues that differ from the positions of others in the same camp. In other words, a person's political ideology may well have several attitudinal dimensions, which produce typically liberal responses on some items and typically conservative or moderate responses on others.

The importance and import of specific issues in American politics change from election to election and from era to era. And the meaning and location of specific issues within a larger ideological spectrum may shift from time to time. To take an example, Vietnam was a salient issue in 1968 and 1972, as we will show, but no longer plays a major role as an issue.

Nevertheless, in a larger perspective there has been in recent years considerable stability in the nature of the underlying issues that are salient for political elites. The role of government vis-à-vis the marketplace, the protection of civil liberties, support for the welfare state, and U.S. foreign and defense policies have all tended to divide party leaders along liberal versus conservative ideological lines in the postreform era. In our empirical assessment of the issue positions of the party elites during the years from 1968 to 1980, we hope to demonstrate the systematic relations between the delegates' issues positions and their support for various candidates.

1968: The Vietnam Division

In their study of delegates to the 1968 Democratic convention Soule and Clarke used an index of nine statements with which the respondents were asked to agree or disagree.[27] These items covered a broad spectrum of foreign and domestic policy issues. According to their analysis, in which they developed a scale of *issue-oriented ideology*, these authors found that 15 percent of the delegates were conservatives, 22 percent were moderates, and 63 percent were liberal.

In correlating amateurism and professionalism with the policy statements, Soule and Clarke found that three of the issue items differentiated between the two types of political activism at the 1968 convention. In particular, the researchers found that amateurs were much more likely than professionals to agree with the following three statements:

1. "Communism today has changed greatly and we must recognize most wars and revolutions are not Communist inspired."
2. "Vietnam is historically and geographically an Asian country and should be allowed to develop autonomously within the Asian sphere of power."
3. "One has a moral responsibility to disobey laws he believes are unjust." [28]

Thus, on communism, on Vietnam, and on civil disobedience there were serious differences of opinion between the professionals and the amateurs at Chicago in 1968. The amateurs tended to be more discriminating in their views toward various communist movements and toward the conflict in Vietnam, and they were generally more tolerant toward civil disobedience.

Soule and Clarke determined that most amateurs supported Eugene McCarthy, whereas professionals tended to support Hubert H. Humphrey. And, as expected, they found that issue-oriented ideology was significantly related to candidate support: the issue-oriented liberals were divided between McCarthy and Humphrey; but McCarthy got almost all of his support from these liberals, while Humphrey did extremely well among the moderates and very well among the conservatives. To emphasize their points, these authors concluded:

> The liberal amateur delegate was the most typical supporter of McCarthy, while Humphrey's most consistent supporters were conservative professional delegates. They were ranked as conservatives almost as often as professionals. We have shown ... that ideology and amateurism are significantly and independently related to candidate preference.[29]

1972: The Liberal Anomaly

Jeane Kirkpatrick's research established the degree to which Vietnam was a salient issue during the 1972 prenomination and campaign seasons.[30] The Democrats in particular had been deeply divided over Vietnam in 1968, and those divisions remained in 1972. In both years that internal division was closely related to the party's inability to unify for the general election campaign.

Kirkpatrick showed that a near-consensus existed regarding Vietnam among McGovern supporters at the convention in 1972: a total of 91 percent of them agreed or strongly agreed that all American troops should be withdrawn from Southeast Asia. In addition, a total of 85 percent of the McGovern supporters were opposed or strongly opposed to continued American military and economic aid to Southeast Asia.[31] Opinions were much more ambivalent and deeply divided among all of the other candidate support groups in both parties. Among Humphrey, Muskie, Wallace, and Nixon supporters in 1972 there was marked division over these two issues related to the war in Vietnam. While the data are not available for strict comparisons, we can infer that the political elites supporting these other candidates probably represented reasonably well the divisions and ambivalence among the American people at that time regarding the U.S. role in Southeast Asia. Here is yet another indication of just how remarkably homogeneous and unique the McGovern delegates were in 1972.

Kirkpatrick used three other items to assess attitudes toward additional foreign and defense policy issues in 1972. These issues were more general and enduring and are still with us today:

1. "American military superiority should have priority in American foreign policy."
2. "The United States should give more support to the United Nations."
3. "The use of nuclear weapons by the United States would never be justified." [32]

Again there were divisions within the Democratic party, with the McGovern delegates the most opposed to any attempt to maintain military superiority, the most opposed to the use of nuclear weapons, and the most supportive of the U.N. On these items, however, the Humphrey and Muskie delegates were not markedly different from the McGovern delegates, although they took a somewhat more centrist position. The major differences on these three issues were between the delegates of the three major Democratic candidates and those of Nixon and Wallace. Nixon's and Wallace's delegates were much more likely to support the maintenance of U.S. military superiority and the potential use of nuclear weapons and much less likely to support the U.N. than were the McGovern, Humphrey, and Muskie delegates.

Kirkpatrick also evaluated issues of domestic policy—particularly the welfare and economic issues. These, too, have current relevance. In the area of attitudes toward welfare and the work ethic, the McGovern delegates were again the most distinctive group. Table 5.6 provides Kirkpatrick's comparisons between all Democratic candidate support groups, all Democratic identifiers, all Republican delegates, and all Republican identifiers.[33]

Table 5.6 indicates that the Humphrey delegates and, to a lesser extent, the Muskie delegates in 1972 were fairly reflective of the party's mass base, which was a good deal less liberal than were the McGovern delegates. The Republican delegates were close to a true representation of their mass base on this issue. Taking all the issues into account, Kirkpatrick found the Democratic rank and file to be closer to the middle of the political continuum than were the political elites who represented them at the national conventions.

Kirkpatrick's general finding on the relationship between the rank and file and the political elites is consonant with Herbert McClosky's classic 1956 study.[34] However, Kirkpatrick parts company with McClosky in her specific finding: whereas McClosky found that the Republican delegates in 1956 were far more conservative than their party's mass base and the American electorate, Kirkpatrick identified the Democratic delegates in 1972 as straying in the liberal direction. McClosky's generalizations about the ideological orientation of political elites and masses were conventional wisdom in the discipline until Kirkpatrick's study. Her view of the ideological alignment in the Democratic party in 1972 has been widely accepted and very influential.

Finally, Kirkpatrick combined a wide variety of specific foreign and domestic issues into what she called a political culture index. From the scores on this index she derived a *cultural liberal* and a *cultural conservative* typology, which she compared with support for specific candidates, partisanship, and amateur-professional status. She characterized her results as follows:

> The cultural liberal was more likely to be under 40, highly educated, and urban in origin.... Politically, the cultural liberal was almost surely a Democrat and very probably a McGovern supporter. His political experience was likely to be relatively brief, and the little experience he had in party office was probably at very low levels. A strong liberal or radical, he came to politics out of intense interest in issues and remained relatively unconcerned with party organization....

Table 5.6 Rank-and-File Identifiers and Elite Compared on Attitudes and Welfare Policy

	Democrats						Republicans	
	Identifiers	All delegates	McGovern delegates	Humphrey delegates	Muskie delegates	Wallace delegates	Identifiers	All delegates
Abolish poverty								
1	12% } 22	28% } 57	38% } 75	15% } 33	19% } 46	0% } 2	8% } 13	3% } 10
2	6	17	24	6	17	2	2	2
3	4	12	13	12	10	0	3	5
4	9	15	12	21	21	3	8	15
5	7	6	4	11	10	9	6	13
6	12 } 69	7 } 28	3 } 12	12 } 45	12 } 33	8 } 95	13 } 79	22 } 75
Obligation to work 7	50	15	5	22	11	78	60	40
Weighted N =	(1,040)	(2,532)	(1,281)	(411)	(277)	(145)	(604)	(1,070)

Question: "Some people believe that all able-bodied welfare recipients should be compelled to work. Others believe that the most important consideration is that no American family should live in poverty whether they work or not. Suppose the people who stress the obligation to work are at one end of this scale, at point number 7, and the people who stress that no one should live in poverty are at the other end, at point number 1, where would you place yourself?"

Notes: Data on rank and file identifiers (voters) were taken from the pre-convention study. Data on elites are from the interviews. Percentages do not necessarily add to 100 due to rounding.

Source: Jeane J. Kirkpatrick, *The New Presidential Elite: Men and Women in Politics*, 299. © 1976 by the Russell Sage Foundation. Reprinted by permission of the publisher.

In background and style, ideological and organizational perpectives they [cultural liberals] closely resembled Wilson's "amateur," Polsby and Wildavsky's "purist." [35]

It always does some violence to individual cases to develop such typologies and broad generalizations. Nevertheless, in political science we seek such typologies as a convenient way of communicating complex concepts and we strive for such broad generalizations as the building blocks of a maturing and more systematic science. We will have occasion to use these typologies and generalizations again as our chronological and conceptual argument unfolds. Based on the data from 1964 through 1972, Figure 5.1 illustrates the intersection of these types and concepts.

1976: The Role of Factions

Everett Carll Ladd has provided empirical data comparing the 1976 party elites to their mass bases and to the American public as a whole. In his book *Where Have All the Voters Gone?* he contends that in 1972 and 1976 the national convention delegates for both parties—but especially the Democrats—were drastically unrepresentative of the party's followers and of the American public.[36] We have already encountered that theme for the 1972 convention in Kirkpatrick's work. Ladd contends that the same thesis holds for the 1976 Democratic convention delegates, even

Ideology

	Liberal	Conservative
Amateur	McCarthy delegates in 1968 McGovern delegates in 1972	Goldwater delegates in 1964 Some Nixon delegates in 1968 and 1972 Wallace delegates in 1968 and 1972
Professional	Humphrey delegates 1968 and 1972 Muskie and Jackson delegates in 1972	Most Nixon delegates in 1968 and 1972

Party Orientation (left margin label)

Figure 5.1 Elite Ideology and Party Orientation

though they chose Jimmy Carter, who was popularly believed to be the most moderate Democratic candidate that year.

After examining the delegates' policy preferences compared to those of Democratic party identifiers, Ladd found that the delegates were invariably more liberal than their grass-roots counterparts on several specific issue items. From busing to defense spending, these party elites were far out of step with the rank-and-file Democrats that year. The same was true for the delegates' self-identified political philosophy. Only 8 percent of the delegates called themselves conservatives, whereas 36 percent of Democrats identified themselves that way.

In addition, Ladd divided the Democrats into two major factions. One he labeled the *old class Democrats*, the lower-middle- and working-class, blue-collar people who are usually thought of as the backbone of the Democratic party. Wilson would probably call the activists from this group professionals. These people are now considerably less liberal than they once were, according to Ladd, although they are still highly representative of the Democratic party's mass base. Indeed, because of their numbers, they *are* the Democratic party's mass base.

Countering the old class Democrats is the other major faction, which Ladd labeled the *new class Democrats*. These people are the well-educated, upper-middle-class elite—products of the universities, the mass media, and the modern welfare state. As Ladd defines them, they are the leading advocates for—and beneficiaries of—the reforms and changes that have taken place in the Democratic party. The activists drawn from this faction are more likely to be the amateurs we discussed earlier. They are the ones who now win the primaries and who manipulate the caucuses and conventions in such a way as to increase their own numbers and gain advantages for their own favored candidates, according to Ladd.

In an article published in 1978 Ladd expanded on his typology and analyzed the implications of the issue and ideological differences within the two major parties by emphasizing the parties' class polarization. He contends that during the 1960s and 1970s American society became much more deeply divided along class lines, with the gulf between the lower-middle and upper-middle classes becoming increasingly pronounced.[37] The lower-middle and working classes are quite concerned about their economic futures and protective of the traditional goals and gains of labor unions; however, they are increasingly conservative on lifestyle and family-oriented values and on national defense issues. In contrast, the upper-middle class is increasingly comprised of elite groups in high-tech and professional occupations. They are also likely to have adopted lifestyles and personal values that reflect the recent easing of social mores. This class polarization is particularly focused within the Democratic party and has led to a deep division between what Ladd calls the *old fashioned liberals* based in the working class and the labor unions and the *new liberals* based in the upper-middle class. Not surprisingly, the elites of the Democratic party are increasingly divided along these lines as well.

Ladd dilineates the divisions within the Republican party similarly. He says that while most Republicans are also conservatives, modern conservatism has two sides. Both emanate from roughly the same class base—the upper and upper-middle classes—but they are divided by major geographical and economic differences. *Moderate conservatives* are often business and industrial leaders located predominantly in the Northeast and upper Midwest who have generally made their peace with the New Deal and the more active role for government it defined. *Orthodox conservatives* today are the owners of newer, more entrepreneurial businesses generally located in the Sunbelt, and they are rather aggressively opposed to active government in general and the federal government in particular. In Ladd's words:

> These two major camps are most deeply divided over the service state, that still-growing offspring of the New Deal. As noted, moderate conservatives accept the service state and the governmental intervention that accompanies it. Even though they may inveigh against it at Rotary luncheons and convention banquets, back in the privacy of the boardroom they try to shape its uses, especially in promoting economic development and in advancing the immediate interests of the business middle-class. Orthodox conservatives, in contrast, remain profoundly and genuinely uncomfortable with the New Deal state.[38]

While there are many variations on the pure versions of each party's two ideal types, Ladd's descriptions offer a convenient shorthand for summarizing the factions within the parties. Those factions are also reflected in the candidates who seek the presidential nominations within the two parties. For the Republicans the orthodox conservatives are the most likely base of support for Ronald Reagan, whereas in 1976 the moderate conservatives would probably have supported Gerald Ford. In 1980 the moderate conservatives initially supported Bush, while the orthodox conservatives continued to form Reagan's core of supporters. In the Democratic party the old fashioned liberals would have been most likely to support Humphrey in 1968 or Henry Jackson in 1972, while the new liberals would likely have been found in the camp of McCarthy in 1968 or McGovern in 1972. One should not overdo these divisions just for the sake of symmetry, but they do seem to characterize the general tendencies prevailing within each of the parties.

In the end Ladd offers only limited data to buttress his claims about the 1976 delegates. Research done by Jackson and his associates on the delegates to the 1976 Democratic National Convention casts some doubt on just how far out of step they were in comparison to the party's mass base and the American public.[39] Their data show that the 1976 Democratic delegates were predominantly moderate to liberal in their ideological self-identification. In comparison to the 1972 delegates, there were very substantial reductions in the ranks of the very liberal delegates who had helped nominate George McGovern. In 1976 Carter received the support of the majority (57 percent) of the self-identified moderate delegates, and he received a plurality of the votes of those who termed themselves either liberals or conservatives.[40] This research indicated that the 1976 delegates were not as markedly unrepresentative of their party's mass base as the 1972 delegates were.

1980: Delegates and Other Elites

The national convention delegates are not the only party elites who count in the nomination process, although the studies cited so far have concentrated on these people. Seen from a broader perspective, the delegations are a cross section of the parties' national, state, and local leadership. While the conventions actually make the nominations and conduct important party business (discussed in more detail in Chapter 8), other segments of party leadership at every level are equally concerned with the outcome of the nominating season.

In light of the role these other party leaders play, John S. Jackson III, Barbara Brown, and David Bositis in 1980 conducted a study of political elites in which they expanded the definition of party elite to include party leaders at every level in addition to convention delegates. Jackson and his associates included each of the following groups in their study:[41]

A sample of all delegates to the 1980 Democratic and Republican national conventions

A sample of all Democratic and Republican county chairs nationwide

The total population of Democratic and Republican state chairs

The total population of members of the Democratic and Republican national committees

The research was an attempt to build on and extend McClosky's work, which defined the left-to-right ideological continuum and the place of party elites on it. The authors took into account research on the 1968-1976 elections, as reviewed in this chapter. The Jackson et al. study of

1980 also made use of survey data from the Center for Political Studies to assess the positions of the parties' mass bases and the American public on a series of policy issues.

The data collected on a self-identified ideological scale are reproduced in Table 5.7. As expected, the Democratic elites were on the left of the political continuum; the Republican elites were on the right; and the parties' bases and the American public were generally in the middle. This array fits the classic McClosky finding for the 1956 party elites and mass public. However, there were a number of interesting and useful variations discovered about differences *within* the parties. For example, the Democratic county chairs were found to be by far the most moderate group within the Democratic elite strata, and the national convention delegates were by far the most liberal group.

This result generally agrees with the findings from other studies; yet the data for recent years indicate a decrease in self-identified liberal delegates at the national conventions and an increase in delegates calling themselves moderates. Only 53 percent of the delegates to the 1980 Democratic convention considered themselves to be liberal, a figure far below the 79 percent of the 1972 convention. Self-identified moderates made up 43 percent of the 1980 delegates. The 1980 figures are comparable to Jackson and his associates' findings of 51 percent liberal and 45 percent moderate for delegates to the 1976 convention.[42]

Thus, it is evident that in 1976 and 1980 the Democratic convention delegates had, in the aggregate, moved to a somewhat more moderate position on the political continuum. In addition, it is clear from these results that other Democratic party elites in 1980 were reasonably close to the political middle and reasonably representative of their party's identifiers and the mass public. A study conducted by Robert S. Montjoy, William R. Shaffer, and Ronald E. Weber of the 1972 Democratic county chairs indicates that they also may have been more representative of the political center that year.[43] Montjoy found that the Democratic county chairs in 1972 were quite moderate in comparison to the individuals studied by Kirkpatrick—the national convention delegates who nominated McGovern.

Jackson's team went on to explore the self-identified positions of the Republican elites vis-à-vis their identifiers and the mass public in 1980. As was expected, the Republican leaders stood to the right on the continuum. What was surprising about the Republican elites was how little they differed from each other. For instance, 68 percent of the Republican county chairs called themselves conservatives, compared to 64 percent of the national convention delegates and 56 percent of the Republican National Committee and state chairs. By comparison, 67

Table 5.7 Party Elites, Identifiers, and Mass Public Compared on Ideology

Ideology	DNC and state chairs	Democratic National Convention delegates	Democratic county chairs	Democratic identifiers	Mass public	Republican identifiers	Republican county chairs	Republican National Convention delegates	RNC and state chairs
Liberal	48%	53%	22%	29%	21%	15%	1%	2%	1%
Moderate	50	43	63	29	30	19	32	34	43
Conservative	2	4	15	42	49	67	68	64	56
N =	(132)	(493)	(531)	(348)	(863)	(233)	(538)	(492)	(89)
Mean	1.55	1.51	1.93	2.13	2.27	2.52	2.67	2.62	2.55

$\chi^2 = 1045.5$ $p < 0.001$

Note: Data for the mass public and the party identifiers are drawn from the Center for Political Studies 1980 survey, January/February wave.

Source: John S. Jackson III, Barbara L. Brown, and David Bositis, "Herbert McClosky and Friends Revisited," American Politics Quarterly 10 (April 1983): 158-180.

percent of the Republican mass identifiers called themselves conservatives, so the party elites were not substantially different from their mass base on self-identified ideology.

By 1980 the Republican party had become a very conservative organization in terms of its ideological self-perception. This generalization was true of all three of what Key called the major components of a political party: the party organization, the party-in-the-electorate, and the party-in-government.[44] The former liberals who had misidentified with the Republican party, such as Jacob Javits, Edward Brooke, and Nelson Rockefeller, were gone from the Republican leadership ranks and for the most part from the party's rank and file. Perhaps never before in American history had there been a major American party more self-consciously homogeneous in ideology than the 1980 Republicans. It should have come as no surprise that they nominated an avowedly conservative candidate like Ronald Reagan and adopted a strongly conservative platform in 1980. Certainly the ideological image aspects of the Republican elites' actions were faithful representations of what their mass identifiers supported that year. In 1984 the actions of the Republican National Convention and the platform it adopted showed that the conservatives were still dominant in the national party.

In addition, the 1980 Jackson study assessed a number of important domestic and foreign policy issue stances taken by the Republican party leaders compared to party identifiers and the mass public. For instance, one question posed the possibility of cutting federal programs in order to try to balance the budget. Table 5.8 provides the comparisons for each of the groups. There are numerous within- and between-party comparisons afforded by this table. For instance, from the right side of the table one can easily see that the Republican leaders were committed to cutting welfare, education, and health/Medicare programs. They were also the largest group willing to take a look at cutting Social Security, although here their numbers ranged only between 12 and 20 percent. On the other hand, the Republican *identifiers* did not provide large levels of support for cutting anything except welfare. In addition, the American mass public provided only minuscule support for cuts in any of the program areas—again with the notable exception of welfare. Thus, on matters of domestic spending, even including welfare to some extent, the Republican elites were highly unrepresentative of American public opinion.

The same is true in reverse for the Democrats on domestic programs and defense spending. The Democrats—both the leadership and the rank and file—were consistently more liberal toward domestic programs, although 65 percent of the Democratic county chairs wanted to

Table 5.8 Party Elites, Identifiers, and Mass Public Compared on Preferred Places to Cut the Federal Budget

Programs to be cut	DNC and state chairs	Democratic National Convention delegates	Democratic county chairs	Democratic identifiers	Mass public	Republican identifiers	Republican county chairs	Republican National Convention delegates	RNC and state chairs
Defense	52%	58%	30%	35%	29%	18%	6%	6%	5%
Social Security	4	8	11	4	7	10	20	27	12
Health/Medicare	15	14	22	8	9	17	57	57	59
Education	17	15	26	6	8	12	43	61	62
Welfare	36	38	65	48	54	66	94	89	89
$N =$	(113)	(460)	(500)	(670)	(1,500)	(335)	(534)	(488)	(85)

Note: These data drawn from the February 1980 Gallup Poll. The data were coded so 1 = "Yes," i.e., checked *do* cut this item and 2 = "No."

Source: John S. Jackson III, Barbara L. Brown, and David Bositis, "Herbert McClosky and Friends Revisited," *American Politics Quarterly* 10 (April 1982): 158–180.

look at welfare spending as their first choice of a place to cut spending. (One clearly gets the sense that welfare spending is highly unpopular with all segments of American society, even among those who are probably its most consistent supporters.) While the Democratic leaders were rather faithful reflections of the priorities of their mass base and of the American public on domestic issues, they were highly unrepresentative on defense spending. Here the Democratic convention delegates and the Democratic National Committee and state party chairs provided the only significant numbers willing to take a look at potential cuts in defense spending. The Democratic county chairs again proved to be an exception and were quite representative of the public on this matter.

In general, this was the pattern that held throughout an analysis of several specific issue items. On domestic issues, the Democratic party elites were fairly close to their base and to the American public, the Democratic county chairs were the most faithful reflection of the general electorate, and the Democratic National Convention delegates were the most liberal group. On the other side, the Republican elites were far out of step with public opinion on domestic matters and fairly reflective of public opinion on foreign and defense policy. Here the Republican county chairs tended to be the most conservative group (though often not significantly), while the national committee and state party chairs group was the least conservative.

Conclusion

The American talent for political compromise and adaptation has produced a mixed system for presidential nominations. Not surprisingly, the variety of state practices produces a demographically and ideologically diverse set of delegates to the national conventions.

In regard to demographic representativeness the parties differ markedly. As a result of their well-directed efforts, Democrats in recent conventions have more faithfully represented blacks and women in the population. Republicans in the postreform era include more women in their convention delegations than they once did; blacks make up little of the Republican rank and file and little of the party elite. Thus the conventions have come closer to Standing For the parties' bases on the matter of demographic representation.

Socioeconomic representativeness is more difficult to assess and achieve. Both parties recruit delegates predominantly from their upper-middle-class activists and party leaders. In the reform era both parties witnessed a dramatic (and not unintentional) decline in the participation of party and elective officials in convention delegations. Between 1972 and 1980 the participation of officials in the Democratic conventions remained low, to the point where many felt the survival of the party might be endangered; both the Winograd and the Hunt commissions have addressed the problem by creating some form of special status for selected officials. The Republican party also suffered a decline in the number of party and elected officials participating in its conventions, although these numbers seem to have returned to their earlier strength.

Ideology and issue positions are currently a source of major differences between the parties' elites: the Democratic elites are moderate to liberal and the Republican elites are predominantly conservative. Both are somewhat more extreme than their mass bases, and convention delegates stand out more than any other segment of the parties' elites. Nonetheless, convention delegates do Act For their constituents by supporting candidates they consider most likely to win the general election. The demands of the ballot box discipline elite behavior throughout the electoral process.

It is no longer accurate, if it ever was, to say the parties are alike as tweedledum and tweedledee. In fact, the parties may now offer more systematic philosophical differences at the elite level than ever before in their history. Some academic literature suggests that these differences will lead to a realignment of the parties along conservative versus liberal lines, but we feel it is still too early to tell whether this tentative change will mark a permanent realignment.

NOTES

1. See Hanna F. Pitkin, *The Concept of Representation* (Berkeley: University of California Press, 1967), chap. 4-6.
2. Ibid., 142.
3. Paul T. David, Ralph Goldman, and Richard C. Bain, *The Politics of National Party Conventions* (Washington, D.C.: Brookings Institution, 1960), 327.
4. Frank J. Sorauf, *Party Politics in America* (Boston: Little, Brown, 1968), 260.
5. Commission on Party Structure and Delegate Selection (McGovern-Fraser Commission), *Mandate for Reform* (Washington, D.C.: Democratic National Committee, 1970), 40.
6. John S. Jackson III, "Some Correlates of Minority Representation in the National Conventions, 1964-1972," *American Politics Quarterly* 3 (April 1975): 171-188.
7. Warren J. Mitofsky and Martin Plissner, "The Making of the Delegates, 1968-1980," *Public Opinion* 3 (October/November 1980): 37-43.
8. See Robert Dahl, *Who Governs?* (New Haven: Yale University Press, 1961).

9. *Proceedings: 1980 Official Report of the Democratic National Convention* (Washington, D.C.: Democratic National Committee, 1980), 463, 453.
10. Barry Sussman and Kenneth E. John, "The Delegates Are Not the Democratic Rank and File," *Washington Post Weekly Edition,* July 23, 1984, 9-10.
11. Steven V. Roberts, "Rules of Party Playing Desired Role," *New York Times,* July 15, 1984, 26.
12. See Philip Converse, "The Nature of Belief Systems in Mass Publics," in *Ideology and Discontent,* ed. David E. Apter (New York: Macmillan, 1964), chap. 6.
13. Jeane J. Kirkpatrick, *The New Presidential Elite* (New York: Russell Sage Foundation, 1976).
14. See Walter D. Burnham, *Critical Elections and the Mainsprings of American Politics* (New York: W. W. Norton, 1970); Everett Carll Ladd, with Charles D. Hadley, *Transformations of the American Party System* (New York: W. W. Norton, 1975).
15. John S. Jackson III, Barbara L. Brown, and David Bositis, "Herbert McClosky and Friends Revisited," *American Politics Quarterly* 10 (April 1982): 158-180.
16. Warren E. Miller and Teresa Levitin, " 'Move to the Right': Tracing the Rumor," *Public Opinion* 1 (September/October 1978), 39.
17. See James Q. Wilson, *The Amateur Democrat: Club Politics in Three Cities* (Chicago: University of Chicago Press, 1962).
18. Aaron Wildavsky, "The Goldwater Phenomenon: Purists, Politicians, and the Two Party System," *Review of Politics* 27 (July 1965): 386-413.
19. John W. Soule and James W. Clarke, "Amateurs and Professionals: A Study of Delegates to the 1968 Democratic National Convention," *American Political Science Review* 64 (September 1970): 888-898.
20. John W. Soule and Wilma McGrath, "A Comparative Study of Presidential Nominating Conventions: The Democrats 1968 and 1972," *American Journal of Political Science* 19 (August 1975): 501-517.
21. See Austin Ranney, "Comment," *American Political Science Review* 68 (March 1974).
22. Kirkpatrick, *The New Presidential Elite,* 126-127.
23. Robert A. Hitlin and John S. Jackson III, "On Amateur and Professional Politicians," *Journal of Politics* 39 (August 1977): 786-793.
24. This information was taken from Jackson's current, long-term research on party elites and convention delegates covering the Democratic conventions since 1972 and the Republican convention in 1980. The question on working for the party has come to be one of the most often used of the original Soule and Clarke index items. See John S. Jackson III, "A Decade of Reform: The Perspective of the Democratic Delegates" (Paper delivered at the annual meeting of the American Political Science Association, Washington, D.C., September 1979).
25. Thomas H. Roback, "Motivation for Activism among Republican National Convention Delegates: Continuity and Change 1972-1976," *Journal of Politics* 42 (February 1980): 181-201; Peter B. Clark and James Q. Wilson, "Incentive Systems: A Theory of Organizations," *Administrative Science Quarterly* 4 (September 1961): 129-166.
26. Roback, "Motivation for Activism among Republican National Convention Delegates," 195.
27. Soule and Clarke, "Amateurs and Professionals," 888-898.
28. Ibid., 894.

29. Ibid., 897.
30. Kirkpatrick, *The New Presidential Elite,* 179-185.
31. Ibid., 180-181.
32. Ibid., 182-183.
33. Ibid., 299.
34. Herbert McClosky, Paul J. Hoffman, and Rosemary O'Hara, "Issue Conflict and Consensus among Party Leaders and Followers," *American Political Science Review* 56 (June 1960): 406-429.
35. Kirkpatrick, *The New Presidential Elite,* 208.
36. Everett Carll Ladd, *Where Have All the Voters Gone? The Fracturing of America's Political Parties,* 2d ed. (New York: W. W. Norton, 1982), 65.
37. Everett Carll Ladd, "The New Lines Are Drawn: Class and Ideology, Part II," *Public Opinion* 1 (September/October 1978): 14-20.
38. Ibid., 15.
39. John S. Jackson III, Jesse C. Brown, and Barbara L. Brown, "Recruitment, Representation, and Political Values," *American Politics Quarterly* 6 (April 1978): 187-212.
40. Ibid., 199.
41. Jackson, Brown, and Bositis, "Herbert McClosky and Friends Revisited," 163.
42. Jackson, Brown, and Brown, "Recruitment, Representation, and Political Values," 198-208.
43. Robert S. Montjoy, William R. Shaffer, and Ronald E. Weber, "Policy Preferences of Party Elites and Masses: Conflict or Consensus?" *American Politics Quarterly* 8 (July 1980): 319-344.
44. See V. O. Key, Jr., *Politics, Parties, and Pressure Groups,* 4th ed. (New York: Thomas Y. Crowell, 1958).

Voting Behavior and Candidate Strategy | 6

The interaction of voters and candidates could be considered the most important element of the entire presidential election process. As we have seen, party rules governing preconvention processes can encourage certain voters to participate and can favor certain candidates. But in many respects these actors are beyond party influence. Voters decide whether to participate and for whom to vote; candidates decide how to approach the voters. In this chapter we examine these two interrelated groups of decision makers.

Voting Behavior

How do voters decide for whom to vote in the primaries? This is one of the most intriguing questions behind any investigation of the prenomination processes. The answer is found in a complex set of influences, including some characteristics of the voters and some of the candidates.

Studying Voting Behavior

The General Election. Voting behavior has been an object of extensive study in the field of political science. Especially since the impetus provided by the research on voter decision making compiled beginning in the 1950s by the University of Michigan, staggering amounts of data as well as books and articles have become available.[1] But most of the research has concerned the general elections; the primaries have been studied in detail only recently. Accordingly, we must still base some of our generalizations here on the research developed from the general elections.

The classic contribution in the field of voting behavior is *The American Voter*, by Angus Campbell, Philip E. Converse, Warren E. Miller, and Donald E. Stokes.[2] These scholars established what has come to be the dominant paradigm in the discipline for explaining voter decision making. Their model, in essence, rested on the three crucial attitudinal factors of party identification, issues, and candidate image, which tell us most of what is important about how most voters make up their minds most of the time in most elections. If a voter holds particular attitudes toward the parties, the issues, and the candidates, the researcher can predict, with a high degree of accuracy, how that person will vote. Behind these most proximate attitudes stand other relevant factors, such as demographic characteristics and group memberships. These factors also affect voting behavior, but their influence is usually more indirect and distant from the voting decision and is mediated through the voter's attitudes.

Of the three basic attitudinal factors, party identification was presented as the most important among equals in the work of Campbell and his associates. They viewed party identification as central because it acted alone and colored the voters' views of the issues and the candidates. Their findings corresponded with a host of earlier studies on political socialization, which showed that party identification was acquired early in life by many people.[3] Party identification was considered to be a very stabilizing influence on American politics, by providing a setting for assessing the issues and the candidates' personalities in a particular election. Indeed, as long as approximately three-fourths of the American people identified with one of the two major parties and most voted accordingly, there *was* much stability in American electoral politics.

Events in the political arena have combined with more recent scholarship to raise questions about the role of party identification in the behavior of American voters. In Chapter 3 we illustrated the extent of recent social and political change and the resultant instability that has become a recurring element on the political scene. The approach of voting age Americans to politics has changed a good deal, even since the 1960s. As politics and politicians began to change, research scholars noticed different patterns emerging from their empirical data. At the aggregate level the proportion of the population who identified with one of the two major parties declined to about 65 percent. The proportion of people who called themselves independents increased to between 30 and 35 percent. There was a dramatic increase in the number of people who split their ticket in voting. The percentage of the eligible electorate who actually bothered to vote in presidential elections declined.[4] The levels of distrust of all major American political institutions, including the presidency, the Congress, and the political parties, increased steadily after 1964, although there has been a modest rebound in political trust levels since 1980.[5] All of these were convincing indicators that some important changes were under way in the American system.

Research into voting behavior began to reflect some of those changes. Some researchers, like Gerald Pomper, began to stress the apparently growing influence of issues and ideology in the voting decision, while others documented the increasing influence of candidate images and the mass media.[6]

As we showed in Chapter 3, social and political instability have overlapped to a great extent in recent years. The voters changed, the candidates changed, the parties changed. And, as we explained in Chapter 2, the rules of the presidential nomination system have changed. Since primaries have—not coincidentally—grown in importance in the postreform era of the 1970s and 1980s, some researchers have begun to pay more attention to the voters and how they reach their decisions in these prenomination elections.

The Primaries. In some respects a primary is like a general election for the voter. The manner in which the voter weighs the candidates, the issues, and ideology may not be fundamentally different in the context of the two types of elections. The major difference between the general election and the primaries is that all the candidates facing the voter on the primary ballot are from the same party. (Another important difference is that the primary voter often has more than two candidates to choose among, rather than just the two major party candidates who dominate the general election.) Clearly, if the voter's cue of party identification is not available, our explanation must focus on the other major factors that help the voter make a choice. In addition, the increased involvement of the media and the average voters and the increased emphasis on the personalities of individual candidates have resulted in a decreased role for the party organizations in the nominating process.

Issues may not be very important in primaries; as Malcolm Jewell has argued, the field is often crowded, the time is short, and the media shift their attention predominantly to the candidates and their images.[7] Mark Wattier designed a study to test the relative importance of the factors that influence decisions in the context of presidential primaries.[8]

The study employed the *Kelley-Mirer* rule of the voting calculus, developed to examine voting behavior during general election campaigns, which posits that the voters will assess their positive and negative feelings toward the candidates (that is, image) and vote for the one for whom the voter holds the most positive feelings. If this does not produce a decision, the voter turns to ideology and tries to vote consistently with his or her own ideological position.[9] Wattier's study used empirical data drawn from 8,607 exit interviews conducted by CBS News/*New York Times* pollsters on primary election day in 10 Democratic presidential primaries in 1980. The study found that the Kelley-Mirer rule worked in 85.4 percent of the cases. Wattier concluded that primary voters make up their minds in the following way:

> Voters in primaries canvass their likes and dislikes of the leading candidates. Weighing each like and dislike equally, they vote for the candidate toward whom they have the greatest net number of favorable attitudes. If no candidate has such an advantage, the voter votes consistently with his ideological identification.[10]

In the terminology of voting behavior studies this assessment stresses simply candidate image. Although there may be many different dimensions to the voters' likes and dislikes of the leading candidates, the factors are all subsumed analytically under the rubric of image; a complementary role is played by ideology.

Another recent study does not disagree with Wattier's position, but does provide additional data on the behavior of voters in the primaries. Political scientists Scott Keeter and Cliff Zukin did an extensive analysis of individual voting behavior during the primary campaigns. They emphasized the fact that the primary stage is where the field of contenders for the presidential nomination is narrowed down to the two candidates with the most realistic chance of becoming president and that the reform era has elevated the role of the mass voters in this process. Obviously, then, those researchers see the primaries as important to the presidential nomination process.[11]

Those authors examined in some detail national data from surveys conducted in 1980 by the Center for Political Studies, CBS News/*New York Times* Poll data, and their own data for the state of New Jersey (gathered by the Eagleton Poll at Rutgers University). They looked at how the voters were introduced to the various candidates running for the nominations, when and how they learned about the candidates, how much interest they had in the primaries, how much and what kind of information they had about the candidates and the primaries, and how they decided for whom they would vote.

After examining their extensive data collections Keeter and Zukin reached some fairly pessimistic conclusions. They concluded that the behavior of the voters falls far short of the informed-choice criteria demanded by ideal democratic standards. They blamed not the voters but the structure of the primary campaigns and the quality of information offered to voters by the media and the candidates. The authors were particularly critical of the serial nature of the primary season and the almost random spacing of the various state events that allowed the early contests—especially the Iowa caucuses and the New Hampshire primary—and the momentum the victors could build from them to dominate the initial phase of the process. In essence Keeter and Zukin are quite critical of the reforms and their consequences, which, they feel, fall far short of producing interested and well-informed voters.

We are not inclined to be as critical as Keeter and Zukin are of the levels of issue awareness and voter education during the primary season. The voters in Keeter and Zukin's study of the primaries seem to be very much like the voters in general elections; in fact, their study found very few significant differences between the two types of voters. If classic democratic theory holds the ideal voter to be highly informed about his electoral choices and extremely enthusiastic about exercising his right to choose, then the shortcomings of the average American voter are real enough; these shortcomings, however, are not restricted to the primaries. Certainly levels of information are inadequate during the primaries and candidate images and campaign trivia are exaggerated by the media; however, the same must be said about the general elections when measured against our demanding democratic ideals.

Candidate Image and the Voters

In the largest sense every presidential election is fundamentally about candidate image.[12] The major contenders spend years, sometimes their entire adult lives, developing their records, moving up through the ranks, creating an image, and positioning themselves for those one or two rare instances when they will have a realistic chance of gaining their party's nomination and becoming president of the United States. They and their supporters spend months and even years before and during the election year primary season trying to convince both the party activists who will become convention delegates and the party identifiers and ordinary voters who will participate in the primaries that they should be nominated.

Candidates and their images have always been important in American politics. One can imagine that George Washington might have been very impressive on television and that Thomas Jefferson might have sparkled in debates sponsored by the League of Women Voters. Nevertheless, the personal qualities of the candidates have achieved unusual prominence during recent campaigns. Richard Nixon's perceived difficulties in handling the televised debates in 1960 illustrate how quickly the elusive quality of candidate image can become a significant factor in a primary or general election campaign: Nixon presented a new, more confident image in his 1968 bid for the presidency; McGovern appeared indecisive in his handling of the Eagleton affair in 1972; Carter projected candor and trustworthiness in his 1976 campaign, qualities that seem to have won the early primaries for him that year. In 1980 Carter again won the early primaries, this time over Edward Kennedy, partly as a result of his initial handling of the Iranian hostage crisis. By the 1980 general election, however, Carter was perceived to lack leadership qualities in comparison with Reagan. In 1984 Gary Hart surprised many political pundits with his victory in New Hampshire's Democratic primary. His initial image was of the ideal modern candidate, goodlooking, touting his theme of "new ideas," and exuding confidence and excitement.

All these bits and pieces coalesce to form a picture of the candidate, which emerges before and during the primary season and must be fleshed out during the general election campaign. Some of these elements are within the control of the candidate and his organization, who attempt to fashion as much as possible the image being projected. A desirable image usually includes the semblance of experience, competence, honesty, intelligence, courage, toughness, and leadership ability, among other qualities.[13]

Other aspects of the candidate's image are beyond the control of the candidate. Friends, family, enemies, and the media all contribute their own pieces to the mosaic. The mass media probably play the most influential role: early on they develop their own perceptions of the potential candidates and winnow out the ones who do not seem to measure up to some ill-defined set of standards.[14] In the mass media age of American politics, the candidates' personal qualities and image are becoming increasingly important in determining who will receive each party's nomination and who will ultimately win the presidency.

Candidate Ideology and the Voters

When image is not the most important aspect of a campaign or the image qualities of two candidates cancel one another out, as sometimes happens, the remaining element influencing the voters is ideology, as

Wattier points out in the passage quoted earlier. In fact, some possiblity exists that ideology is the other important variable in the analysis of voting behavior.

There is much debate in the scholarly literature about how committed the mass public is to particular ideologies; however, even those who see ideology as the dominant aspect of today's political environment will admit that the incidence of well thought out, systematic ideology is considerably lower among the mass public than it is among political elites.[15] Ideology is less important to the mass public than is party identification. But whereas party identification plays almost no role in the primary season, ideological symbolism has the potential for great significance.

Whatever significance one attributes to ideology, it can have its uses for voters. Ideology can perform a cue-giving function that helps the voter make up his or her mind without the necessity of extensive information gathering, regardless of whether the voter holds a sophisticated and well thought out ideology. Campbell and his associates found party identification to be the most important factor—to fulfill what they called a *master cue function*—for most voters in the general election. For some of today's primary voters, ideology can be a type of shorthand used to match individual voters' views with the multiple candidates running in the primaries.[16] If the candidate adopts the label of conservative or liberal, or if others (including the media and the opposition) consistently apply one of these terms to the candidate, the campaign gains an important, information-lending dimension. If the individual voters judge themselves to be more sympathetic either to conservative or to liberal candidates and policies, the label becomes an important factor in their decision making, no matter how knowledgeable the voters or how well-defined the candidates' positions.

In 1980 the Republicans nominated Ronald Reagan, their most conservative presidential candidate since Goldwater in 1964. The nomination of an archconservative seemed to be contrary to the conventional wisdom and the experiences of 1964 and 1972, which suggested that political parties should nominate middle-of-the-road candidates in order to avoid defeat. Reagan, of course, went on to win by a large electoral margin in the general election. The symbol of conservatism was crucial to his getting the nomination: conservative party members contributed disproportionately to his winning the party's primaries and caucuses, and conservative delegates dominated the national convention.[17] Ideology and its symbolic significance were not the only factors in Reagan's primary and general election victories, but they were very important.

In a similar vein, Walter Mondale's long-time reputation as a consistent supporter of liberal causes made him widely acceptable to the Democratic party activists who nominated him in 1984. Mondale epitomized the Democratic coalition in 1984; and his liberal credentials were essential to his success in gaining the nomination. On the other hand, Mondale's liberalism was not expected to be advantageous in the general election. Mondale's acceptance speech at the convention, in which he appealed to a "new realism" in the Democratic party, was apparently an attempt to position himself more moderately in a bid for the support of the general electorate.

The conservative/liberal label affects congressional and gubernatorial candidates as well. On balance, 1978 and 1980 were bad years to be identified in the popular mind as a liberal and good years to be known as a conservative—whatever the ambiguity of those labels to the American public. In the off-year elections in 1982 the recession dominated political discourse; the Democrats increased their majority in the House, and the Republicans maintained their majority in the Senate. Considering the severity of the recession, which many blamed on the conservative administration, these mixed results indicated that conservatism as a symbol had not yet lost its appeal. By mid-1984 the public opinion polls showed President Reagan enjoying relatively high levels of job approval, with excellent prospects of defeating Mondale in November. Reagan's conservatism does not seem to have denied him the opportunity of becoming the first president since Richard Nixon to be elected to a second term.

According to James David Barber, large-scale ideological trends tend to run in patterns and cycles.[18] If so, we can expect some form of liberalism to eventually make a comeback in public opinion. But for now one must conclude that it is much safer and much more popular in most constituencies, including the presidential constituency, to be a symbolic conservative than to be a symbolic liberal. In the presidential primaries the application of the ideological labels and the divining and definition of fine gradients of differences among the candidates within the parties is stressed by media and candidate camps alike. The voters' responses validate such an approach.

In sum, both candidate ideology and image influence voters in determining for whom they will vote in the primaries. Some proportion of the primary voters locate themselves on the ideological continuum and then attempt to vote in the primaries for the candidate who they perceive as ideologically closest to their own position. Other voters rationalize voting for the candidate whose image they like best by perceiving that candidate as being ideologically closest to their own views, regardless of the objective evidence.[19] In many ways, then, the voters' ideology and the candidates' image and ideology are important themes in the decision making of everyone involved in the elections, from voters to candidates to the media.

Candidate Strategy

We have identified candidate image and ideology as the most important influences on the primary voter's decision. The candidate's strategy must be established before the primary season begins so that he will be ready to take advantage of organizational resources, project the desired image, bring up appropriate issues, and identify with a certain ideological position. The context and the competition are within one of the parties; thus the range of issues and ideology to choose from is necessarily limited. Candidates face the complex task of appealing not only to the party's electorate but to the potential delegates and to the influential party elites (who can attract and provide money and endorsements); the general election voter is continually in the background. Media attention is also crucial. The best-run campaigns try to understand these factors, take advantage of them, and shape the circumstances to increase their chances of victory.

Considering the complexity of today's contests, it is no wonder that an entire industry has grown up around presidential campaigns. The candidate who has or can obtain sufficient funding can find a whole stable of experts to employ in preparation for the primary election. There are mass media consultants, marketing experts, pollsters, direct-mail fund raisers, and public relations specialists, among others.[20] Such people work directly for the candidate, independent of the parties—although some of the experts offer their services only to candidates with certain philosophies or in the party they support. One of the most important functions these consultants fill is to help the candidate project a certain image and find a niche in the field.

Image, Ideology, and Positioning

One of the candidate's most difficult tasks—and a source of considerable but unavoidable tension—is to appeal both to the party's voters and to the political elites. In the prereform era the elites were the most important audience, and the primaries more or less validated their choices. The postreform era is more fluid. As we mentioned earlier, party service is not a prerequisite to the nomination. Both elite and mass appeal can easily be made on the basis either of ideological fervor or of personality alone.

Some candidates are especially successful in attracting issue and ideological enthusiasts to their cause. McCarthy in 1968 and McGovern in 1972, both running against the Vietnam War, are good cases in point. Goldwater's and Reagan's conservative enthusiasts also fit this mold. Other candidates seem to attract personal followings, which are influenced to a degree by the candidates' ideological and issue positions; but such candidates transcend those qualities by using their own personalities and images and creating an enthusiastic response among dedicated followers. Reagan has always enjoyed this advantage and type of following, as have Robert Kennedy and, to some extent, Edward Kennedy.

John H. Aldrich has written about the constant strain on candidates created by the differences in ideological position between party elites and mass voters. Our discussion of voters in Chapter 4 showed that party elites tend to identify themselves as farther from the center than mass voters. Therefore, if a candidate moves too far toward the left or the right to pick up the party activists, he may risk alienating the more moderate voters. This problem was encountered by Goldwater on the right in 1964 and McGovern on the left in 1972. At the same time, if the candidate is positioned in the center of the ideological continuum, influential party activists may feel that the candidate is too moderate and not differentiated enough from the candidates of the other party. Carter had this problem with the liberal Democrats in 1980. Aldrich offers the following postulate about the candidates' ideal strategic placement:

> The best position for a candidate is some place between the policy center of his party and that of the electorate as a whole. The candidate cannot stray too far from the preferences of the party without becoming vulnerable to a candidate at the party's center. At the same time, a candidate who is directly at the party's center can be defeated by a rival who is a bit less ideologically pure, but a more likely winner in the general election. . . . Candidates must often stray from the center to win their party's nomination. This explains, in large part, why the Democratic and Republican candidates are more liberal and more conservative, respectively, than each other.[21]

It might seem as if candidates on the parties' ideological extremes would be the most favored by a primary system. Certainly, George Wallace's successes in the 1972 Democratic primaries were partly attributable to the fact that he was the conservative in a moderate-to-liberal field. While a case can be made that ideologically extreme candidates and candidates who are not the favorites of the party establishment *may* have some advantages, particularly in early primaries, their standing in the race depends on many factors. It is the relative positioning, the ideological distance between the candidates, and individual personalities and images that really count. If a candidate shares many personal characteristics as well as ideological and issue proximity with other candidates, that candidate will be disadvantaged.

For instance, the liberals in the Democratic party were hurt when faced with the perceived moderate, Carter, in 1976. Again in 1984 the liberals seemed to be dividing up a good deal of the same turf, and Glenn appeared to be the moderate who would gain votes; things did not work out that way, however, and Glenn dropped out of the race early in the primary season. Among the Republicans, a more moderate candidate could hope to win if the rest of the field were badly divided among only conservatives; George Bush in 1980 benefited briefly from such a situation with his victory in the Iowa caucuses, though he did not go on to gain the nomination.

While the ideological candidates do have the advantage of a ready-made ideological constituency, moderates can also stand out under certain circumstances, as our examples show. The importance of ideology in any particular nominating season will depend on how many candidates of what type enter the race and on how well each of the candidates organizes and funds a campaign.

We have seen that broadening participation in the nominating processes, as the party reforms have done, does allow different groups to gain power in the system (Chapter 2), and some of those groups are committed to a particular ideological position. Critics of the reform era maintain that the postreform delegate selection processes generally favor the candidate with a strong personal and ideological following. Such a candidate can unexpectedly stack a caucus with his followers and take a quick victory; he may be able to win a party primary no matter what his past record of party fidelity and political experience may be. These antireformers see the party regulars—who have deep ties with the party organization and who are more likely to be the party moderates—as the major losers under the new reform rules, and they decry the loss of the careful party recruitment and long periods of party organization apprenticeship that they associate with the prereform system.

These critics have perhaps overlearned the lesson of the 1972 McGovern nomination. Certainly, one or two cases do not solidify a trend. Ford in 1976 was the obvious choice of his party's rank and file as well as the American public. Carter and Reagan in 1980 were their parties' most popular choices for the nomination both among the parties' bases and the public in general. Mondale was unquestionably the choice of Democratic party regulars in 1984. Furthermore, no matter who comes into a convention ahead, ideologue or moderate, the delegates can still act to maximize their party's chances in November if they choose to do so, although it may be more difficult than ever to put aside their own ideological motivations.

The importance of ideological position comes down to how the voters and the party elites actually behave. Primary voters do identify themselves as more ideologically committed than the rest of the population (Chapter 4). And those elites who become delegates to the conventions are more sophisticated and ideologically oriented than the parties' bases or the mass public (Chapter 5). Certain segments of the parties' elites are more representative on ideology and issues, but they have only limited influence in the nominating system. Delegates to the national conventions have often acted in what they perceived as the interest of the party rather than in line with personal ideology; we have identified this as Pitkin's Acting For representation. The amateurs of a few years ago are the professionals of today, and they understand the importance of winning elections.

On the basis of the recent evidence, one must conclude that personality and ideology have importance only relative to other factors and the field of candidates. A candidate's positioning cannot be established mechanically to satisfy some formula for success. For the political scientist the concept is useful for explaining results but not for predicting outcomes. The context of the entire race remains to condition the candidate's strategy.

Timing

Each election year the race for the presidential nomination seems to begin earlier. Reagan is said to have devoted six years of continuous work to achieving the Republican party's nomination: two years in preparation for his 1976 race against incumbent president Ford and four years devoted to the successful pursuit of his party's 1980 nomination. Philip Crane announced his candidacy for the 1980 Republican nomination 27 months before the presidential election. At the time some might have considered that announcement early, yet in 1980, when a number of Democrats—Mondale, Kennedy, Cranston, Glenn, Hollings, Bumpers, Askew, and Hart—began to position themselves for their 1984 run, no one seemed surprised. In 1982, two years before the presidential election, Kennedy formally announced his withdrawal from the race for personal and family reasons. In early 1983 Udall formally announced his intention not to seek his party's nomination, in part because he believed it was too late to put together an adequate campaign. By this time, apparently no one thought it odd that a candidate should withdraw from a race that he had not formally entered and that would not formally begin until early 1984. There is more. In 1982 California Democrats held a state convention with no immediate relevance to the presidential delegate selection that would begin two years later. Nonetheless, a number of the prospective presidential contenders appeared to test their strength. For many in the party and the media, this marked the informal beginning of the very long nominating season.

The need to attract funds and supporters, to build name identification, and to field an organization *before* any of the primaries or caucuses begin forces candidates to commit themselves early. The process is long, arduous, and uncertain. Nonetheless, in the present system it is not unusual for a prospective candidate to do the necessary groundwork for a campaign in the two years following a presidential election; by the third year he is ready to formally announce a candidacy for the next election and is prepared to move into the field. As an example of this sort of preparation, here is an excerpt from a letter one of the campaign organizations mailed to many voters in January of 1983:

> I want you to be among the first to hear from me personally that I have finally and firmly decided to announce my candidacy for the Democratic Party nomination for President. . . .
>
> The assessment of my advisory committee and the encouraging response to my year of exploratory activities convince me that the race in 1984 is wide open. I intend to run long, hard and effectively to win the nomination and the election. . . .

Candidates must be prepared to do well in the early primaries and caucuses; the importance of these early contests can hardly be overstated. Their importance results from the compelling need to develop a sense of momentum. That is, the perception must be fostered that the candidate is winning primaries, is winning pledged delegates in the caucuses, is picking up steam, and can ultimately go on to take the nomination—preferably on the first ballot. Of course, the role of the media in shaping expectations and defining who has momentum, who is developing it, and who is lagging behind is all important.[22] Indeed, it is possible for a candidate to take advantage of victories in the early primaries and caucuses to capture national attention and appear to have a mandate, as Carter did in 1976. Theoretically the early winner could sweep to the nomination; the 40 percent of the delegates that some researchers have said will ensure convention victory may be had within a rather short time.[23]

A related point from the candidate's strategic perspective is the sequencing of the primaries and caucuses. Most of the early primaries and caucuses are held in the East and Midwest. Candidates who are recognized, who have built an organization, and who have won support in these geographical areas may be in a more favorable position than those who count most of their support where most of the important contests come later, in the West and, to a lesser extent, in the South. Ronald Reagan found that the sequencing deck seemed to be stacked against him for a while in his 1976 battle against Gerald Ford, for instance. When the primaries shifted to the South and West, Reagan started winning and gaining on Ford in the delegate count. After early successes in Iowa and New Hampshire, Gary Hart encountered the same problem in 1984. Hart's strength was in the West, but the fact that the majority of these contests occurred relatively late in the campaign season hurt his candidacy. By the time Hart got to his areas of strength, Mondale's lead in the total delegate count was virtually insurmountable.

Candidates and their managers must choose very carefully which primaries and caucuses to enter and how much of their time and scarce resources to expend when and where. If a candidate happens to get into a situation where he stumbles or does less well than expected, he can be written off very early. This is, for example, what happened to Edmund Muskie in the 1972 primaries; he went into the season as everyone's front-runner, but he was finished as a viable candidate after the New Hampshire, Florida, and Wisconsin primaries. In each case, Muskie did less well than the media and many of his supporters expected, and the verdict was swift. The same thing happened to Morris Udall in the 1976 primaries and caucuses. Udall had mistakenly decided not to contest the Iowa caucuses vigorously; when he belatedly tried to enter them he did not do as well as he had hoped. He later made the same mistake in Wisconsin by not spending adequately, and by then Carter was the candidate with the victories and momentum. Glenn appeared to repeat this pattern in 1984; he was stymied by organizational problems.

It pays for the candidate to organize well and early under the current nominating system. But as a consequence the process of presidential nomination has become virtually continuous, and it seems unlikely that party rules and restrictions will be able to reverse this trend.

The Strategic Environment

Aldrich has argued convincingly that candidates are rational actors, that they are pragmatic campaigners with resources at their command, objectives to be realized, and a choice of alternative strategies calculated to achieve their goals.[24] With the changes of the reform era—making primaries the dominant form of delegate selection—those strategies came increasingly to emphasize the winning of the maximum number of convention delegates possible in the primaries.

The strategic environment before the convention and as the convention begins is much different for the front-runner than it is for the challengers. The front-runner must make every effort to hold on to the potential majority of delegates and protect his position. During the convention credentials challenges, rules changes, and potential platform divisions all must be viewed in light of the delegate count. As the convention's first ballot draws near, the front-runners tend to become very conservative in their strategies and very protective of the rules under which they won. Their desire is for peace, stability, and the semblance of a party unified behind their candidacy at virtually any cost; candidates know how important party unity is to their general election campaigns. Walter Mondale's maneuvering along these lines immediately prior to the 1984 Democratic convention is only the most recent illustration of this phenomenon. Meanwhile, in the weeks before and at the opening of the convention the challengers must do everything and anything to create confusion and sow the seeds of uncertainty. They must inject doubts about the inevitability of victory for the front-runner, and they strive to create as fluid a convention as possible. In their efforts they often are both aided and thwarted by the mass media.

Because of the increased use of the primaries and the emphasis on publicly committed delegates, it is possible for the media and the candidates' organizations to develop comprehensive and rather accurate counts of delegate strength as the nominating season unfolds. Thus, there is rarely any doubt about who is the front-runner. Nevertheless, the media thrive on conflict and drama. They often fasten on any rumor, any straw in the wind to get a story. If at any time a delegate even seems to consider going over to the other side, he or she can gain an interview on national television. As the convention nears, any chance that a rules change or credentials dispute could affect the delegate count becomes a major news event. The challengers readily exploit this characteristic of the media in their effort to create confusion and uncertainty about the nomination. Naturally, their fondest hope is to start a stampede of delegates away from the front-runner and into their own camps at the convention. Challengers have not been deterred by the reality that most recent conventions have turned out as foreordained by the primaries and caucuses.

Conclusion _____

Throughout this chapter we have barely touched the complexity of presidential nomination campaigning. And we have not directly addressed the crucial question of how the right candidates can be encouraged in a nominating system, for that question is not readily addressed by empirical means. Many of those who oppose the changes of the reform and postreform eras believe that certain types of candidates (especially the ideologues, as we discussed earlier in this chapter) have undue advantages under the current system. Clearly, we do not fully agree with that assessment. The success of a candidate depends on a number of factors, both environmental and individual, including these:

1. The relative position of one candidate versus the others in the field on any given primary or caucus day
2. The sequencing of the primaries and caucuses
3. The amount of resources each candidate chooses to focus on a particular primary or caucus (see Chapter 7)
4. The attention given by the media to an event and their interpretation of the outcome
5. The winnowing effect that takes place as a result of all these factors

There are times when the political forces simply overwhelm the official rules. There is no way the rules alone can select the candidates, and each party in each election year will have a unique set of candidates representing an unpredictable array of images and ideologies. Some rules—for example, the provision of federal financing for primary candidates—allow candidates to remain in the race longer than might otherwise be possible; but the size of the original field is determined by a host of personal and political factors. The formal rules provide some general perimeters within which national candidates must work to maximize their own chances of being nominated. Large-scale changes in the nominating system would no doubt bring in a different number of candidates, and perhaps encourage a different type, as we will discuss in Chapter 9.

In the end, no matter how good our assessment tools in the discipline of political science may become, our capacity to analyze and unravel what happened in the past election will always be superior to our ability to predict the next election. The drama, pathos, and excitement of American politics stem from these intersections of time, personalities, and circumstances that are ever changing.

NOTES

1. See Angus Campbell et al., *The American Voter* (New York: Wiley, 1960); Norman H. Nie, Sidney Verba, and John R. Petrocik, *The Changing American Voter* (Cambridge, Mass.: Harvard University Press, 1976); Gerald M. Pomper, *Voters' Choice* (New York: Dodd, Mead, 1975). These are just some of the more important works that offer a sampling of the variety of voting behavior studies.
2. See Campbell et al., *The American Voter.*
3. See Herbert Hyman, *Political Socialization* (Glencoe, Ill.: Free Press, 1959); Fred I. Greenstein, *Children and Politics* (New Haven, Conn.: Yale University Press, 1965); Robert D. Hess and Judith V. Torney, *The Development of Political Attitudes in Children* (Chicago: Aldine, 1967).
4. *The Gallup Report* 195 (December 1981): 32-39; Walter Devries and V. Lance Tarrance, *The Ticket Splitter* (Grand Rapids, Mich.: Eedermans, 1972). See also William H. Flanigan and Nancy H. Zingle, *Political Behavior of the American Electorate*, 5th ed. (Boston: Allyn and Bacon, 1983), chap. 1; Gary C. Jacobson, *The Politics of Congressional Elections* (Boston: Little, Brown, 1983), chap. 5; Jack Dennis, "Changing Public Support for the American Party System," in *Paths to Political Reform*, ed. William Crotty (Lexington, Mass.: Lexington Books/D. C. Heath, 1980), 36-66.
5. Arthur H. Miller, "Political Issues and Trust in Government," *American Political Science Review* 68 (September 1974): 951-972; Jacob Citrin, "Comment: The Political Relevance of Trust in Government," *American Political Science Review* 68 (September 1974): 973-988; David B. Hill and Norman R. Luttbeg, *Trends in American Electoral Behavior*, 2d ed. (Itasca, Ill.: F. E. Peacock, 1983), chap. 4.
6. Nie, Verba, and Petrocik, *The Changing American Voter*, is perhaps the most thorough documentation of recent trends in voting behavior; Pomper, *Voters' Choice*, chap. 8; Dan Nimmo and Robert L. Savage, *Candidates and Their Images* (Pacific Palisades, Calif.: Goodyear, 1976), chap. 2; Dan Nimmo, *Popular Images of Politics* (Englewood Cliffs, N.J.: Prentice-Hall, 1974). Hill and Luttbeg, *Trends in American Electoral Behavior*, provides an excellent synopsis of the recent research in this field and a judicious assessment of the influence of each of the important independent variables involved in voting behavior.
7. Malcolm Jewell, "A Caveat on the Expanding Use of Presidential Primaries," *Policy Studies Journal* 2 (Summer 1974): 279-284. For an argument that issues are important in primaries, see Steven J. Brams, *The Presidential Election Game* (New Haven, Conn.: Yale University Press, 1978), chap. 1.
8. Mark J. Wattier, "The Simple Act of Voting in the 1980 Democratic Presidential Primaries," *American Politics Quarterly* 11 (July 1983): 267-292.
9. Stanley Kelley and Thad Mirer, "The Simple Act of Voting," *American Political Science Review* 68 (June 1974): 572-591.
10. Wattier, "The Simple Act of Voting in the 1980 Democratic Presidential Primaries," 267.
11. See Scott Keeter and Cliff Zukin, *Uninformed Choice: The Failure of the New Nominating System* (New York: Praeger, 1983).
12. Nimmo and Savage, *Candidates and Their Images*, chap. 2.
13. See David A. Leuthold, *Electioneering in a Democracy* (New York: Wiley, 1968).

14. Donald R. Matthews, "Winnowing": The News Media and the 1976 Presidential Nominations," in *Race for the Presidency: The Media and the Nominating Process,* ed. James David Barber (Englewood Cliffs, N.J.: Prentice-Hall, 1978), 55-78.
15. Herbert McClosky, Paul J. Hoffman, and Rosemary O'Hara, "Issue Conflict and Consensus among Party Leaders and Followers," *American Political Science Review* 54 (June 1960): 406-427; John S. Jackson III, Barbara L. Brown, and David Bositis, "Herbert McClosky and Friends Revisited," *American Politics Quarterly* 10 (April 1982): 158-180.
16. Nimmo, *Images of Politics,* chap. 2. See also Murray Edelman, *The Symbolic Uses of Politics* (Urbana: University of Illinois Press, 1964).
17. See Jackson, Brown, and Bositis, "McClosky and Friends Revisited."
18. See James David Barber, *The Pulse of Politics: Electing Presidents in the Media Age* (New York: W. W. Norton, 1980).
19. See Keeter and Zukin, *Uninformed Choice.*
20. See Larry Sabato, *The Rise of the Political Consultants* (New York: Basic Books, 1981); Dan Nimmo, *The Political Persuaders* (Englewood Cliffs, N.J.: Prentice-Hall, 1970).
21. John H. Aldrich, *Before the Convention: Strategies and Choices in Presidential Nomination Campaigns* (Chicago: University of Chicago Press, 1980), 167.
22. Thomas R. Marshall, *Presidential Nominations in a Reform Age* (New York: Praeger, 1981), 3.
23. William A. Gamson, "Coalition Formation at Presidential Nominating Conventions," *American Journal of Sociology* 68 (September 1962): 157-181. Of course, Gamson formulated his theory before the current era, and it is uncertain as to whether the rule holds in the era of one ballot conventions decided by the primaries.
24. See Aldrich, *Before the Convention.*

7

The funding of electoral contests has always been a subject of controversy and one of the most difficult tasks for candidates and their organizations. Hubert H. Humphrey, who ran a number of campaigns in his long political life, was oppressed by the financial aspects of candidacy:

> Campaign financing is a curse. It's the most disgusting, demeaning, disenchanting, debilitating experience of a politician's life. It's stinky, it's lousy. I just can't tell you how much I hate it. I've had to break off in the middle of trying to make a decent, honorable campaign and go up to somebody's parlor or to a room and say, 'Gentlemen, and ladies, I'm desperate. You've got to help me....' [1]

Introduction

Raising money is a necessary evil in any political campaign, especially in the age of expensive television advertising and huge professional campaign staffs. Charges of corruption or misconduct have accompanied numerous political campaigns; as in any situation where large amounts of money change hands, temptation is often present. Abuses and inequities have from time to time sparked reforms in campaign financing, beginning in the early 1900s. Several federal laws eventually addressed a number of aspects relating to campaign financing, including sources of contributions, limits on contributions, limits on spending, financial disclosure, and enforcement (the specific laws are reviewed later in this chapter).

The intent of campaign finance reforms was to have politicians appear as Caesar's wife, beyond reproach, which is an impossible task. In practice, most financial reforms were aimed at mollifying public opinion in the wake of political scandal. But whether fair campaigns can be effectively encouraged through funding legislation is an important question that is beyond the scope of this book. Here we will examine the issues of prenomination fund raising and campaign spending and how recent legislation has affected these tasks.

Campaign Reform Legislation

The most recent round of campaign reforms culminated with the passage of several important pieces of legislation in the early 1970s: the Revenue Act of 1971, the Federal Election Campaign Act (FECA) of 1971, and the Campaign Reform Act of 1974 (the formal title of which is the Federal Campaign Act Amendments of 1974). Together these acts provide the basis for contemporary campaign regulation. The most important innovation of this reform legislation was the provision of federal funding for presidential prenomination and general election campaigns (which the candidate is free to apply for or not). In 1976, the first election year for which the laws were in effect, $10.9 million and $21.8 million were allowed per candidate for the prenomination and general election races, respectively; the amounts have risen with each election year to allow for inflation. In 1984 the primary expenditure limit was $20.2 million and the general election expenditure limit was $40.4 million.

To provide a source for these federal funds, a special check-off system was set up in the Revenue Act of 1971. On the income tax forms, taxpayers were allowed the option of earmarking one dollar for the presidential campaign. In addition, taxpayers were allowed income tax credits for 50 percent of their political donations up to a maximum of $12.50 on a single return and $25.00 on a joint return. That amount has now been increased to $50 and $100, respectively. In effect, the federal government will subsidize half of small donations. The campaign finance bills instituted specific and exacting financial disclosure standards to prevent campaign abuses and created the Federal Election Commission (FEC) to oversee the new requirements.

In regard to the financing of prenomination campaigns, the rules are quite specific, and we will review them here in outline before proceeding in more detail later in the chapter. (Our discussion centers on 1980 figures since those are the latest complete figures available.) Candidates for their party's nomination who apply for federal financing must agree to a specified ceiling of expenditures for their prenomination campaigns ($14.7 million in 1980 and $20.2 million in 1984). In addition, there is a limit imposed on how much a candidate may spend in each state. (In 1980 this ranged from $29,400 for the states with the least population to just under $3.9 million for California.) To qualify for federal funds the candidate must raise by other means the initial sum of $100,000 in at least 20 states (with a $5,000 minimum for each state). Individual contributions to this sum cannot exceed $250. To defray the costs of fund raising the candidate is allowed to spend up to 20 percent beyond the specified campaign ceiling.

Once the candidate has raised the initial $100,000, the first $250 of all contributions is matched by federal funds, up to the specified maximum for prenomination races. Individuals are limited to a maximum contribution of $1,000, and political action committees (PACs) may contribute up to $5,000. Detailed financial disclosure reports on both receipts and expenditures must be filed periodically during the campaign period with the FEC. All contributors or recipients of funds in excess of $200 must be identified by name, address, and business affiliation; the disclosure information is available to the media and the public.

To remain eligible for the federal funds, a candidate must receive a minimum of 10 percent of the vote in each of two consecutive primaries or caucuses. This provision is intended to establish minimum criteria for eligibility so that federal funds will not be used to prolong hopeless candidacies.

As in general election campaigns, PACs or individuals may spend their own funds to independently promote or attack a candidate; any money spent this way does not count against a candidate's limit, provided that the independent efforts are not coordinated with the candidate's campaign.[2] The Supreme Court in *Buckley v. Valeo* (1976) has upheld the legality of such spending as an exercise of the First Amendment freedom of expression. In 1980, for example, $2.2 million was spent independently by unaffiliated groups and individuals to promote candidates, and an additional $0.5 million was spent independently in advertising directed against specific candidates. Labor unions and corporations, in addition, invested $0.8 million in partisan activity during the prenomination period (a quarter of this in campaigning against); they spent another $0.5 million in drafting presidential candidates.

All candidates, whether they accept public funds or not, must observe the contribution limits and meet the disclosure requirements. Those who do not accept federal funds are allowed to spend whatever they can raise. But in spite of the attached strings, public financing has proved attractive to almost all potential nominees.

In our discussion of prenomination funding and expenditures in this chapter, we will return to these and other provisions of the reform legislation. The campaign finance reforms have been amended and refined during the last decade, but the original legislation remains the basis for fund raising and spending in presidential campaigns. So far, only John Connally (in his 1980 quest for the Republican nomination) has rejected federal funding, preferring instead to raise all of his funds privately and thus avoiding the spending limits.

The 1980 Campaign

The broadest measure of campaign spending is derived from the total receipts and expenditures of the candidates as a group. Table 7.1 presents the total figures for campaign expenditures among candidates who received federal matching funds in 1976 and in 1980. This table and the others in this chapter are based on *adjusted* figures, which are roughly 6 percent lower than gross amounts; the FEC revises campaign totals to account for refunds to contributors, loan payments, and similar changes. The ten candidates who received matching federal funds in 1980 raised $94.2 million and spent $92.3 million. Compared with the 1976 amounts, the 1980 expenditures represent a rise of almost 140 percent; considering that fewer campaigns qualified for matching funds in 1980, the costs of each individual campaign roughly doubled. Six candidates in 1980 did not receive federal funds: five did not qualify,

Table 7.1 Presidential Prenomination Campaign Costs, 1976-1980 (in millions of dollars)

	1976		1980	
Number of candidates	(15)		(10)	
Adjusted receipts	$67.9	100.0%	$94.2	100.0%
Individual contributors	42.5	62.7	61.0	64.8
PAC contributions	0.8	1.1	1.4	
Federal matching funds	24.3	35.8	30.9	32.8
Adjusted disbursements	66.9		92.3	

Note: The difference in the number of campaigns, plus inflation, should be taken into consideration before any comparison is made.

Source: Federal Election Commission

Table 7.2 Presidential Prenomination Candidate Receipts and Expenditures, 1980 (in millions of dollars)

	Net receipts per *Report*[a]	Adjusted receipts[b]	Individual contributions[c]	PAC contributions	Matching funds[d]	Net disbursements per *Report*	Adjusted disbursements[b]
Brown (Dem.)	$ 3.21	$ 2.65	$ 1.71	$ .04	$ .89	$ 3.21	$ 2.65
Carter (Dem.)	19.59	18.55	12.93	.46	5.05	19.56	18.52
Kennedy (Dem.)	16.74	12.29	7.75	.23	3.86	16.72	12.27
LaRouche (Dem.)	2.23	2.14	1.55	.008	.53	2.23	2.15
Anderson (Rep.)	7.25	6.63	3.91	.02	2.68	7.05	6.52
Baker (Rep.)	9.08	7.14	4.20	.13	2.64	9.01	7.07
Bush (Rep.)	22.21	16.71	10.87	.13	5.72	22.20	16.71
Crane (Rep.)	5.42	5.24	3.47	.002	1.75	5.40	5.22
Dole (Rep.)	1.56	1.43	.90	.045	.45	1.52	1.39
Reagan (Rep.)	28.32	21.39	13.76	.285	7.29	26.75	19.82
Subtotal	$115.60	$ 94.17	$61.05	$1.35	$30.86	$113.75	$ 92.32
Connally (Rep.)	$ 13.80	$ 12.72	$ 11.64	$ .205	0	$ 13.70	$ 12.62
Fernandez (Rep.)	.26	.25	.19	.002	0	.25	.25
Stassen (Rep.)	.12	.11	.006	0	0	.14	.12
Clark (Lib.)	1.10	1.09	.57	0	0	1.03	1.02
Hunscher (Lib.)	.15	.15	.01	0	0	.10	.10
Pulley (SWP)	.16	.13	.10	0	0	.15	.12
Grand total	$131.19	$108.62	$73.57	$1.56	$30.86	$129.12	$106.55

[a] Net receipts or net disbursements per *Report* total reported receipts or disbursements minus any transfers received from or disbursed to affiliated committees.

[b] Adjusted receipts or adjusted disbursements are total reported receipts or disbursements minus transfers from or to affiliated committees, loan repayments, contribution refunds, and refunds or rebates received.

[c] Individual contributions are total reported contributions minus itemized contribution refunds. Unitemized refunds are not included in the net calculation.

[d] Matching fund figures are taken from the total reported by the campaigns through December 31, 1980. Total matching fund certifications totaled $31.3 million. Additional funds were certified to Carter, Crane, and Kennedy in 1981.

Source: Federal Election Commission

and Connally did not apply. Overall, the 16 candidates in 1980 (a figure that includes the six candidates who did not receive federal matching funds) raised $108.6 million and spent $106.5 million, as Table 7.2 shows.

A breakdown of contributions also appears in Tables 7.1 and 7.2. The relative proportions of funding sources changed little from 1976 to 1980. The principal source of funds for the candidates as a whole was individual contributors (nearly 65 percent in 1980). The federal government was the next largest contributor, with about 33 percent in 1980. And it may come as a surprise that PACs, the fastest growing and most significant source of campaign funds in congressional elections,[3] made negligible direct contributions to the presidential prenomination campaigns (less than 2 percent of the total reported in 1980).

Sources of Funding

Individuals

Individuals are the single largest source of prenomination funding, as the campaign financing legislation intended. One purpose of the campaign financing reforms was to spread the financial burdens of the campaign among a large number of givers, in hopes of lessening a candidate's dependence on big money and allowing candidates without access to corporate or individual wealth to compete for the presidency. It is useful to examine differences among the candidates regarding the types of donations they received and from where they received them.

Size. The results from 1980 (Table 7.3) illustrate that small individual donations played a large part in many campaigns.

Minor party and long-shot candidates tend to depend overwhelmingly on grass-roots funding and small donations to finance their efforts (in 1980, Anderson, LaRouche, Baker, Crane, Clark, Fernandez, and Pulley). There are exceptions: Connally, who based his entire campaign on private donations, received over 44 percent of his funds from donors of $750 or more; and Dole and Brown obtained 38 percent and 32 percent, respectively, of their funds through large donations (that is, $750 or more).

Among the other candidates, incumbent president Jimmy Carter did best among the big contributors (50 percent of his total), far outdistancing Kennedy, Reagan, and Bush. Conversely, Carter's ability

Table 7.3 Contributions by Individual Donors, 1980 Prenomination Races

	Under $500			$500–$749			$750 and up		Total	
	($)	(%)	(N)	($)	(%)	(N)	($)	(%)	($)	(%)
Democrats										
Brown	938,086	54.73	430	217,597	12.69	565	558,425	32.58	1,714,108	100.00
Carter	4,200,997	32.31	4,521	2,294,069	17.65	6,603	6,505,870	50.04	13,000,936	100.00
Kennedy	4,540,456	58.50	1,596	816,108	10.52	2,460	2,404,295	30.98	7,760,859	100.00
LaRouche	1,399,874	89.90	174	92,379	5.93	68	64,901	4.17	1,557,154	100.00
Republicans										
Anderson	3,391,422	86.75	439	220,710	5.65	304	297,430	7.61	3,909,562	100.00
Baker	2,783,617	65.48	1,189	597,898	14.06	889	869,705	20.46	4,251,220	100.00
Bush	6,228,267	56.99	3,983	2,000,878	18.31	2,795	2,700,268	24.71	10,929,413	100.00
Connally	5,027,980	42.67	3,084	1,556,084	13.20	5,308	5,200,534	44.13	11,784,598	100.00
Crane	3,177,824	91.29	254	129,075	3.71	175	174,035	5.00	3,480,934	100.00
Dole	390,748	43.31	324	162,200	17.98	354	349,326	38.72	902,274	100.00
Fernandez	167,712	87.67	17	8,695	4.55	15	14,900	7.79	191,307	100.00
Reagan	8,172,918	58.86	2,945	1,489,726	10.73	4,231	4,222,713	30.41	13,885,357	100.00
Stassen	3,003	46.18	1	500	7.69	3	3,000	46.13	6,503	100.00
Other										
Clark	508,605	88.32	48	24,518	4.26	43	42,722	7.42	575,845	100.00
Hunscher	7,591	60.55	2	1,000	7.98	4	3,946	31.47	12,537	100.00
Pulley	98,405	100.00	0	0	0.00	0	0	0.00	98,405	100.00
Totals	41,037,505	55.41	19,007	9,611,437	12.98	23,817	23,412,070	31.61	74,061,012	100.00

Source: Federal Election Commission

to attract smaller donors fell well behind the other three, all of whom received over 50 percent of their funds from these sources.

Geographical Sources. To qualify for federal matching funds, as 10 candidates did in 1980, money must be raised initially in at least 20 states. But contributions are not evenly distributed among the states. Table 7.4 lists the top 10 states contributing to each of the major contenders in the 1980 prenomination contests (Carter and Kennedy for the Democrats; Reagan and Bush for the Republicans). Better than 70 percent of Kennedy's, Reagan's, and Bush's contributions came from the states listed. Even the incumbent, Carter, whose contributors were distributed somewhat more broadly than the others, received 65 percent of his contributions from the top 10 states.

Table 7.4 Top 10 State Contributors to Major Contenders, 1980 Prenomination Races

Democrats			Republicans		
Candidate	State	Percent of total	Candidate	State	Percent of total
Carter	Florida	11.7%	Reagan	California	31.1%
	New York	11.1		Texas	10.3
	California	10.3		New York	6.9
	Georgia	5.8		Florida	5.7
	Ohio	5.6		New Jersey	4.8
	Texas	5.5		Michigan	4.6
	New Jersey	4.9		Illinois	4.4
	Delaware	3.7		Pennsylvania	2.9
	Illinois	3.4		Ohio	2.8
	Pennsylvania	2.9		Oklahoma	2.0
Kennedy	California	16.5%	Bush	Texas	19.4%
	Massachusetts	15.5		New York	15.9
	New York	15.0		Illinois	7.8
	Illinois	9.2		California	7.3
	Florida	5.6		Connecticut	6.5
	Delaware	4.9		Florida	5.4
	New Jersey	2.8		Massachusetts	2.9
	Pennsylvania	2.7		Pennsylvania	2.8
	Maryland	2.7		Ohio	2.5
	Puerto Rico	2.3		New Jersey	2.5

Note: Percentage represents proportion of total of individual contributions given by people living in the state.

Source: Federal Election Commission

Certain large states appear in each candidate's top 10: California, New York, Illinois, Pennsylvania, New Jersey, and Florida; Texas and Ohio contributed heavily to all these candidates but Kennedy. Each candidate received a good percentage of his contributions from his home state. Bush, for example, has family ties with Connecticut and currently calls Texas home; both states contributed heavily to his campaign.

Kennedy's support was heavily from Eastern states; Reagan's list shows the most Midwestern and Western states, areas that have been the bedrock of his political career. Carter's largest bloc of contributions came from Florida, followed in turn by the large states of New York and California and then by his home state of Georgia. In general the larger, wealthier states were on the top 10 lists for almost all candidates, but the home state and home region advantages show up in the data for each candidate as well.

Beyond these general trends, the contributions seem to reflect certain idiosyncratic appeals. For instance, Puerto Rico is on Kennedy's top 10, which may reflect his appeal to the Hispanic population. Tiny Delaware appeared on both Kennedy's and Carter's top 10 list, perhaps reflecting the fact that the state is corporate headquarters for many national companies. In general, these regional differences reflect to a limited degree the varying geographical and personal appeal of the candidates.

Candidates

Another side of campaign financing is the candidates' use of their personal financial resources. Under present laws, an individual's giving to his or her own campaign is unrestricted if the campaign accepts no federal matching funds. If it accepts public funds, the limit for personal spending by a candidate under the 1976 law is $50,000.[4] Nonetheless, most candidates do not contribute significantly to their own campaigns. As Table 7.5 shows, only 4 of the 16 campaigns in 1980 received any donations from the candidates. Only the Libertarians used candidate donations as the main source of campaign funds, and that party accounted for 96 percent of the entire amount of candidate contributions; Clark, its presidential candidate, gave $490,000 of his own money and Hunscher, its eventual vice presidential candidate, gave $141,935 of his. Stassen, a Republican, gave $24,000 to his own campaign. Among the major candidates, only Carter made a direct contribution, and that was negligible ($1,000).

Table 7.5 Candidate Contributions to Their Own Campaigns, 1980 Prenomination Races

	Personal contributions	Personal loans
Democrat		
Brown	0	0
Carter	$ 1,000	
Kennedy	0	$ 40,000
La Rouche	0	3,000
Republican		
Anderson	0	0
Baker	0	0
Bush	0	0
Connally	0	578,883
Crane	0	15,375
Dole	0	0
Fernandez	0	0
Reagan	0	0
Stassen	24,414	74,509
Other		
Clark	490,000	0
Hunscher	141,935	0
Pulley	0	0
Democratic subtotal	1,000	43,000
Republican subtotal	24,414	668,767
Other subtotal	631,935	0
Grand total	$657,349	$711,767

Source: Federal Election Commission

Personal loans from candidates to their campaigns were more common. Connally was forced to extend a loan of over $500,000 dollars to his faltering effort, a sum that accounts for the bulk of the personal loans in the 1980 races. Stassen lent his campaign an additional $75,000 and Kennedy lent his $40,000. Smaller loans were made by Crane and by LaRouche. But for the most part, it appears that candidate contributions and loans to their own races were not significant factors in funding the 1980 contests.

Political Action Committees

As we mentioned earlier in this chapter, contributions by PACs accounted for an insignificant proportion (less than 2 percent) of the direct

Table 7.6 Contributions by Political Action Committees (PACs), 1980 Prenomination Races, by Type of PAC

	Party	Corporation	Labor	Noncon-nected	Trade associations	Cooperatives	Corporations without stockholders	Nonparty
Democrat								
Brown	$ 0	$ 5,500	$ 18,050	$ 4,000	$ 10,000	$ 0	$ 0	$ 37,550
Carter	5,800	260,301	81,350	9,450	78,950	21,100	9,500	460,651
Kennedy	7,300	38,634	162,056	9,750	19,934	0	2,000	232,374
LaRouche	0	50	0	8,150	0	0	0	8,200
Republican								
Anderson	0	8,620	0	2,000	12,675	0	1,200	24,495
Baker	0	94,056	500	4,200	23,685	5,000	2,000	129,441
Bush	0	120,204	200	3,291	1,840	0	4,500	130,035
Connally	0	177,530	700	1,850	12,025	5,000	8,000	205,105
Crane	0	775	0	0	1,050	0	0	1,825
Dole	100	31,939	150	3,375	9,850	0	0	45,314
Fernandez	0	2,000	0	0	0	0	0	2,000
Reagan	2,000	221,858	0	15,281	31,800	10,000	6,500	285,439
Stassen	0	0	0	0	0	0	0	0
Other								
Clark	24,300	0	0	0	0	0	0	0
Hunscher	0	0	0	0	0	0	0	0
Pulley	0	0	0	0	0	0	0	0
Democrat subtotal	13,100	304,485	261,456	31,350	108,884	21,100	11,500	738,775
Republican subtotal	2,100	656,982	1,550	29,997	92,925	20,000	22,200	823,654
Other subtotal	24,300	0	0	0	0	0	0	0
Grand total	$39,500	$961,467	$263,006	$61,347	$201,809	$41,100	$33,700	$1,562,429

Note: Nonconnected PACs are primarily policy- or ideology-oriented PACs not connected with any corporation, trade association, union, or political party.

Source: Federal Election Commission

contributions to prenomination campaigns in both 1976 and 1980. PACs make a heavy investment in congressional campaigns, for which their contributions have increased remarkably over the 10 years between 1974 and 1984. But in presidential campaigns they have a much more limited impact.[5] Keeping that in mind, it is useful to examine how the PAC contributions were divided among the candidates. As Table 7.6 shows, the Republicans enjoyed disproportionate support from corporations, the Democrats from labor unions (with corporations spending over 3.5 times what unions spent). PACs representing cooperatives, trade associations, and health groups divided their funds equally between the parties.

It is revealing to compare corporate and labor contributions by candidate (Table 7.7). Some of the differences between the two major parties, as well as information about the relative standings of the candidates, emerge clearly from the results. The incumbent does well, as is expected throughout American politics. Jimmy Carter ranked first in corporate contributions and second in labor contributions in 1980. And not surprisingly, the Republicans Reagan, Connally, Bush, and Baker accounted for 64 percent of the corporate expenditures in the

Table 7.7 Corporate and Labor Union Contributions, 1980 Prenomination Races

Corporate giving			Labor giving		
Candidate	Amount	Percent of total corporate contribution	Candidate	Amount	Percent of total labor contribution
Carter	$260,301	27%	Kennedy	$162,056	62%
Reagan	221,858	23	Carter	81,350	31
Connally	177,530	18	Brown	18,050	7
Bush	120,204	13	Others (4)	388[a]	—
Baker	94,056	10			
Kennedy	38,634	4			
Dole	31,939	3			
Others (5)	3,389[a]	2			
Total	$961,467	100		$263,006	100

[a] Average each candidate.

Source: Federal Election Commission

prenomination race. On the other hand, Kennedy, as a nonincumbent liberal Democrat, received over 60 percent of the labor total and only 4 percent of the corporate contributions. Brown got some labor support (mostly from California unions) but managed to obtain only $5,500 from corporations, 0.5 percent of the overall total.

As we have shown so far in this chapter, the sources of campaign funding are diverse but follow several patterns and show some party differences. Equally important for an understanding of campaign financing is an examination of how the money is spent.

Expenditures

The amount of money each candidate receiving federal matching funds may spend in each state is limited by law in proportion to the state's population; the figures are modified in accordance with inflation each election year. The second column of Table 7.8 presents the 1980 limit for each state. The state by state expenditures of the four major candidates—Carter and Kennedy for the Democrats, Reagan and Bush for the Republicans—are listed and compared to the legal limits in columns 3 through 10 of Table 7.8. Candidates rarely spend the allowable limit in a state, in part because the total of the state limits far exceeds the national limit.

As one would expect, states receive different amounts of attention from the candidates, ranging from no expenditures at all to beyond the limit (for example, by Carter in Alaska and Iowa, respectively). What concerns us here is understanding why candidates approach different states as they do. In fact, how candidates allocate prenomination campaign funds depends on several elements of their overall strategy (see Chapter 6).

The candidates are all striving to obtain enough convention delegates to clinch their party's nomination on the first ballot. But if that were the only basis for their spending, they could concentrate on the largest states alone: the 10 largest states accounted for more than enough delegate votes to win the Democratic party's nomination and 88 percent of the delegate votes required to win the Republican party's nomination. The figures in Table 7.8 show that size was not the basis of the candidates' spending strategy. Although such large states as Florida, Illinois, and Massachusetts were fairly well covered by candidate expenditures, other large states, such as California, New Jersey, and Ohio, were not. The candidates invested on the average one-quarter of the financial resources allowed by law.

Table 7.8 Expenditures of Major Candidates in 1980 Prenomination Races, by State

State	Expenditure limit	Democrats				Republicans			
		Carter	Percent spent	Kennedy	Percent spent	Reagan	Percent spent	Bush	Percent spent
Alabama	622,715	75,452	12	48,863	8	180,372	29	443,637	71
Alaska	294,400	0	0	2,654	1	61,009	21	13,901	5
Arizona	399,677	77,241	2	49,495	12	48,021	12	3,660	1
Arkansas	363,172	8,986	2	2,839	1	44,320	12	31,571	9
California	3,880,192	204,202	5	307,041	8	482,276	12	70,693	2
Colorado	464,445	17,863	4	53,102	11	61,419	13	24,370	5
Connecticut	540,518	150,393	29	69,466	13	231,449	43	412,023	76
Delaware	294,400	35	*	4,137	1	11,049	4	2,705	1
D.C.	294,400	10,312	4	37,702	13	9,105	3	32,940	11
Florida	1,562,204	673,003	43	134,648	9	1,171,146	75	1,302,739	83
Georgia	838,687	45,090	5	13,857	*	259,849	31	19,925	2
Hawaii	294,000	20	*	4,361	1	43,511	15	10,953	4
Idaho	294,400	2,761	1	9,797	3	10,961	4	1,151	4
Illinois	1,883,453	1,050,838	56	215,905	11	673,325	36	1,315,526	70
Indiana	896,625	128,344	14	35,979	4	112,840	13	14,821	2
Iowa	489,882	493,067	101	442,848	90	466,088	95	462,382	94
Kansas	406,036	28,282	7	6,759	2	55,187	14	100,405	25
Kentucky	585,267	3,190	1	269	*	53,801	9	26,160	4
Louisiana	641,321	31,497	5	278	*	38,478	6	23,009	4
Maine	294,400	286,039	97	141,536	48	84,761	29	60,583	21
Maryland	706,560	68,933	10	57,806	8	76,180	11	127,890	18
Massachusetts	1,001,667	310,075	31	306,579	31	608,840	61	796,281	79
Michigan	1,523,814	153,762	10	84,890	6	159,196	10	376,420	25

Minnesota	681,124	176,089	26	66,475	10	92,268	14	118,257	17
Mississippi	382,484	11,125	3	3,263	1	107,137	28	7,686	2
Missouri	829,972	69,556	8	20,034	2	53,136	6	0	0
Montana	294,400	3,057	1	15,367	5	17,089	6	1,847	1
Nebraska	294,400	43,685	15	41,658	14	30,914	11	15,764	5
Nevada	294,400	1,144	*	7,911	3	44,323	15	1,513	1
New Hampshire	294,400	285,201	97	264,479	90	280,748	95	264,851	90
New Jersey	1,255,793	46,059	4	122,614	10	165,590	13	137,350	11
New Mexico	294,400	5,414	2	16,387	6	34,993	12	2,817	1
New York	3,037,737	1,196,782	39	487,481	16	739,065	24	354,646	12
North Carolina	940,196	18,797	2	4,625	*	80,338	9	62,828	7
North Dakota	294,400	697	*	3,366	1	22,700	8	920	*
Ohio	1,800,550	273,260	15	206,531	11	144,166	8	72,781	4
Oklahoma	488,940	63,143	13	33,193	7	56,471	12	4,862	1
Oregon	430,531	64,479	15	24,643	7	68,765	16	191,823	48
Pennsylvania	2,030,182	722,272	36	215,050	11	250,128	12	1,369,807	67
Rhode Island	294,400	5,202	2	27,254	9	4,912	2	20,314	7
South Carolina	477,164	16,035	3	21,677	5	434,413	91	228,934	48
South Dakota	294,400	10,527	4	9,355	3	31,469	11	1,971	1
Tennessee	738,120	15,280	2	8,302	1	56,179	8	60,505	8
Texas	2,188,216	162,786	7	88,477	4	216,498	10	695,299	32
Utah	294,400	1,987	1	26,676	9	39,474	13	5,535	2
Vermont	294,400	87,376	30	40,202	14	153,596	52	100,065	34
Virginia	885,084	33,003	4	54,519	6	143,637	16	75,196	8
Washington	666,286	59,557	9	60,013	5	57,498	9	48,900	7
West Virginia	315,361	157,716	50	27,534	9	11,192	4	4,457	1
Wisconsin	794,173	214,816	27	59,683	8	193,130	24	574,471	72
Wyoming	294,400	6,212	2	6,736	2	3,591	1	8,134	3

* Less than 0.5%.

Source: Federal Election Commission

In some contests a candidate may spend more heavily to weaken an opponent. For example, Reagan successfully eliminated Connally in South Carolina, where he spent 91 percent of the limit. (Bush spent heavily in South Carolina also, perhaps because the stakes had been raised by Reagan, whereas the Democrats paid little attention to the state.) Other states where one candidate spent disproportionately more than his opponents may have had similar strategic importance to a campaign. Candidates may have several reasons for wanting to look good in a certain state. Credibility may be important, as it probably was for Bush in his native state of Connecticut—where he also had reason to believe his money would be well spent; for Reagan in Georgia—where by garnering Deep South support he might indirectly have a chance to make Carter look bad; and for Carter in Maine—where his win in a New England state would damage Kennedy.

The campaign financing laws also help determine candidate strategy in terms of influencing decisions on which contests to enter. Anyone who fails to get 10 percent of the vote in two successive contests is disqualified from receiving federal matching funds. If the candidate fears a poor showing, he may choose not to enter a certain state's contest at all. This provision does not affect the major candidates as much as the minor ones, but every organization has to be aware of the consequences of misjudging the candidate's chances. As another consequence of the laws, the candidate must keep state-by-state strategy always in mind, since the total allotment is so much smaller than those of all the states taken together.

None of these explanations accounts for the most dramatic state expenditures. The highest state expenditures were in Iowa and New Hampshire, the states with the first two presidential nomination contests, where each of the candidates spent over 90 percent of the state limits (Table 7.8). In only four states—Iowa, New Hampshire, Florida, and Massachusetts—did the major contenders even average over 50 percent of the legal maximum, and all four held their delegate selection events during the early weeks of the season. Obviously, these states are perceived as critically important by anyone with a serious interest in securing a party's nomination. In Chapters 2 and 3 we identified the front-loading phenomenon, in which states pushed their contests earlier and earlier to attract media and candidate attention and enhance their influence on the nomination process. As a result the front-loading phenomenon works into the candidates' strategy more than any other single element: candidates must do well in the earlier contests to generate momentum and enthusiasm for their campaigns, and doing well means spending money.

Table 7.9 Cost per Vote in Selected Contests in Prenomination Races, 1976 and 1980

		Cost per vote	
State	Month	1976	1980
Iowa	January	$9.46	$13.89
New Hampshire	February	7.22	8.90
Florida	March	2.02	2.21
Wisconsin	April	1.15	1.36
Nebraska	May	1.30	0.45
California	June	0.68	0.23

Source: Congressional Quarterly Weekly Report, December 26, 1981, 2566.

A comparison of the cost per vote statistics for various contests—calculated by dividing expenditure by population—dramatically illustrates the difference timing makes. As Table 7.9 shows, in both 1976 and 1980 progressively less money was spent per vote as the season developed. In 1980, 60 times as much money was spent to secure an Iowan's vote in January as to get a Californian's vote in June.

It would be hard to argue that the top 10 states in candidate spending—a list (Table 7.10) that includes the small states Maine, Vermont, and Connecticut as well as New Hampshire and Iowa—are among the most critical states either for winning the general election or for contributing delegates to the parties' national conventions. Yet, among the top 10 states in electoral importance (Table 7.11), only Illinois, Florida, and Massachusetts received a significant proportion of the spending limit. Those states had early primaries. California, New Jersey, and Ohio—which had their delegate selection events in the last weeks of the prenomination season—were relatively neglected in terms of candidate spending.

In the 1980 contests Reagan spent so heavily in the early state primaries and caucuses that he was in danger of running out of funds during the later stages of the delegate selection process, as was Walter Mondale in 1984. Had George Bush, or one of the other contenders, presented a more formidable challenge, he (or they) would have had a clear financial advantage in later races. Reagan (who had the resources to spend 97.1% of the national limit) had spent almost two-thirds of his legal limit by the end of February. Reagan may have been an extreme example. But a number of the other contenders had the resources to spend over 70 percent of the assigned maximum in seeking their party's

Table 7.10 States Receiving Most Candidate Attention, in Percentage of Limit Spent, 1980

State	Percent of limit spent	Number of delegates to national conventions		Percentage of national convention vote		Number of electoral votes	Percentage of electoral college vote
		Democrats	Republicans	Democrats	Republicans		
Iowa	95%	50	37	2%	2%	8	1%
New Hampshire	93	19	22	6	1	4	1
Florida	53	100	51	3	3	17	3
Massachusetts	51	111	42	3	2	14	3
Maine	49	22	21	1	1	4	1
Illinois	43	179	102	5	5	26	5
Connecticut	40	54	35	2	2	8	1
South Carolina	36	37	25	1	1	8	1
Wisconsin	33	75	34	2	2	11	2
Vermont	33	12	19	3	1	3	1

Source: Federal Election Commission

Table 7.11 States with Greatest Political Importance, Based on Electoral College Representation

	Number of electoral college votes	Percentage of electoral college vote	Number of delegates to national convention		Percentage of national convention vote	
			Democrats	Republicans	Democrats	Republicans
California	45	8%	306	168	9%	8%
New York	41	8	282	123	8	6
Pennsylvania	27	5	185	83	6	4
Texas	26	5	152	80	5	4
Illinois	26	5	179	102	5	5
Ohio	25	5	161	77	5	4
Michigan	21	4	141	82	4	4
New Jersey	17	3	113	66	3	3
Florida	17	3	100	51	3	3
Massachusetts	14	3	111	42	3	2

Source: Federal Election Commission

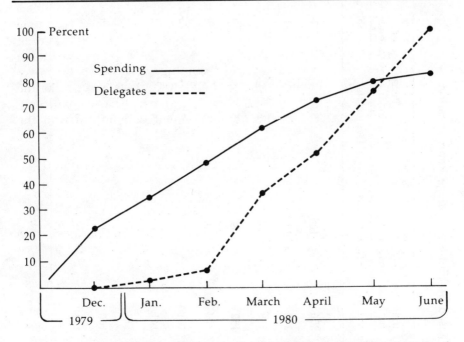

Figure 7.1 Cumulative Percent of Delegates Apportioned and of Spending Limit Reached by Top Four Candidates (1980), by Month. (From F. Christopher Arterton, "Dollars for Presidents: Spending Money under the FECA," in *Financing Presidential Campaigns,* Campaign Finance Study Group, John F. Kennedy School of Government, Harvard University [Cambridge, Mass., 1982], 3.24. Reprinted by permission.)

presidential nomination as well: Carter had 93.7 percent, Bush had 91.8 percent, Connally had 72.8 percent, and Kennedy had 72.3 percent; these candidates had spent an average of 57 percent of their total by the end of February.

The expenditure of money and the number of delegates at stake in a given state bear little relationship (Figure 7.1). Although one-half of all the money to be spent in the nominating campaign had been committed by the end of February, only 7 percent of the national convention delegates had been selected.

A campaign strategy based on timing might seem one-sided, but it accomplished for both Reagan and Carter exactly what they intended: each was virtually able to eliminate the other serious contenders and make his party's nomination all but inevitable by the end of the Illinois primary. Such results serve to reinforce the same pattern next time around: go all out in the early tests and then let the rest take care of themselves. In fact, the data on Table 7.9 show that the gap between the the early and late states in per vote spending increased in 1980 over 1976. The attention of the media to the early contests helps make the candidates' strategy pay off. As Thomas R. Marshall has convincingly shown, the media *verdict*—the pronouncement of who has won the nomination and who is out of the picture—was made very early (by March) in both parties in 1976 and 1980.[6]

The main conclusion we can draw from our examination of the patterns of candidate spending is that the importance of a state in the candidates' decision making depends largely on the scheduling of its primary or caucus. Attention is not paid in relation to the size of a state's convention delegation or to the significance of the state's vote in the electoral college. A state's prenomination political importance bears no apparent relationship to the size of its population or its contribution to the nation's economy.

Many observers are critical of this aspect of the current nominating system, which ties in with the sequencing of the nomination contests and the role of the media. Clearly, the importance accorded the early states, which are for the most part unrepresentative, is not fair to the larger states, which carry more votes but less influence. As we will show, this is one area where further reform may be called for; indeed, the Democrats' rules changes tried to address the problem by shortening the season in 1984.

The State of Campaign Financing

The campaign finance legislation that culminated in the 1974 Campaign Finance Act drastically changed the way presidential races are funded as, for the first time, the federal government became involved in campaign fund raising and expenditures. More candidates became able to afford the prenomination contests, which in theory has resulted in a greater range of policy choices for the voters. On the whole, candidates and the public have accepted the utility of public financing of presidential campaigns. Most candidates do apply for federal matching funds; some, like John Connally in 1980, choose instead to rely on private contributions, and others never qualify for public funds.

Potential candidates should not have to rely on personal wealth and rich friends to mount a campaign. The present system, with its reliance on public funding, is intended to encourage small contributions in qualifying for federal funds as a sign of widespread popular support for a candidacy. Requirements of the laws, both for certification and enforcement, have resulted in unprecedented amounts of paperwork; at the same time, large amounts of data have become available to scholars and the media, documenting the precise costs of presidential campaigns.

Some disadvantages are built into the laws as they are currently formulated. Most candidates find that raising funds in small individual donations is very time consuming and takes a well-managed campaign organization. The limits on spending force candidates to make choices that must shortchange some voters and restrict the candidates' activities. Independent group spending is not at all evenly distributed among the candidates, so it works to great advantage in some campaigns and damages others. So far the more conservative candidates, such as Ronald Reagan, have benefited from the independent spending of such groups as the Moral Majority, the National Conservative Political Action Committee (NCPAC), and the Fund for a Conservative Majority; liberal groups have not approached their track record.

Fund-Raising Difficulties

Gary R. Orren in his review of the campaign financing legislation notes several areas in which the reforms have accomplished their goals. The low contribution limits (especially the $1,000 limit on individual contributions) have minimized the impact of private wealth on presidential campaigns. Further, by encouraging small donations, the legislation has reduced the opportunity for individuals to buy influence through large or strategically timed donations. These are significant achievements.

Nonetheless, a price has been paid. Orren suggests that the importance of money in campaigns may actually have increased. He points out that the demands of bookkeeping—disclosure requirements and certification of donations for the FEC—force candidates to begin their fund raising early (one or more years before the first primary) and to devote a good deal of time and attention to the raising and handling of funds.[7] Thus one of the unintended consequences of the reform laws has been a lengthening of the nominating season.[8] The need to begin raising money early—and thus to declare a candidacy and set up an organization—in combination with the party rules limiting the window in which states may hold their primaries and caucuses, has effectively shut out late starters.[9] Therefore, the field of candidates is for the most part established before the first state caucus or primary, a factor that lends additional weight to the outcomes of the early tests. While these circumstances might seem to favor the well-established party favorite, in fact the reverse can be the case: when there were no limits on fund raising and expenditures, the nationally known candidates could quickly raise and spend large sums of money; the equalization that has taken place gives long-shot candidates a more even chance.

Unreasonable Spending Limits

Most of the controversy and criticism regarding campaign funding is directed at the spending limits. Gallup Poll data show that the American public favors putting even tighter limits on campaign expenditures. The people favor public financing of congressional campaigns by a margin of 57 percent to 30 percent. In general the public seems to feel that further reduction of the campaign spending limits is the most important campaign reform available.[10] On closer examination, though, we find that such an attitude may represent an inappropriate ordering of priorities. The choosing of a president is one of our most important national activities, and how we accomplish it affects everyone in the United States. Yet we limit presidential campaign spending to a fraction of corporate media advertising (less than 1 percent in 1976). In fact the *total* amount spent on all political campaigns in 1976 amounted to less than the advertising budget of two large corporations, Proctor and Gamble and General Motors.[11] Values aside, even in absolute terms the spending limits may be too low for well-rounded, effective campaigns.

In 1980 and 1984 the following provisions applied to campaign spending:

> The prenomination campaigns were limited to a national spending total of $14.7 million in 1980 and $20.2 million in 1984.
>
> The general election campaigns for the parties' nominees were limited to $29.4 million each in 1980 and $40.4 million in 1984.
>
> Expenditures in each state were limited to 23.55 cents per eligible voter, with a minimum limit of $294,400 for the smallest states.
>
> A campaign's legal and accounting fees incurred in connection with requirements of the legislation were not counted against the limits.
>
> A campaign's fund-raising costs could extend the limits by up to 20 percent.
>
> State and local parties could spend unlimited amounts for the expenses of volunteers, voter registration activities, and get-out-the-vote campaigns.

Table 7.12 Expenditures for 1980 Prenomination Campaigns (in millions of dollars)

Candidate	Campaign costs	Legal and accounting fees	Total costs	Percent of authorized limit spent
Reagan	$15.54	$5.15	$20.69	106%
Carter	13.87	4.67	18.54	94
Bush	13.51	3.20	16.71	92
Connally	10.41	2.27	12.67	71
Kennedy	10.65	1.62	12.27	71
Baker	3.29	3.74	7.03	47
Anderson	6.52	0.00	6.52	44
Crane	5.22	0.00	5.22	35
Brown	2.15	0.57	2.72	18
Dole	1.22	0.17	1.39	9

Source: Data from Federal Election Commission, reported in F. Christopher Arterton, "Dollars for Presidents: Spending Money under the FECA," in *Financing Presidential Campaigns,* Campaign Finance Study Group, John F. Kennedy School of Government, Harvard University (Cambridge, Mass., 1982). Reprinted by permission.

A major source of friction in these provisions, as we have mentioned earlier in this chapter, is the fact that the sum of the state limits ($40.8 million) is well above the national limit of $14.7 million. Even if the state limits did reflect the cost of running a representative campaign in each state (and many believe they do not), the candidates could not come close to spending the necessary amount in each state. Nonetheless, in 1980 only Reagan utilized (exceeded, actually) the entire amount authorized for prenomination campaigns; just four of the others spent over $10 million of the almost $15 million they were allowed (Table 7.12). According to Orren the realistic costs of campaigning have risen to exceed the limits:

> The evidence suggests that the permissible level of campaign spending throughout the pre-nomination period has been insufficient for running a national campaign for the presidential nomination of one of the major parties. Moreover, the situation is getting worse. In essence the expenditure limits simply have not kept pace with the rising cost of waging an effective national campaign since the passage of the law. . . . The costs of campaigning (travel, media advertising, polling) respond immediately to technological advances and improving campaign strategies; and thus they have been rising at a significantly swifter rate than the Commerce Department's market basket of consumer goods. Furthermore, the overall spending limit does not take into account increases in the size of the electorate over time. Yet many campaign

expenses, such as media costs and phone banks, climb directly in proportion to increases in the size of the population.[12]

Several other factors, connected with reforms of the prenomination system, have changed the nature of campaign spending in recent decades, forcing candidates to spend more money in more states. First, primaries are more expensive than caucuses—according to one estimate, a candidate's costs are increased 15 times in each state that replaces its caucus system with a primary. Primaries, which have more than doubled in number since the 1960s, require expensive media campaigns and large organizations to reach a large number of individual voters. Second, the assignment of delegates in proportion to popular vote tends to divide a state's delegation and require victories in more states to gain the necessary number of delegates; thus the candidate must enter many contests.[13] In contrast, under the old party system caucuses were widely used; proportional distribution of convention delegates was rare, with winner-take-all contests being the rule; and individual contests were less important because the nominee was often decided in the convention.

In today's elections candidates must allocate resources carefully. Grass-roots spending has suffered as candidates have been forced to use mass campaigning techniques rather than selected local activity. Although local and state party organizations are permitted to engage in unlimited activity, in practice they have done little to assist presidential candidates.

The money goes primarily to television, the most efficient way to reach large numbers of voters. James Baker, manager of Bush's 1980 prenomination campaign and later a top White House aide to President Reagan, succinctly expressed the candidate's decision: "The first thing you cut are the grass roots items—pamphlets, buttons, bumper stickers. You save for the tube." [14] Curiously, one result of funding reform laws was to increase the reliance on media campaigns, even though the original objective may have been the opposite. When there is a limit on the amount of money which can be spent and the spending must be closely monitored, the campaigns turn to their highest priority—which is television. As Baker suggests, other things may suffer in the campaign's priorities.[15]

The Influence of Independent Spending

Independent spending by groups (mostly PACs and labor unions) on behalf of a candidate has been interpreted by the Supreme Court in *Buckley v. Valeo* to be an expression of free speech, as we have mentioned earlier in this chapter, and campaign finance laws allow for unlimited spending by such groups. In practice, such spending magnifies differences between candidates. Orren reports that as the Reagan campaign reached its legally mandated spending limit in the pivotal 1980 New Hampshire primary, the Fund for a Conservative Majority invested more than $60,000 in the state on Reagan's behalf.[16] Reagan was to enjoy this advantage repeatedly during the 1980 election year: of the $13,732,855 spent independently on behalf of the candidates, over $12 million, about 90 percent of the total, went to promote Reagan's candidacy (Table 7.13). Conversely, less than $50,000 of the independent money was spent in opposition to Reagan. In contrast, nearly $500,000 was used in negative campaigning against Kennedy, and nearly $250,000 was spent in opposition to Carter.[17]

Clearly, the current laws are not accomplishing all they were drafted to do. Many feel they do not take into account the nature of today's presidential nomination system. Unfortunately, they may often act as a hindrance to, rather than a facilitator of, the type of well-funded, national campaign that would best serve the broader interests of candidate and voter alike.

Table 7.13 Independent Spending in the Presidential Election, 1980

Candidate	For	Against
Reagan	$12,242,535	$47,868
Carter	45,869	245,611
Kennedy	77,189	491,161
Connally	288,032	0
Anderson	199,438	2,635
Kemp	62,497	0
Baker	3,433	0
Bush	0	17,172
Ford	0	8,415
Total	$12,918,993	$812,862
	$13,732,855	

Source: Xandra Keyden, "Independent Spending," in *Financing Presidential Campaigns,* Campaign Finance Study Group, John F. Kennedy School of Government, Harvard University (Cambridge, Mass., 1982), 7-3. Reprinted by permission.

Proposals for Change
in Campaign Financing

Although the basic commitment to the public funding of presidential prenomination campaigns is not often questioned, there have been a number of proposals for modifying present funding laws. Most of these are relatively modest calls to amend present procedures.

The Campaign Finance Study Group of the Kennedy School of Government at Harvard University has monitored the workings of the campaign laws. In a report prepared for a committee of the U.S. Senate after the 1980 election, the study group recommended that a number of incremental changes be made in the laws that apply to the prenomination phase of the presidential campaign, including the following:[18]

1. That the amount of public money made available to candidates for prenomination campaigns be substantially increased.
2. That the first $5 million of smaller contributions (redefined as $500 or less) be matched at the rate of $2 to $1 and that the second $5 million be matched at $1 to $1. (Currently, public funds match contributions up to $250 at $1 to $1.)
3. That the threshold test by which candidates qualify for federal funds be raised, for example to $500,000 to be raised in 25 states.

The report of the study group concluded that should things remain as they are, "current trends will render . . . campaign funding acts increasingly ineffective and potentially harmful."[19]

Not all of the study group's proposals may be workable or wise—and indeed the Congress has so far rejected most of these changes. But they do set an agenda for discussion that works within the context of the present law. And, like other observers, the study group recognizes that the prenomination campaign is a significant public act that deserves public financial support and needs close regulation.

The cost of running for the nomination remains an issue of great national importance and debate. Money—the ability to raise it, the timing of its availability, and the sources from which it will come—continues to be a significant factor in the ability of a candidate to compete successfully for the nomination.

NOTES

1. Herbert Asher, *Presidential Elections and American Politics*, rev. ed. (Homewood, Ill.: Dorsey, 1980), 279.

2. See Herbert E. Alexander, *Financing Politics*, 3d ed. (Washington, D.C.: CQ Press, 1980).
3. William Crotty and Gary C. Jacobson, *American Parties in Decline* (Boston: Little, Brown, 1980), 108-116, 175-179.
4. Michael J. Malbin, *Money and Politics in the United States* (Washington, D.C.: American Enterprise Institute, 1984), 8.
5. On PACs in congressional campaigns, see M. Margaret Conway, "PACs, the New Politics, and Congressional Campaigns," and Marjorie Randon Hershey and Darrell M. West, "Single-Issue Politics: Prolife Groups and the 1980 Senate Campaign," in *Interest Group Politics*, ed. Allan J. Cigler and Burdett A. Loomis (Washington, D.C.: CQ Press, 1983), 126-144 and 31-59, respectively.
6. Thomas R. Marshall, *Presidential Nominations in a Reform Age* (New York: Praeger, 1981), 83-84.
7. Gary R. Orren, "Presidential Campaign Finance: Its Impact and Future," *Commonsense* 4, no. 2 (1981): 52.
8. On the unintended consequences of reform in general, see Kenneth Janda, "Primrose Paths to Political Reform: 'Reforming' versus Strengthening American Parties," in *Paths to Political Reform*, ed. William Crotty (Lexington, Mass.: Lexington Books/DC Heath, 1980), 309-347.
9. Orren, "Presidential Campaign Finance," 52.
10. *Gallup Opinion Index* 183 (December 1980): 58-61.
11. Orren, "Presidential Campaign Finance," 54. The figures are those of Herbert E. Alexander, of the Citizens' Research Foundation.
12. Ibid., 54-55.
13. Ibid., 55.
14. Quoted in Ibid., 57.
15. William Crotty, *Political Reform and the American Experiment* (New York: Thomas Y. Crowell, 1977), 168-190.
16. Orren, "Presidential Campaign Finance," 57.
17. See Xandra Kayden, "Independent Spending," in *Financing Presidential Campaigns*, Campaign Finance Study Group, John F. Kennedy School of Government, Harvard University (Cambridge, Mass., 1982).
18. Campaign Finance Study Group, *Financing Presidential Campaigns*, 1.21-1.31.
19. Ibid., 5.

The National Conventions | 8

The national nominating conventions play a unique role in American political life. Once every four years the two major political parties gather to select their presidential nominees, one of whom is almost certain to be president of the United States. For four intense days, the nation's collective attention is focused on one of the conventions, then, a few weeks later, on the other. The intensity, excitement, and drama of the conventions are unparalleled by any other scheduled political event.

The Nature of the Conventions

In the national conventions we see an embodiment of the American tendency to incorporate seemingly incompatible goals and philosophies into a single institution. On the one hand, the conventions, being representative bodies, are characterized by elite decision making; on the other hand, democratizing reforms have opened up the entire nominating system, including the conventions, to greater participation by the rank-and-file party members. Since the 1960s politics in the United States has been profoundly affected by divisions in the society on matters of war, economics, ethics, race, and sex. Most of these divisions have found their way into the convention halls, often in the form of debates over who the candidates should be and what should be in the party platforms. The 1964 Republican convention, the 1968 and 1972 Democratic conventions, the 1976 Republican convention, and the 1980 Democratic convention dramatically reflected strains in the American polity. Yet, in spite of the controversy that continues to surround individual conventions, the institution survives.

The Functions of the National Conventions

National nominating conventions survive because they perform necessary functions for the political parties and for the larger political system. Those functions can be readily identified and classified, and a number of political scientists have done so.[1] We will adopt here the classification of Marian D. Irish and James W. Prothro, which is in keeping with most such listings.[2] In their terminology—based on the theoretical approach known as *structural-functionalism*[3]—the functions of conventions are of two types: manifest and latent. *Manifest* functions are the direct and intended consequences of conventions; *latent* functions are indirectly performed. Irish and Prothro classify the functions as follows:[4]

Manifest functions
Nominating the candidates
Creating enthusiasm for the candidates and the party
Suggesting, implicitly through the nominees and explicitly in the
    platform, the party's position on the key issues of the day

Latent functions
Democratizing the choice of a president
Creating or ratifying a party consensus on the nominees
Celebrating through ritual the democratic nature of the political
    parties
Reinforcing the existence of the national parties

These lists of functions express the theoretical meaning of the national conventions in the political culture and the roles they perform for the political system.

The official business of the convention is rather straightforward. The convention must accept the credentials of the state delegations, seat the delegates, ratify the rules, elect the officers, adopt the platform and resolutions, nominate candidates for president and vice president, and serve as the highest governing authority for the national party.

Each day of a convention has its own rhythm and its own main event. The first day is devoted to organization, reports of the national committee, the introduction of convention officers, and the keynote address. The second day is devoted to accepting the report of the credentials committee, adopting the rules for the nomination, and working on the platform and resolutions. The third day is the climax with the nominating speeches, roll-call votes, and anticipation of the announcement of the vice presidential candidate (if his or her identity is not already known). The final day is given over to the acceptance speech by the presidential nominee, the nomination of a vice president, and the national party's official business.

Setting Up the Convention

The work of a national convention actually begins about two years before the convention meets. National party committees must begin planning far in advance to be ready on time. Cities must prepare to deliver a wide variety of basic services. National news organizations must mount a huge logistical operation. A large number of people besides candidates and delegates are involved in planning a convention and operating it smoothly.

Choosing the Site

The party's national committees invite applications from big cities that would like to host their conventions. Relatively few cities can handle the thousands of delegates, media people, and visitors who flock to the conventions. A city must have sufficient hotel space, a large, well-equipped convention hall or arena, good transportation, and plenty of restaurants and entertainment opportunities; a city must also spend a lot of money, especially on security arrangements. Although the city must put up with crowds and extra expenses, there is usually no shortage of applicants for the honor of hosting a party's convention. Millions of dollars are spent in the host city; jobs for the inhabitants and free publicity for the city usually more than make up for the bother.

There are political considerations in the choice of a site for the convention. The incumbent president's party must choose a site that is acceptable to him; often the city is one with some meaning for him personally. For instance, in 1972 Richard Nixon chose Miami Beach, although the RNC's first choice had been San Diego, since besides being near one of his houses, the site was considered less vulnerable to demonstrations. If the party does not have a sitting president, the national chair's wishes may also affect site selection. It was reported that the Democratic national chair, Charles Manatt of California, was instrumental in the choice of San Francisco for the Democrats in 1984.

The party may attempt to make a symbolic statement through its choice of site. For example, the Democrats in 1976 and 1980 chose New York both to help the city financially and to recognize the city as a bastion of party strength; for the Republicans in 1980 Detroit reflected their attempt to reach out to the industrial heartland; in 1984 Dallas reflected the Republicans' growing Sunbelt base. In short, both logistical and political considerations must be weighed carefully.

Once the national committee has announced the final site decision, the detailed logistical planning begins in earnest. It takes thousands of planning hours and millions of dollars to mount a national convention. Party officials, federal, state, and local agencies, the media, the hotels, and all the support service officials must carefully mesh their planning and work to create the convention. Finally, everything is in place, and opening day arrives: the convention is called to order, the flags are presented, and the national anthem is sung.

Committees of the Conventions

As is the case in Congress, much of the important work of the national conventions is done in committees. Skeletal organizations for the standing committees are put in place months before the convention. As more and more states choose their delegations, the committees gain members. By late spring the rosters are usually complete. The committees hold several meetings and develop their positions on most matters before the conventions even open.

In recent years the conventions have had three major standing committees. Their common names and major functions are listed below, in approximate order of importance.

Platform Committee.   As the name suggests, the platform committee writes the major draft of the platform. The platform sets the party's agenda for the next four years: in the platform the party celebrates its own past accomplishments, identifies the problems facing the nation—most of which are blamed on the opposition party—offers its own vision of the future, and outlines its plan for attaining that vision. The platform committees of both parties hold hearings about what the platform should contain. They may also develop resolutions addressing issues that are of immediate concern to the convention but that are not incorporated into the main body of the platform. The prevailing view among the American people and the mass media seems to be that platforms are not worth much. But Gerald Pomper and his associates have done research indicating that the parties do take platforms seriously and that the president and party members in Congress use their party's platform in developing legislation.[5]

Rules Committee. The rules committee, through the procedural rules it develops, defines the entire conduct of the convention, including the decorum required for floor demonstrations and the length of speeches. The committee's major order of business is to establish the rules for choosing the nominees. In their work on convention rules the Democrats in particular are coming increasingly to incorporate the extant party law and the work of the reform commissions.

Credentials Committee. Someone must accept the bonafides, the credentials, of the delegates. For each state the convention delegation and each individual delegate must be recognized as legally chosen. The credentials committee is the source of this official recognition. If there is no controversy, this is a routine matter of certifying the winners of a state primary or caucus. The official delegate lists are then made up and the entrance badges are prepared from those names. On the other hand, if there is conflict, two different sets of delegations may claim the same seats and only one, or perhaps a combination of both delegations, can be seated. The credentials committee tries to work through all the conflicts and reach a settlement although ultimate authority for deciding the outcomes of disputed delegations rests with the convention as a whole.

The credentials committee of the 1972 Democratic convention had plenty to do. As we explained in Chapter 3, this convention was the scene of the fight between two delegations from Chicago: Mayor Daley's regular delegation and the Singer-Jackson insurgent delegation. Within the convention there was simmering resentment against Daley because of his handling of events at the 1968 Chicago convention; on the other hand, the regulars feared that the McGovern forces would not play by the usual rules. By a majority vote of the full convention the Singer-Jackson delegation was seated; by this vote the McGovern delegates knew their candidate would ultimately get the nomination.[6]

All of the standing committees make very important decisions, and those decisions can help set the tenor of the entire convention and affect the potential for party harmony. The conventions themselves are too large and unwieldy to accomplish the kind of work committees do in advance. The assembled delegates react to what the committees present to them. They respond to the work of the committees by (1) accepting the report of the committee as presented, (2) adopting a minority report worked out by some faction within the committees, or (3) slightly modifying the work of the committee through suggestions from the floor. Most of the time, conventions accept the work of the committees. When there is controversy, one party faction or candidate support group may be able to demonstrate control of the convention by prevailing, as we saw in the case of the Singer-Jackson challenge in 1972.[7]

Although the standing committees may seem on the surface to do rather mundane work, they often deal with issues of great political importance. For example, challenges by candidates made on ostensibly procedural grounds may in fact be power struggles that will be resolved on the convention floor in favor of the likely nominee. Such floor fights can be the climax of the entire convention.

The Media at the Conventions

The mass media are a force to be reckoned with at the national conventions, since they will filter and interpret the events of the conventions for the public. Television, especially, has clearly transformed our national conventions since the 1950s.[8] And the parties are aware that in some respects the conventions are staged for the home audience. But what the media *say* about what is happening on the convention floor is at least as important as the events themselves.

There were 10,000 media representatives accredited to the 1980 national conventions and 14,000 to the 1984 conventions, several times the number of official delegates. People connected with the media are everywhere: in the aisles, in the outer halls, in makeshift studios, in bars, in hotels, and anywhere else they sense a story can be developed. In fact, the media have themselves become part of the conflict and the drama of the conventions. The media not only carry the story, they help generate it and they are a part of it. Walter Cronkite's 1980 interview with Gerald Ford about the former president's becoming Ronald Reagan's vice presidential running mate became part of the play. When Republican delegates shouted their disdain for the media during Barry Goldwater's 1964 convention and when journalists found themselves in the middle of the Grant Park riots in Chicago in 1968 the media entered the political context.

Most media organizations are in business to make a profit by selling advertising, and their income depends on the size of their audience. The need to attract and hold a fickle audience encourages the media to emphasize drama, competition, speed, and accuracy; they look for the stars, the unusual events, the human interest story. Television, the medium from which most people get their information, plays up visual messages—movement, excitement, color—and the entertainment values that are at the heart of television news.[9] Only the most dramatic speeches from the podium are given more than cursory attention; the speaker who delivers a careful, cerebral discourse offering complex solutions to the nation's ills is not likely to be heard at home. Those who create and perpetuate conflict and uncertainty are given constant coverage; those who quietly go about the main business of the convention are largely ignored. The leaders of the intense minorities are instant celebrities, while the less colorful leaders of the state delegations are ignored unless they threaten to do something extreme. Actually, a smooth, conflict-free convention, which both the Democrats and Republicans tried desperately to achieve in 1984 and which is viewed as the greatest success from the party's viewpoint, is likely to be considered boring by the media.[10]

The imperatives of holding an audience and advertisers force the media in effect to slant the news. There is no particular liberal or conservative, pro-Mondale or pro-Reagan conspiracy in convention reporting. Given the heterogeneity of the people covering the conventions, and their sheer numbers, such a conspiracy theory of media coverage is quite unrealistic. But the media—like other industries—do share certain patterns of socialization and recruitment as well as some professional norms and evaluations of news.[11] Thus the voter at home may end up with a distorted picture of the convention and its results, a picture that may affect the way the voter approaches the general election.

The Delegates at the Conventions

The delegates are the heart of the conventions. In this section we examine how the delegates behave at the convention, with particular emphasis on the groups they form. As we showed in our personal and political profile of Chapter 5, delegates come from all strata of the population. Even though all are political activists by definition, their political behavior at the convention varies widely. We will adopt the terminology of Lester Milbrath to describe in the following paragraphs the types of delegates in terms of their political participation.[12]

Apathetics, who are relatively few in number, do not participate at all and pay little attention to the events surrounding them at the convention. Some apathetic delegates devote most of their time and attention to the social and entertainment opportunities readily available during the convention.

Spectators, on the other hand, are quite conscientious about attending to their convention duties. They go to most, if not all, of the required meetings; they listen and learn from the debates and conversations going on around them; and they cast relatively well informed votes, when they are asked to vote. Spectators do not, however, aspire to a more active role; they do not seek positions of leadership within their delegations; they do not participate in the making of key decisions aside from casting their votes on the prominent roll-call ballots, such as the nomination votes; and they do not often try to influence other delegates. Instead, they respond to the events and choices created by others. Probably most delegates fall into this intermediate category. Although most delegates are political activists on the home front, few will stand out in a group of three thousand.

Gladiators are the delegates who do stand out for their exceptional involvement. They are deeply enmeshed in the affairs of the convention and they help make things happen. Gladiators are the people at the center of the party's communications networks; they have some power to negotiate when bargains are to be struck; and they influence the decisions that are made at the convention.

While the ranks of the gladiators are necessarily limited, their numbers probably grew during the reform era. The party leaders who dominated in the prereform era now have to compete and share power with other party activists who have their own political resources to use at the conventions. Many gladiators are candidate-centered delegates, who have become far more important in the postreform era. Their power resources are at least as formidable as the resources of individuals whose credentials stem from their involvement with local and state party organizations. (Some delegates are both local leaders and candidate centered.)

Some gladiators represent other interests and pursue other agendas at the conventions. Labor unions at the Democratic conventions and business interests at the Republican conventions have traditionally been centers of power. While their power has been diluted somewhat by the reforms and related events, both groups are still active and influential in the conventions. Other groups, such as the National Education Association (NEA) and women's organizations for the Democratic party and evangelical groups (for example, the Moral Majority) and antiabortion groups for the Republican party, have in recent campaigns and conventions become forces to be reckoned with. Indeed, a variety of conservative interest groups appeared to control the 1984 Republican convention in Dallas; their social and economic agenda became the party's conservative platform that year.

Interest Groups and Caucuses

Although gladiators are the most visible of the delegates, all the delegates are to some extent representatives of group interests of various sorts: their home states, their candidates, demographic interests, economic interests, and so on. Some of these interests organize into temporary caucuses that meet before and during convention week and dissolve afterward.[13] A national convention would typically include the following types of caucuses:

General purpose caucuses
State delegations
Candidate-centered caucuses

Special purpose caucuses
Black caucus
Hispanic caucus
Women's caucus
Youth caucus
Others, such as NEA, Ripon Society, gays

General Purpose Caucuses. All delegates are automatically members of a state (or District of Columbia or territorial) delegation. With the exception of the few delegates who are truly uncommitted at the beginning of the convention, all delegates are also members of a candidate-centered caucus. Because of their near-universal applicability we have labeled these the general purpose caucuses.

The state delegation is for most delegates the primary organizing force in the convention. Many of the delegates are already friends or acquaintances, and the convention is an excellent opportunity to expand their political and personal networks. Each delegation is organized, with a chair and other officers. The state delegations provide for most of the logistical needs of the delegates each day. Their hotel rooms are booked together. They travel to the convention site together. Candidates or their representatives come to the state caucuses and ask for support, often in terms of state interests and shared political history; interest group representatives make similar appeals. In short, the state delegation caucuses serve many logistical, procedural, and political purposes that are not duplicated elsewhere.

The candidate-centered caucuses are the next most pervasive. These caucuses proliferated during the reform era as delegates became more independent from local and state party leaders, who had in the past bargained with candidates on behalf of entire delegations. The candidates and their staffs need to communicate with their delegates, and they hold formal and informal caucuses to do so. The communication works both ways: sometimes a candidate may approach his or her caucus for support; at other times the caucus may extract promises from the candidate. Most often the caucuses are a means for the candidates to explain their strategies on rules, credentials, or platform issues and to create enthusiasm among their rank-and-file delegate supporters.

Candidates reach as far as they can into the state delegations, hoping to get supporters into leadership spots. Then they supplement the formal leadership positions with informal appointments of, for example, the Reagan coordinator for a particular state, the Mondale coordinator for a congressional district's delegation, and so forth. The candidate-centered convention organizations develop a hierarchy with top leaders, middle-echelon leaders, and front-line leaders to manage the party and the delegates; the hierarchy also demands complex technical facilities. The candidate who cannot communicate instantly with his supporters is at a decided competitive disadvantage during the convention.

Special Purpose Caucuses. The special purpose caucuses are organized to provide representation, communications networks, and a decision-making arena for various subgroupings of delegates. The reform era encouraged the participation of previously excluded groups (see Chapter 2). The most visible of these have been blacks, Hispanics, women, the young, and the old. Naturally, these groups wanted to share the power and the limelight at the national conventions, and they formed temporary organizations to further their goals.

In the reform era, especially in the Democratic party, the black and women's caucuses received the most attention and were probably the most active. These convention caucuses overlapped to some extent with several permanent political organizations, such as the congressional black caucus and the National Organization for Women (NOW), which has increased their effectiveness. In the postreform era many other groups have formed at the conventions. The proliferation of special purpose caucuses is a sign of the fragmentation evident in conventions during the postreform era.

The activities of special purpose caucuses sometimes reinforce those of candidate-centered caucuses. Most special purpose caucuses seek to promote candidates who are considered especially sympathetic to their cause. For example, as Denis G. Sullivan and his associates showed, the black caucus at the 1972 Democratic convention was central to Rep. Shirley Chisholm's candidacy. At the same convention women bargained with McGovern, offering their support in the South Carolina and

Illinois credentials challenges in return for his support on issues important to them.[14]

Special purpose caucuses may attempt to influence party policy as well as the candidates. In 1980 the Democratic women's caucus was instrumental in getting a plank inserted into the party's platform prohibiting the national party from financially aiding any candidate who did not support the Equal Rights Amendment (ERA).[15] In the same year some Republican women delegates tried to persuade their convention to include an endorsement of the ERA in the platform, but they were unsuccessful.

Sullivan and his associates studied the different caucuses as a focus of decision making during the 1972 Democratic convention.[16] They found that members of particular candidate-centered caucuses and special purpose caucuses more often expected their caucus to be the most important arena of convention decision making than did nonmembers. They also found that involvement in the special purpose caucuses generally declined as the convention week wore on and that the delegates' perceptions of the importance of the special purpose caucuses generally declined over the week. The McGovern caucus was widely perceived to be the site of the most crucial decision-making activities. In some cases McGovern's supporters were able to rally their caucus to vote against the black and the female caucuses when they deemed it necessary to protect McGovern's interests.

When a particular demographic group has a large number of delegates, their caucus can exert some leverage on rules, platforms, and credentials disputes if they are united and if they determine that an issue impinges on their interests. However, in most cases the special purpose caucuses are divided by both candidate and state loyalties, and these divisions prevent them from making common cause on any but the most highly salient issues. Largely because of overriding state and candidate loyalties, the special purpose caucuses have not been successful as bargaining agents on the most important decision, that of naming the nominee. Nonetheless, they have enjoyed limited success in extracting some promises from the candidates, and they have been able to some extent to gain rules changes and platform planks favorable to their views. Thus, the special purpose caucuses must be regarded as supplements to the state delegations and candidate-centered caucuses.

The Goals of the Delegates

So far we have implied a good deal about what many delegates want the national conventions to accomplish. Now we will examine that matter explicitly. Perhaps the most direct statement of delegate goals was made by Nelson Polsby and Aaron Wildavsky in a 1960 article: "The major goals of most delegates to national conventions may be simply described: to nominate a man who can win the election; to unify the party; to obtain some claim on the nominee; and to strengthen state party organizations." [17]

Certainly this statement still describes the pragmatic goals of most national convention delegates in the postreform era. Delegates do want their party to win the presidency; after all, those who ran in primaries and caucuses survived several tests of their party loyalty. Most delegates recognize the importance of party unity in winning the presidency. It is in the nature of politics that supporters like to be recognized by the winner they helped and that it can be useful to grant favors that will be repaid. And many delegates are aware that a good nominee can help the party at all levels.

In other respects the goals of delegates have changed in the postreform era as the conventions have become less deliberative and more likely to ratify decisions made by the rank and file in primaries and caucuses. Two views of the party and conventions have emerged in this period: the pragmatic party approach and the responsible party approach.

The *pragmatic party* approach stresses the goals related to winning the general election,[18] as Polsby and Wildavsky's list does. This approach is associated with the professional attitude that predominated among delegates in the prereform era, as we discussed in Chapter 5. The health and survival of party organizations tends to be a foremost consideration in this view.

Those who take the *responsible party* approach are concerned more with policy goals and party programs.[19] Such delegates focus their energy during the convention on the platform and on resolutions and rules that will aid their policy goals. They may be active in the special purpose caucuses. Although they want their party to win the general election, they will base candidate loyalty on issue positions more than pragmatic electoral goals. Advocates of the responsible party position see the proper role of the political party and of the national convention as being to advance policy and program proposals that can be voted on in the general election and eventually enacted into law if the election is won.

Certainly not all delegates can be fitted neatly into one or the other of these categories. Indeed, most delegates have a complex mixture of goals. But most delegates will choose at the convention to pursue one of these approaches more than the other. And both approaches have their place in the manifest and latent functions a convention performs. As is the case in most U.S. political institutions, these competing approaches coexist in a system that allows for the necessary ambiguities and trade-offs.[20]

The Candidates at the Conventions

Candidates are the stars of the convention, even though one of them is reasonably assured of the nomination before the convention begins (having obtained enough committed delegates through the primaries and caucuses). The probable nominee and other candidates may still find themselves leading their caucuses into battle over platform planks, procedures, and rules. Often the losing candidate who challenges the leader is hoping to gain policy influence through the platform or trying to test the waters for the next election year.

Several recent conventions have been the scene of strategic battles between candidates. We will look here in detail at three instances of the strategic behavior of candidates at recent conventions: Reagan's 1976 challenge to Ford, Kennedy's 1980 challenge to Carter, and Hart and Jackson's challenge to Mondale in 1984.

In 1976 President Gerald Ford was understandably the Republican front-runner for the nomination. He was running for president for the first time, having come into office upon the resignation of Richard Nixon. Ronald Reagan mounted a strong primary challenge. Near the end of the primary season the delegate counts showed that although at that time Ford was not assured of the nomination, he was definitely ahead, having 47.9 percent to Reagan's 45.4 percent.[21] Naturally, Reagan's campaign challenged the delegate counts and claimed more for their man. Two weeks before the convention, Reagan named Sen. Richard Schweiker of Pennsylvania as his running mate. Reagan challenged Ford to name his vice presidential candidate, ostensibly so that the convention could judge a team rather than an individual. Under the banner of good government, the Reagan forces proposed a change in the national party rules that would have required a presidential candidate to reveal his choice of running mate before the roll call on the presidential nomination. The maneuvers were designed both to throw the Ford camp off balance and trigger mistakes from them and to create confusion and uncertainty among the delegates.

Reagan's maneuvers did create uncertainty. On the second night of the convention it became clear that Ford would prevail when the vote on the vice presidential rules change went his way by 1180 votes to 1068. On the roll-call vote for the nomination, Ford won by about the same margin (1187 to 1070). In his losing effort, Reagan did not even gain the support of the Pennsylvania delegation. In the end Reagan lost to an incumbent president by just over 100 votes. But he had gained a great deal of national exposure, which served him well in his 1980 campaign.

In 1980 President Carter was in a very strong position going into the Democratic convention. He had well over the majority of delegate votes he needed, and his delegates were bound by party law to vote for him on the first ballot (see Chapter 2).[22] Kennedy's forces seized on this rule as being fundamentally unjust, as depriving the convention delegates of the opportunity to change their minds in light of the amount of time that had passed between the earliest primaries and the convention. They also argued that the rule helped eliminate the decision-making and bargaining ability of the delegates, especially on the question of the nomination.

From the Kennedy camp came talk of how the delegates had become automatons. From the Carter camp came appeals to the principle of being faithful to the wishes of the voters. Underneath the conflict were the differing strategic needs of the two campaigns. Carter needed to protect his position and what he had already won. Kennedy needed to create confusion and cast doubts on the delegate counts and commitments. To that end, Kennedy's delegates introduced a rules change to undo the bound delegate rule. In the end the president's position prevailed in a dramatic roll call on Monday night. Carter won the nomination on Wednesday night by almost exactly the same margin of victory he had enjoyed on Monday.

In 1984 Walter Mondale ended the primaries and caucuses with the nomination seemingly assured. After a long and hotly contested pre-nomination season, Mondale could claim 2,067 delegate votes on the eve of the convention, 100 more than the 1,967 needed for nomination. But Mondale was unable to increase his lead during the preconvention maneuvering, leaving some lingering doubts as to his eventual success. In their attempts to test Mondale's strength and to push their policy agenda, Hart and Jackson at first refused to concede the nomination; then, before the convention, each decided to support minority positions in formulating the platform: for example, Hart wanted a plank opposing the use of force in Central America, and Jackson wanted stronger civil rights guarantees. Their stances were probably partly a matter of principle and partly an attempt to win over some Mondale and uncommitted delegates.

Mondale's announcement just before the convention of his vice presidential candidate, Rep. Geraldine Ferraro of New York, was a bold move that solidified Mondale's position as the party's leader. After that decision, Hart and Jackson's platform maneuvering took on the appearance of a symbolic quest with no real chance of breaking Mondale's grip on the nomination. Mondale went on to compromise on the platform issues, pushing some aside, giving in on others. The intent was to avoid splitting the convention and putting his strength to a vote. He also agreed that Jackson and Hart, in that order, should be allowed prime time television exposure to address their constituencies and receive the attention they earned during the long campaign period. These were shrewd moves. Everyone was mollified; the convention and party were unified; and Mondale got what he wanted, the nomination.

The parallels among the cases are striking. The preconvention front-runners tried to protect their leads; the challengers tried to create confusion and uncertainty among delegates and the media, using challenges to the proposed rules or to the platform as a central instrument of that strategy; the failure of the procedural challenges presaged the outcome of the nomination roll call; and the front-runners won the nomination, but had no clear path to the presidency.

Selection of the Vice Presidential Candidates

In many conventions, the naming of the vice presidential nominee is one of the most eagerly anticipated events. Very few people actively seek the vice presidency, which is widely considered a ceremonial position. Actually, being a current or former vice president is one of the best springboards into the presidency. Since the 1940s four presidents (Truman, Nixon, Johnson, and Ford) had previously served as vice president. Two other vice presidents (Humphrey and Mondale) obtained their party's nomination for president.

Given the importance of the office, it is somewhat surprising that so little prior thought and planning usually go into the selection of the vice presidential nominee. In general, the presidential nominee has an almost free hand in selecting the vice presidential candidate, who must then be ratified by the convention. Usually the nominee and his campaign carefully choose a person who they consider an asset and a complement to the president, in an exercise known as *ticket balancing.* The vice presidential candidate ideally lends geographical or ideological strength where the presidential nominee may be weak. For example,

Johnson, a Texan who was well connected to the Democratic party's more conservative wing, was chosen to lend wider appeal to Kennedy's ticket in 1960. In light of the 110,000 vote margin by which Kennedy won the general election, the choice of Johnson (who surely helped the Democrats carry Texas) proved to be wise.

In 1980 the Reagan campaign looked for a ticket-balancing vice presidential candidate, though the choice was by no means foreordained. For a time during the convention it seemed that Reagan would choose former president Ford as his running mate. But after Ford asked for guarantees of real vice presidential power in the administration, Reagan turned to Bush, who was considered a moderate with ties to the Sunbelt and the East. Although a former president would have lent prestige to the campaign, Bush was apparently a good choice, helping Reagan with the more moderate wing of the Republican party.

Some recent candidates have rejected the classic ideological and geographical ticket-balancing strategy in favor of presenting a solid ideological front. For example, in 1964 Republican nominee Barry Goldwater chose Rep. William Miller of New York, a person almost as conservative as himself, for his running mate. Similarly, McGovern in 1972 selected a liberal in-law of the Kennedy's, Sargent Shriver, to be his vice presidential candidate. It may be that ideological and personal compatibility are becoming more important in the minds of some of the presidential candidates as they weigh the advantages and disadvantages of the ticket-balancing strategy.

Walter Mondale's choice of Ferraro in 1984 was a historic political first and probably represented a blend of ideological compatibility and a particular brand of ticket balancing. Ferraro had a record quite consonant with Mondale's brand of New Deal liberalism. Being from New York, Ferraro balanced the ticket geographically (Mondale's home state is Minnesota) and could be expected to increase the Democrats' appeal in the East and in urban areas, where they usually have to do well to win the general election. And the fact that Ferraro was both the first Italian-American and the first woman on a major party ticket made her choice a ticket-balancing bargain for Mondale.

The vice presidential nominee can harm a campaign as well as help it. During the 1972 convention McGovern named Sen. Thomas Eagleton of Missouri to be his running mate. The decision was apparently made under pressure at the last minute, with the aid of very little systematic research. When it was revealed 10 days after the convention ended that Eagleton had undergone shock therapy for the treatment of severe depression, Eagleton was removed from the ticket. In a special meeting of the Democratic National Committee on August 8, 1972, three weeks after the convention, Eagleton was replaced by Sargent Shriver, McGovern's new choice. The damage to McGovern's candidacy was swift and severe.

Another type of potential harm in the choice of a vice presidential candidate is illustrated by the case of Nixon and Spiro Agnew. In 1968 Agnew was the little-known governor of Maryland; he was named to the ticket partly as a balancing act and partly because the polls showed that he would do little harm to Nixon's candidacy. During Nixon's second term, in 1973, Agnew was forced to resign from office after charges involving tax evasion and graft. Clearly, Agnew's case damaged Nixon both in his work as president and in his struggle for political survival in the aftermath of the Watergate break in.

One of the most carefully considered and orchestrated choices of a vice presidential nominee in recent history was probably Carter's choice of Mondale in 1976. After Carter wrapped up the nomination before the convention, he went on a well-publicized search for his vice presidential candidate. Carter and his advisers invited senators Muskie, Glenn, and Mondale to meet them in Plains, Georgia, for interviews and an intensive screening session. Several other leading candidates were interviewed in New York. According to Carter, political and personal compatibility, as well as Mondale's ideas about how the vice president should function, were the key ingredients in the selection of Mondale.[23] Carter's choice of Mondale was also a ticket-balancing exercise, since Mondale's credentials with liberals and with labor and civil rights groups were very strong and clearly complemented Carter's strengths, which lay elsewhere. In 1984 Mondale, who was perhaps influenced by Carter's 1976 approach, went through his own elaborate series of interviews with a variety of candidates, including women, blacks, and a Hispanic, from many different states and levels of government, before choosing Geraldine Ferraro. The precedents set by these candidates may increase the pressure for public auditioning sessions for potential vice presidential candidates in the future.

Presidential nominees always tout their vice presidential choices in phrases such as "the best person for the job of president should the need arise." If presidential candidates were candid, they would say something like, "This is the best person I can find who will run with me and who will help bring some balance to the ticket or at least not hurt me in the campaign." Such candor is not likely to become a trend in presidential campaigns, but it would have the virtue of giving us an inkling of what actually went into the strategic calculations.

In an exceptional move, Democrat Adlai Stevenson in 1956 left the choice of the vice presidential nominee to the convention. After much debate, the body finally picked Sen. Estes Kefauver of Tennessee over Sen. John F. Kennedy of Massachusetts in a closely fought race (which, incidentally, marked Kennedy's emergence on the national political scene). Stevenson's example of leaving the choice up to the convention is sometimes discussed in political circles but has not yet been emulated in recent national conventions. Presidential candidates apparently feel that the choice is too important to them personally and politically to be left up to the caprice of the national convention and its thousands of delegates.

The delegates usually ratify the presidential candidate's choice as a mark of their respect for him and as a show of party unity. On some occasions, however, competing vice presidential nominations are made from the floor and voted on in the convention. Significant segments of the party, powerful constituencies, or disgruntled factions may choose the vehicle of the vice presidential nomination to air their grievances or to show their political muscle. For example, black people or women among the Democrats or the more moderate elements of the Republican party can use the occasion of the vice presidential nomination to make highly visible statements about their own interests and demands on their party. All this can prove to be an embarrassment to the presidential nominee and it can also be a signal that the wounds of the primary season have not yet healed.

The vice presidential choice can become an instrument for the presidential nominee to achieve party unity and prepare for the general election battle. And the office is an important one. The decision deserves more systematic attention than it has usually received.

The Importance of Party Unity

By the end of the convention, the party must be made ready for the fight against the opposition party. Divisions exacerbated during the primary season must be healed. Otherwise, the convention roll call can become a Pyrrhic victory that leads to defeat in November.

From recent history we can derive a number of generalizations that demonstrate how important party unity is in winning the presidency. As the party considers its strategic position in the general election, it would be well to pay attention to these lessons from history.

1. Disunity within a party is a function of deep factional divisions that are not reconciled during the nominating season or the national convention. Indeed, these divisions are often exacer-

bated by the contest over the presidential nomination. The party that is the most divided at the end of the national conventions has lost each of the elections since 1964, as we see in the following cases: Republicans in 1964; Democrats in 1968 and 1972; Republicans in 1976; Democrats in 1980. This generalization holds whether the party has an incumbent president or not.

2. An incumbent president who wants his party's nomination will ultimately get it, as did Johnson in 1964, Nixon in 1972, Ford in 1976, Carter in 1980, and Reagan in 1984. However, serious internal party challenges to incumbent presidents have become increasingly frequent, as Ford found in 1976 and Carter found in 1980. Such challenges seriously damage the incumbent's chances for reelection. In fact, as Table 8.1 shows, throughout the twentieth century presidents who have been unopposed for the

Table 8.1 The Recipe for Reelection Success

	Incumbent's percentage of		General election result
	Primary vote	Convention delegates	
"Clear Sailing"			
William McKinley (1900)*	—	100%	Won
Theodore Roosevelt (1904)	—	100	Won
Woodrow Wilson (1916)*	99%	99	Won
Calvin Coolidge (1924)	68	96	Won
Franklin D. Roosevelt (1936)*	93	100	Won
Franklin D. Roosevelt (1940)	72	86	Won
Franklin D. Roosevelt (1944)	71	92	Won
Harry S Truman (1948)	64	75	Won
Dwight D. Eisenhower (1956)*	86	100	Won
Lyndon B. Johnson (1964)	88	100	Won
Richard M. Nixon (1972)*	87	99	Won
"Tough Sledding"			
William H. Taft (1912)*	34%	52%	Lost
Herbert Hoover (1932)*	33	98	Lost
Gerald R. Ford (1976)	53	53	Lost
Jimmy Carter (1980)*	51	64	Lost

Note: An asterisk (*) indicates that incumbent was completing first full four-year term. A dash (—) indicates that there were no presidential primaries. Primary vote for Lyndon B. Johnson in 1964 inludes vote for favorite sons and uncommitted delegate slates.

Source: Congressional Quarterly Weekly Report, February 4, 1984, 224.

nomination within their own party have won reelection; presidents who faced significant opposition for renomination have lost the election.

3. The out-party (the party that does not control the White House) is likely to win the presidency if an incumbent is not running. No in-party has offered a successful candidate to succeed their incumbent since Herbert Hoover followed Calvin Coolidge in 1924.[24]

Political scientists must look for political and historical patterns and develop larger generalizations, in spite of the small number of cases the elections give us. We need to learn what we can about the relationship between the nominating season and the general election season.

What we can conclude from these generalizations is that if the primary season does not cause a consensus to emerge regarding the nomination, then the national convention must serve that function if at all possible. Recent divisions within the parties have been too deep and too fundamental to be settled by the national conventions, which are in any event often divided as well. Conflict over personalities and leadership can perhaps be reconciled in the convention. On the other hand, longstanding factional strife is not likely to be resolved there. Only on rare occasions can a particular candidate bring a party together with the election in sight.

It is clear, then, that a workable level of party unity must exist well before November. By the time the final gavel falls at the convention, the party can make a reasonable assessment of party unity, and thus of the party's chances in the general election. The party is well positioned for the race if the convention has been successful in creating enthusiasm for the candidate and in creating or ratifying a consensus; if the party has adopted positions that promise to be attractive to the voters; and if the party has successfully avoided alienating its activists and voters. If problems remain evident after the convention, or if the problems are actually exacerbated by the events of the convention itself, then the nominee and his party are likely to be in trouble in November.

Revitalizing the National Conventions

At the beginning of this chapter we established that the national conventions do perform functions essential to the political system. With changes in the party system in the reform and postreform eras, however, the conventions have lost some of their meaning, as we have seen. Here we will set forth some scholars' observations of the state of the conventions and of how to preserve them as an integral part of the nominating system.

Before the introduction of presidential primaries in the Progressive era, the national convention held undisputed authority over presidential nominations (as well as other party affairs). V. O. Key's description of the national conventions in the "old party" system captures their significance and the sensitive role they played:

> The party nationally tends to be an alliance of state and city leaders who work together most faithfully during a presidential campaign. . . . The basic coalition-forming process occurs in the national convention which nominates the candidate who succeeds in lining up a commanding block of state organizations. The nominee symbolizes the terms of the coalition at the moment; the platform may make them explicit; and, on occasion, the decisions of the convention may leave gaping cleavages indicative of the inability of the politicians to bridge the differences among the elements of the party.[25]

With the shift of power over nominations to the party's rank and file, the national convention's role changed: it became the meeting place for the victorious faction of the party in the nomination battle. It would select its candidate and create the platform it favored. No longer could the national convention be seen as a body representative of all party groups, compromising the differences, airing its grievances, rewarding its supporting coalition, and agreeing on policies and candidates that appeal to the majority of party groups.

Many would like to see the national convention returned to a place of preeminence in party affairs. To do this would mean rearranging the balance of power over presidential nominations in such a way that the real decisions would once again be made by the delegates assembled in the convention.

There is much to be said in favor of the traditional role of the national convention. The classic defense of the national convention has been put forward by Herbert J. McClosky, in a work published at the height of agitation (1968) over convention reform. McClosky notes:

> Most of the discontent with the convention system in the 1960s revolved around questions as to representativeness and their openness to different points of view, rather than behavioral excesses or frivolity, although these have been aspects of concern to some political observers.[26]

McClosky argues that national conventions are democratic institutions that serve the party and the voter better than any proposed alternatives. He lists a number of benefits of conventions, stressing the advantages of a deliberative, representative body over the capricious mass electorate for making the momentous decision on the party's presidential nominee. He fears that the voters as a whole may "fall victim to demagogues and crowd pleasers, matinee idols and publicity seekers, familiar names and celebrities." [27] As have other observers, he favors the moderating influence of those who are committed to the functioning of the parties: the politically sophisticated individuals who predominate in the conventions, who may be able to consider the issues wisely and evaluate the candidates and their policy positions carefully. He sees strong parties as fundamental to an orderly democracy and thus favors allowing them latitude in their nominating systems and decision making.

Others (Jeane Kirkpatrick, for one), who have built on the ideas put forth in another context by Joseph Schumpeter, have argued that any goals of inclusiveness and mass participation in the nomination process are basically irrelevant.[28] In this view, political parties should be closed bodies, free to conduct their own business as they see fit. Mass voters should not be free to take over the parties' functions; they make the final choice in the general election. Choosing the president is the democratic obligation of the voters, but choosing the nominees is the responsibility of the parties alone. We have seen similar expressions of this point of view throughout our examination of the presidential nominating system.

The depiction of the national conventions by its most ardent supporters is somewhat idyllic. All of the points raised in defense of a convention-dominated system can be refuted, or at least answered; counterarguments could be raised about the accessibility and relevance of convention procedures within the changing social climate. Certainly, some earlier conventions—such as the Democratic convention of 1968 and the Republican convention of 1964—were susceptible to serious questions about independence, accountability, and basic procedural fairness. The reform era was a response to problems in the system, and many things have been changed. The electoral system is different today. We cannot turn back the clock.

Restoring the national convention to dominance in the party system is not an explicit issue in the debate between party reformers and party regulars.[29] Most would favor the retention of the national convention as the supreme governing body of the political party in fact as well as theory. Some aspects of the debate continue in regard to the presence of party officials in reserved (ex officio or superdelegate) slots and in the number and role of primaries. There is inherent tension in a system that attempts to reconcile a rank-and-file presence in presidential selection with a truly deliberative national convention, and that tension is not likely to be resolved in the near future.

NOTES

1. Various authorities provide different lists of the specific functions performed by the national conventions; however, these usually boil down to be approximately the same as the one adopted here. For example, see Judith H. Parris, *The Convention Problem* (Washington, D.C.: The Brookings Institution, 1972), 2. For the classic statement see Paul T. David, Ralph M. Goldman, and Richard C. Bain, *The Politics of National Party Conventions*, rev. ed. (New York: Vintage, 1963), chap. 16.
2. Marian D. Irish and James W. Prothro, *The Politics of American Democracy*, 5th ed. (Englewood Cliffs, N.J.: Prentice-Hall, 1972), 312-315.
3. *Structural-functionalism* is a technical term denoting a theoretical approach to the study of political science. The best explanation of this approach, with special emphasis on the functions of political parties, is Gabriel A. Almond, "Introduction," *The Politics of the Developing Areas*, ed. Gabriel A. Almond and James S. Coleman (Princeton, N.J.: Princeton University Press, 1960), 3-64.
4. Irish and Prothro, *The Politics of American Democracy*, 312-315.
5. See Gerald M. Pomper with Susan L. Lederman, *Elections in America*, 2d ed. (New York: Longman, 1980), chap. 7.
6. Theodore H. White, *The Making of the President 1972* (New York: Atheneum, 1973).
7. Frank Sorauf makes this same point and has a useful discussion of the classic case of the 1952 Republican National Convention's contest between Robert Taft and Dwight Eisenhower. That convention decided to seat the disputed delegates from Georgia, Louisiana, and Texas loyal to Eisenhower, thus signaling the strength of Eisenhower's forces in that convention. Frank J. Sorauf, *Party Politics in America*, 4th ed. (Boston: Little, Brown, 1980), 279-280.
8. Theodore H. White, *America in Search of Itself: The Making of the President 1956-1980* (New York: Harper and Row, 1982).
9. William E. Bicker, "Network Television News and the 1976 Presidential Primaries," in *Race for the Presidency: The Media and the Nominating Process*, ed. James David Barber (Englewood Cliffs, N.J.: Prentice-Hall, 1978), 79-110. See also Av Westin, *The Newsmakers* (New York: Ballantine Books, 1982); Timothy Crouse, *The Boys on the Bus* (New York: Ballantine Books, 1974).
10. Barber, *Race for the Presidency*; David H. Weaver et al., *Media Agenda-Setting in a Presidential Election* (New York: Praeger, 1981); Doris A. Graber, *Mass Media and American Politics* (Washington, D.C.: CQ Press, 1980).
11. Jules Witcover, *Marathon: The Pursuit of the Presidency: 1972-1976* (New York: Viking, 1977); Jack Germond and Jules Witcover, *Blue Smoke and Mirrors* (New York: Viking, 1981).
12. Lester W. Milbrath and M. L. Goel, *Political Participation*, 2d ed. (Chicago: Rand McNally, 1977).
13. The term *caucus* here refers to a temporary group meeting at the convention, which should not be confused with the caucus as a nominating device.

14. Denis G. Sullivan et al., *The Politics of Representation: The Democratic Convention 1972* (New York: St. Martin's, 1974).
15. In June of 1981 this decision by the 1980 Democratic convention may have contributed directly to the loss of a potential Democratic seat in Congress. Because of this platform position the Democratic National Committee was prohibited from helping an aspirant in a closely contested race in Ohio. He subsequently lost the race by 378 votes.
16. Sullivan et al., *The Politics of Representation.*
17. Nelson W. Polsby and Aaron B. Wildavsky, "Uncertainty and Decision Making at the National Convention," *Western Political Quarterly* 13 (September 1960): 609-619.
18. Robert A. Hitlin and John S. Jackson III, "Change and Reform in the Democratic Party," *Polity* 11 (Summer 1979): 617-633.
19. Austin Ranney, *The Doctrine of Responsible Party Government* (Urbana: University of Illinois Press, 1964); Evron Kirkpatrick, "Toward a More Responsible Two-Party System: Political Science, Policy Science or Pseudo-Science," *American Political Science Review* 65 (December 1971): 965-990; David H. Everson, *American Political Parties* (New York: New Viewpoints, 1980). Everson's book provides an excellent analysis of contemporary trends in the development of the political party system.
20. For a more complete development of the American eclectic party concept, see Hitlin and Jackson, "Change and Reform," 617-621.
21. "Balloting for Republican Nomination," *Congressional Quarterly Weekly Report,* August 21, 1976, 2313.
22. Gerald M. Pomper et al., *The Election of 1980* (Chatham, N.J.: Chatham House, 1980), chap. 1.
23. Jimmy Carter, *Keeping Faith: Memoirs of a President* (New York: Bantam Books, 1982), chap. 3.
24. James David Barber, *The Pulse of Politics: Electing Presidents in the Media Age* (New York: W. W. Norton, 1980). In a provocative thesis Barber contends that there is a definite, 12-year pattern to presidential politics, which includes phases he calls the "Politics of Conflict," the "Politics of Conscience," and the "Politics of Conciliation."
25. V. O. Key, Jr., *Politics, Parties, and Pressure Groups,* 5th ed. (New York: Thomas Y. Crowell, 1964), 330.
26. Herbert J. McClosky, "Are Political Conventions Undemocratic?" *New York Times Magazine,* August 4, 1968, 10.
27. Ibid., 63
28. Jeane J. Kirkpatrick, *The New Presidential Elite* (New York: Russell Sage Foundation, 1976); Jeane J. Kirkpatrick, *Dismantling the Parties: Reflections on Party Reform and Party Decomposition* (Washington, D.C.: American Enterprise Institute, 1978). For Schumpeter's argument see Joseph A. Schumpeter, *Capitalism, Socialism and Democracy,* (New York: Harper, 1942). For a discussion of these ideas and a different point of view, see William Crotty, *Party Reform* (New York: Longman, 1983).
29. For a discussion of the unintended consequences of reform, see Kenneth Janda, "Primrose Paths to Political Reform: 'Reforming' versus Strengthening American Parties," in *Paths to Political Reform,* ed. William Crotty (Lexington, Mass.: Lexington Books/D. C. Heath, 1980), 309-347; Robert Harmel and Kenneth Janda, *Parties and Their Environments: Limits to Reform?* (New York: Longman, 1982).

Part III

Future of the Nominating System

Where Do We Go from Here? 9

Somewhere in this land ... there are people capable of providing presidential leadership within a democratic context, sensitive to the restraints of power, ambitious to promote the public good, skillful in the exercise of constitutionally given responsibilities, experienced in the management of large undertakings, calm and reassuring in character and style, with a measured view of national needs and world realities. The way Americans go about finding such people is of crucial importance.[1]

In effect these words of Stephen Hess sum up the problem. The burden placed on the mechanisms for screening and choosing presidential nominees is probably beyond the ability of any institution to satisfy. Those unhappy with the results are bound to find fault with the nominating system. When times are difficult or the government appears to lack purpose or ability, that criticism increases. Whatever the quality of leadership, however, many in the society remain displeased with the system, and it is unlikely that there will ever be a period in which the process of presidential selection is not a source of disappointment, displeasure, and concern for some group or other in the society. In this chapter we will discuss the qualities that an ideal candidate (and president) should possess and examine whether or not a nominating system can be designed to ensure that the parties nominate candidates with these characteristics. We will explore ways in which the competing interests of the parties' amateurs and professionals can be accommodated. Finally, we will take a look at the variety of proposals for further reform of the nominating system, weighing their pros and cons and assessing their current political feasibility.[2]

The Candidates
and the System _____

The Ideal Candidate

Stephen Hess, in his examination of the presidential campaign process, has outlined the qualities and experience of an ideal president. Among the attributes of such a person are the following:[3]

A mastery of political processes and proven responsiveness to the needs of divergent groups

Demonstrated managerial and executive talent

The ability to make decisions, establish priorities, delegate responsibility, and seek the best advice possible concerning the nation's problems

The self-discipline to use time effectively and well on the most important problems of the day and the stamina to keep going

The courage to make unpopular decisions when necessary

Historical perspective on the presidency and the implications of an administration's actions

The willingness to become a public person, to surrender privacy, and to conduct all business, including the most sensitive and private, in public view

A strong sense of personal honesty and integrity

High intelligence and the capacity to deal with complexities and new ideas

A highly developed political sensitivity to the hopes and aspirations of the nation's people

A grounding in reality and a clear-headed appreciation that the president's policies and actions intimately affect individuals at all levels of society here and abroad

The ability to dream grandly

The ability to inspire trust through style, honesty, patriotism, and capability

These qualities are demanded by the presidency, as James David Barber has shown in his influential analysis of presidential character and psychology, *The Presidential Character*. Barber begins with the premise that personality is the fundamental characteristic of an individual and influences his behavior and decision making. By beginning with an individual's childhood and examining the development of his personality until the time of his first political achievements, one can begin to identify patterns that relate to the individual's character, world view, and individual style. Barber believes that patterned political behavior can be predicted by certain traits, including an activist orientation to the political world and enjoyment of political life. Among presidents, the effects of personality are tempered by the demands of the time and the balance between the internal and external dynamics of the individual and the society.[4]

Barber characterizes the development of personality as follows:

> Life is experimental; consciously or not, a person tries out various ways of defining and maintaining and raising self-esteem. He looks to his environment for clues as to who he is and how well he is doing. These lessons of life slowly sink in: certain self-images and evaluations, certain ways of looking at the world, certain styles of action get confirmed by his experience and he gradually adopts them as his own. If we can see that process of development, we can understand the product. The features to note are those bearing on Presidential performance.[5]

The personality traits Barber identifies with presidential performance are an individual's style, that is, his habitual way of fulfilling political roles; his world view, that is, an individual's "primary, politically relevant beliefs, particularly his conceptions of social causality, human nature, and the central moral conflicts of the time"; and his character, the manner in which he approaches life.

On the basis of his analysis Barber has grouped presidents into four categories, characterizing the dimensions of political activism (active/passive) and enjoyment of political life (positive/negative). The resulting types are: active-positive, with an emphasis on achieving results; active-negative, typically the desire to hold power; passive-positive, the need to seek to be loved; and passive-negative, an emphasis on civic virtue as an end in itself. As examples, Barber classifies Franklin Roosevelt as active-positive, Lyndon Johnson and Richard Nixon as active-negative, Warren Harding as passive-positive, and Calvin Coolidge as passive-negative.[6] It is clear that Barber considers active-positive individuals as the most likely to make good presidents.

While the approach is broad and its predictive powers essentially based on reconstruction, it seems reasonable enough. But is it possible to design a selection process that will sort through qualities of character and personality in a way that is meaningful to performance in office? Some would argue that it is not possible to accomplish such a goal in any reasonable way, given the democratic constraints of our society. Others would say that the present system, whatever other flaws it may have, accomplishes such a winnowing rather well. The prenomination campaign is a grueling test of an individual's ability to relate to others, to solve problems, to direct a large organization, to inspire trust among the public, to deal with constant media attention, and to understand and shape political realities. In fact, the increasing attention the media, the parties, and political leaders are giving to such considerations should result in the broader availabilty of such personality-based information to future voters. In some ways then, the current system does address, though indirectly, these concerns.

The Political Context

Various scholars have addressed other values the nominating system should emphasize. Nelson Polsby argues that (1) the system should select the candidate who is most likely to win the general election for the party (or who will not damage long-term chances for the party) and (2) the candidates chosen should be able to govern

> with some exceptional degree of distinction. Thus, simultaneously, the process should be in some sense good for the party, good for the system of competition between the parties, good for the Presidency, and good for the successful maintenance, more generally, of democratic government in the United States.[7]

As Polsby notes, there is little controversy over the desirability of these goals. Devising a nominating system to implement the goals is where the controversy begins.

But it is unlikely that any nominating system would be able to satisfy all of these varied political and governmental demands simultaneously. Those who design and implement the system can only attempt to strike a balance among competing demands and pick the institutional alternative most likely to realize the greatest number of benefits. The resulting system should allow the society to select as candidates for the presidency reasonably able and broadly acceptable individuals with personal qualities and political instincts sufficient to provide competent leadership.

Some observers would prefer to return to a system in which party officials and elective office holders screen prospective nominees (through caucuses and other peer review procedures) and determine the eventual winners (in the conventions). In practice, this move would emphasize the role of the party elites and elevate the role of the conventions. The process would not be unlike the old party system. Supporters argue that the political elites are best qualified to make the important decisions and are most likely to choose well-qualified and electable candidates. It is sufficient that the voters be left to choose between parties and candidates in the general election, according to this view.

In our opinion, these goals would best be achieved within a system that allows for a representative choice among policy views reflective of broad segments of the electorate, within a process in which the individual rank-and-file party member has a major say in who receives the party's endorsement. We would like to see the system encourage broad-based participation, representative voters, and readily available, high-quality information. The party elites would be part of the mixture but not its dominant element.

Based on the contrasting tendencies of the two approaches, Robert Nakamura and Denis Sullivan have developed the *organizational* and the *participatory* models of party hierarchy (Table 9.1).[8] The former model, sometimes called the *elite* or *party regular* model, emphasizes the dominance of professional politicians in party deliberations; the winning of elections is the party's main—virtually its only—goal. The latter, also known as the *reform* model, involves a broader and more activist party-based clientele in decision making; educating the public about policy concerns is a major goal of campaigning.

Parties in the United States are something of a cross between these models. Even within a single party, competing organizational arrangements, based on fundamentally different assumptions, coexist; party structure is very loose, and parties are subdivided into many segments (for nominating, in Congress, at various levels from local to national).[9]

Choosing one set of objectives requires playing down the other, although neither set can be entirely ignored. For example, advocates of an organizational party orientation believe that policy distinctions of consequence do exist between the two major parties; but for the most part they deemphasize policy in their strategy of winning elections. Conversely, although proponents of the participatory model obviously know that winning elections is important, their goal is to be able to enact their policy commitments.

The two groups differ in the emphasis and relative weight they give to specific values, and they not unnaturally favor different nominating systems. Those who favor the organizational model look to elite-dominant systems, which include measures such as nonbinding preferential votes and delegate selection processes that are closed or nearly closed and characterized by low participation. Professionals tend to support this approach, in which voters would have an indirect say in party affairs. In the other view, held by proponents of the participatory model, measures such as primaries and open processes for delegate selection allow for the best representation of the voters and promote issue-oriented campaigns.

Table 9.1 Alternative Views of Party Democracy

Organizational model	Participatory model
Voters lack the incentives, information, and interest to formulate consistent or realistic opinions about how they should be governed.	**Voters** have specific and detailed opinions about how they want to be governed. They want and will use the opportunity to make their positions clear to leaders.
Parties should be run exclusively by professional politicians who 1. Are motivated by the desire to win elections 2. Value party as their means of winning elections 3. Use as their standard for judging issues and nominees the usefulness of each for winning the election and unifying the party.	**Parties** should be open to issue-oriented activists who 1. Are motivated by the desire to improve public policy by advancing specific issue positions 2. Place a high priority on advancing principled issue positions and a correspondingly low priority on considerations (such as party unity) that would compromise or distort those principles 3. Use as their standard for judging issues and nominees their "correctness" according to the activists' personal standards.
Participation in party nominations should be limited to ensure the maximum room for maneuver on the part of professional politicians. Great care should be taken to preserve resources for the coming campaign, including unstated or vague issue positions.	**Participation in party nominations** should be open to ensure the widest airing for issue positions and to guarantee the selection of a nominee whose positions have been clarified by an open process.
Campaigns should be waged in terms voters will find meaningful. Nondivisive appeals are best: symbols of party identification, ethnic or interest-group loyalties, issues on which a consensus exists. Elections are a test of candidate and party competence rather than a contest of principle. Parties tend to vary their appeals only incrementally from previous years, a tactic related to party or organizational survival.	**Campaigns** are primarily educational events. Candidates have the obligation to clarify their issue positions and differences between themselves and the opposition. Voters are to be educated about the advantages and disadvantages of each party's offerings. Parties may vary their electoral appeals significantly from past years because they are responding to current concerns.
Democratic choice consists of the voter's picking the party whose current appeal or past performance has most satisfied him. Choice is made easier by the simplification of party appeals and each party's criticism of the other.	**Democratic choice** consists of picking the candidate whose detailed issue positions are most in agreement with the voter's.
Election outcomes decide who gets to exercise governmental power. The party in power has an incentive to act responsibly because it wants to win the next election, and the out-party points out deficiencies for the same reason.	**Election outcomes** are binding contracts between the public and officials. Officeholders are expected to behave according to the issue positions of the campaign.
Conclusion. The quality of democracy is dependent on the organizational strength of political parties.	**Conclusion.** The quality of democracy is dependent on the degree of participation exercised by voters within parties and in the electorate.

Source: Robert T. Nakamura and Denis G. Sullivan, "Party Democracy and Democratic Control," in *American Parties and Public Policy,* ed. Walter Dean Burnham and Martha Wagner Weinberg (Cambridge, Mass.: MIT Press, 1978). Reprinted by permission.

Table 9.2 presents some of the differences in approach that distinguish the organizational/party regular model (favoring elite-dominant measures) from the participatory/reform model (favoring mass participation measures). Most of the reforms of the late 1960s and early 1970s have been in line with the participatory model; the organizational model for the most part represents the prereform system. As we have shown (Chapter 2), some prereform measures have been brought back into the system, but for the most part the current system favors the participatory model. That model emphasizes increased involvement by the American public and by the parties' rank and file in presidential nomination. Representativeness, both demographic and subjective, is a goal, albeit one yet to be realized in some important respects. Coalition building and direct presentation of the candidate to the voter at the

Table 9.2 Elite-Dominant versus Mass Participation Measures in the Nominating System

Elite-dominant measures	Mass participation measures
Caucuses/conventions	Direct primaries
Closed primaries with strict tests of party affiliation	Open primaries or closed primaries with lenient tests of party affiliation
Beauty contest primaries	Delegate selection primaries
Unpledged delegates	Pledged delegates
Unit rule	Individual delegate voting
Acting For representation of the masses in decisions	Direct representation of the masses' views and characteristics
Professional delegates, notably public officials	Self-motivated amateur delegates
Party organization as source of information	Mass media as source of information
Low participation rates	High participation rates
Symbolic and indirect policy representation of groups	Demographic and direct policy representation of groups
National convention as the critical point in candidate selection	State and local processes as the critical point in candidate selection
Campaign financing allowing restricted sources of funds, large gifts, and only private financing	Campaign financing requiring dispersed sources of funds and small gifts, and allowing federal or state financing

grass-roots level are stressed. Policy programs and issues must be thought out and presented in the campaigns. And candidates who are elected must be accountable to the voters on these matters.

No doubt ability to govern once elected is an appropriate criterion for selecting viable presidential nominees. But perhaps the personal qualities cannot be held strictly constant in a changing environment. We believe that the presidential nominating system, and the party system, must be flexible, sensitive, and responsive to changing times, new demands, and an evolving social and technological order. If nothing else, a party's survival depends on such responsiveness. Many of the reforms introduced over the past two decades were intended to meet the concerns of a society and polity in transition. The extent to which they have succeeded in this regard, or whether they have made a bad situation worse, has been the subject of much debate. In the final analysis, it will be up to individuals, and to the political parties, to make their own choice in light of the values they assume to be of greatest importance; the nominating and party system that they believe best serves the national interests; and the qualities and structural arrangements they would like to see emphasized.

Proposals for Further Reform

Although there is no general agreement on how much additional reform the nominating system needs or whether restoration of the old party system would be desirable, many plans have been proposed. In the remainder of this chapter we consider a number of the alternatives and evaluate them in light of what they are intended to accomplish.

The proposals we discuss can be grouped into five broad categories:

A national primary in some form
A national postconvention primary
Regional primaries
Approval voting
Adoption of more standardized and centralized rules

Some of the proposals for changing the presidential nominating system—the national primary, for example—would radically transform the system. Others would require less change in the parties and have fewer effects on other institutions; standardizing the rules would be the least radical change. Figure 9.1 illustrates the relationship of these proposals on a conceptual continuum. On the assumption that what requires the

National primary	Postconvention national primary	Regional primaries	Approval voting	Standardized and centralized rules

Most change				Least change

Figure 9.1   Level of Change Required in Reform Proposals

most change is least likely to be implemented, we will discuss the proposals in the order listed above.

The National Primary

The most venerable of the proposals, the national primary, would institutionalize one nationwide primary as the vehicle for the selection of presidential nominees. The idea has a certain democratic appeal and an element of simplicity that is attractive. As with most such proposals, the concept is more complex and possibly less attractive than it might first appear. Several proposals in relation to a national primary have been considered by Congress. These are outlined in the following paragraphs.[10]

Procedures.   In the most commonly referred to proposal, Congress would establish a single national primary for each party on a designated day. The primary would be open only to party members. Candidates would qualify for the national primary by filing petitions from 17 states with a number of signatures equal to at least 1 percent of the state's vote in the previous presidential election. If no one candidate were to receive 40 percent or more of the vote, a runoff election would be held within a few weeks. The national conventions could still be held. Those bodies would select the vice presidential nominee, adopt the platform, and conduct other party business.

In a similar system, but one requiring more direct action, an amendment might be made to the Constitution establishing a single national primary with uniform rules. Under a plan that would leave the states to establish some of the rules, a constitutional amendment would authorize Congress to set one day for state primaries to be held nationwide. Or Congress might legislate a day on which all state primaries, operating under uniform national rules, would be held. States could be provided with grants from the federal government as incentives to schedule their primaries on the designated day.

In a more radical proposal, the Constitution would be amended to provide for one national primary, much like a general election, in which candidates who filed petitions with a minimum of 1 percent of the nation's electorate could compete. Each of the parties could nominate its candidate in this primary; it would even be possible for the two top vote-getters, without reference to party, to compete in the general election.

Even more proposals are on the table, but the main features of the plans are similar. All involve a constitutional amendment, congressional action, or both to set the time, conditions for participation, and rules governing the process, including those for allocating and binding the delegates selected (where appropriate). Each of the proposals deemphasizes (or eliminates altogether) the role of the political party or the states in the nominating process.

Implications. Arguments about the feasibility and desirability of a national primary reflect the differences between an organizational approach and an extreme participatory emphasis. In addition, the two camps do not agree on the effects of certain provisions.

The national primary would complete the nationalization of the nominating processes. Congress would most likely make the rules, and the parties and states would play a very restricted role. The votes of individuals would count more equally than in any other system, since no weighting in favor of certain states or party elites would occur. Some believe that turnout would increase, and others believe that it would decrease.

Media campaigns would most likely entirely replace grass-roots campaigning, since the candidates would have to make a national appeal. Many people would prefer to see the media play a smaller role in national politics, but the national primaries would almost surely increase it. In addition, money might become even more important, and voters would probably have less access to detailed policy information. There would be no time to test the waters in early states, and there would be no possibility of persuading the voters and emerging victorious toward the end of the primary season.

A larger number of candidates would be on the ballot for both parties, since no winnowing would have occurred in early states. Campaigns might become very nasty as candidates attempted to stand out from the crowd. It is possible that a large field would be disadvantageous to centrist candidates—who might not be well differentiated from one another—and advantageous to ideological candidates, who might be able to make a convincing single-issue appeal. A campaign emphasis on broader issues of policy would thus probably give way to more easily grasped fashionable topics. Nationally known candidates would perhaps do better than political outsiders or less well known individuals, since there would be less time for a new reputation to emerge. Runoff elections seem likely, and they would probably include some less popular candidates who were able to garner bloc votes. The necessity for the runoffs, as well as the two national campaigns, could well lengthen the nominating season—even though the national primary is intended to shorten it.

The national primary has broad popular appeal, and some consider it to be the logical extension of the reform movement of the 1960s and 1970s. The Gallup Poll in 1980 reported that 66 percent of the American public favored the national primary proposal and only 24 percent were opposed. That survey merely repeated the results of others: the national primary proposal has been favored by large majorities since Gallup first asked about it in 1952.[11] An electoral reform proposal with this much popular appeal is likely to remain on the national agenda regardless of its potential problems and pitfalls.

In spite of its appeal, we feel that the potential problems of a national primary outweigh the benefits. One of the main drawbacks is practical: amending the Constitution, which would be necessary for many of the proposed forms of national primary, is in practice very difficult to do; many believe that two-thirds of the Congress and three-fourths of the state legislatures would not be willing to undertake so much change in the system. Even making the change by federal statute would prove to be difficult to get through a Congress jealous of state prerogatives in electoral matters. On its merits alone, the national primary is probably not the best nominating process mainly because it damages the party system, which many feel is crucial to a representative democratic system. It would be very difficult to avoid weakening the party organizations if a national primary were adopted, and certainly the role of the mass media would be further enhanced. The role of the states would probably be further deemphasized. On the whole, we believe the pendulum has swung far enough in that direction.

National Postconvention Primary

Less radical because it leaves the parties in the picture, the national postconvention primary is a type of national primary that deserves special attention. In contrast to most of the other national primary proposals, this one is meant to help rebuild the parties and to give party leaders and the party organization more of a role in the nominating process. The leading proponents of the plan, and the developers of the

223

proposal outlined in the following paragraphs, are Thomas Cronin and Robert Loevy.[12]

Procedures.   The national postconvention primary system is meant to combine the merits of both a national convention and a national primary. It would begin with a fairly complex series of events from May through August of the election year. Each state would be required to employ a statewide caucus/convention system, beginning the first week in May, for the selection of convention delegates. Schedules and rules would be determined by national parties. Any party member who registered for the caucuses would be eligible to vote in the postconvention primary.

National conventions would be held in July. A delegate selected by a party's state convention would be bound to vote for the his or her state convention's choice on the first ballot at the national convention. There would be a bloc of 25 percent of each state's delegation officially uncommitted and reserved for party and elective officials. On the second ballot of the national convention all but the three top candidates would be dropped and all delegates would be unbound.

Any candidate who received 70 percent or more of the national convention vote would automatically be the party's nominee for the general election. Otherwise, the top two or three finishers (a minimum of 25 to 30 percent of the total national convention vote would be required) would appear on the ballot in a national primary to be held after the convention (in early September). A party's voters would decide the nominee by a plurality vote. Then the party's nominee would select his vice presidential running mate from a list supplied by the national convention.

Implications.   The authors of this plan believe the postconvention primary could improve in a number of ways on the current nominating system.

The parties would be more influential than they currently are. Caucus/convention systems tend to draw strong partisans. The reserved seats on state delegations allow for officials to take important roles; allowing these delegates to be uncommitted encourages candidates to court their peers. The national conventions would actually narrow the field for nomination and help select the vice presidential possibilities.

All of a party's voters would have a say in the outcome, which should generate interest and turnout. Further enthusiasm might result from a curtailed preconvention race. National candidates would probably have the advantage, and a national policy agenda could be put forth. Cronin and Loevy believe the media would be encouraged to present the national agenda rather than the horse race aspects currently emphasized.

The plan has disadvantages as well, as even its authors admit. In practice, the conventions would be under some pressure to nominate a candidate with over 70 percent of the delegates' votes to avoid the postconvention primary. Otherwise, party elites would lose some power to the voters and the states would be saddled with a large expense they would rather avoid.

Like other national primary plans, the postconvention primary might actually increase the role of the media by making television the principal means of candidate-to-voter communication. As a further consequence of any national plan, pressures would be built into the system to discourage minority candidates, factional candidates, and candidates expressing unusual opinions or policy options—perhaps to the long-term detriment of the party system. Well-known candidates would have the advantage.

Although the postconvention primary would accomodate parties, it would reduce the role of the states in the nominating process; as Cronin and Loevy admit, the plan may be "too national, too rigid, and too mechanistic." [13]

Similar procedures have been used at the nonpresidential level in some states (Colorado and Connecticut) with some success. But at the national level the postconvention primary plan is still in the discussion stage. We speculate that the plan would ultimately undermine the party system through its many restrictions and its national emphasis; the voters could eventually lose confidence in the plan and the nominating system. The practical problem is that a national postconvention primary would involve a complete overhaul of the nominating procedures in each of the states as well as within the two national parties. State legislatures and Congress are especially unlikely to support a system that so reduces the power of the states. Thus the plan is too different from the status quo to survive the rigors of the political process in the near future. We have to conclude that although the plan is provocative and deserves discussion, it is politically impractical at this time.

Regional Primaries

Broad support exists for proposals based on regional primaries. Republican Sen. Bob Packwood of Oregon is most closely associated with the proposal. As a senator, Walter Mondale also devised a regional primary plan.[14] Proponents hope to maintain the health of the political parties while offering a fair and democratic means for selecting presidential nominees. For convenience we will separate our discussion of the two plans, which differ only in their specifics.

The Packwood Plan. Under this plan the United States would be divided into five regions (Figure 9.2). Within a region each state would be required to hold its primary or initial caucuses on the same date. The dates, once a month from March to July, would be assigned by lot 70 days before the first primary.

All serious candidates would be placed on the ballot by a federal commission; petitioning for inclusion would be possible. To withdraw from the ballot, a candidate would have to file for each region a statement declaring that he was not, and did not intend to become, a candidate for his party's presidential nomination.

Candidates would be voted for directly; delegates to the national conventions would be appointed by candidates in proportion to their strength in each state (above a threshold of 5 percent). Each delegate so chosen would be bound to vote for that presidential candidate at the

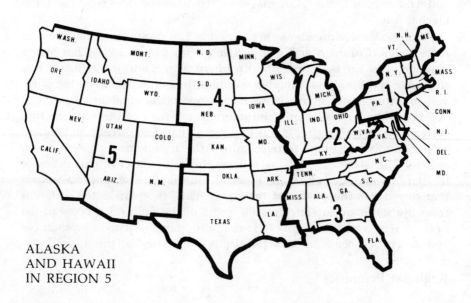

ALASKA
AND HAWAII
IN REGION 5

Numbers do not imply chronological order

Figure 9.2   Packwood's Regional Primary Plan. (From *Congressional Quarterly Weekly Report*, July 8, 1972, 1652.)

national convention for two ballots, until the candidate's vote fell below 20 percent of the national convention total, or until released by the candidate.

The Mondale Plan.   In most important respects, Mondale's plan is like Packwood's. But it would work a little differently.

This plan divides the country into six regions. In October of the year before the election year the regions would be assigned their dates. Primaries and caucuses would be held at two-week intervals from the end of March through the beginning of June. States that chose primaries would be encouraged to restrict them to party members.

The state contests would be used for delegate selection, and delegates could run as committed to a candidate or uncommitted; status would be listed on the ballot. Ballots would thus differ by state. In addition, candidates could choose which contests to enter, as long as they entered at least one state contest in each region.

Both plans retain the national convention and assume that the party will play a large role in the process. And under either plan the states would choose whether to use primaries or caucus/convention procedures.

Implications.   Regional primary plans attempt to resolve some of the difficulties of the current system of scattered primaries while retaining the strengths both of the party system and of reform era democratization. Supporters believe that they would dilute the influence of idiosyncratic early state primaries (New Hampshire, for example) or particular clusters of primaries (as in the southern states). The shifting order of primaries would prevent any long-term influence of early states. All the voters in all the regions would be able to choose among all the candidates, especially under the Packwood plan, although it would still be possible for a candidate to change strategy or drop out based on early results.

Candidates would have to make national appeals, largely through the media, but they would have time to develop policy agendas over the course of a campaign. Idiosyncratic states would have less influence on candidates' agendas. Under the Mondale plan, the nominating season as a whole would be shorter than it is now, meaning less stress on candidates. In addition, regional groupings should make campaigning easier, if not cheaper.

Opponents of regional primaries, like opponents of the other proposals, argue that the new system would have unintended consequences. They see national campaigns as undesirable, for example. National campaigns today are media campaigns, which often means less grass-roots campaigning at higher costs; higher costs mean a longer period of fund raising. Not only would fund raising take longer; the Packwood plan would require a longer series of contests than the 1984 nominating season. And the political parties, although the plan intends them to gain in importance, would not actually have a larger role than they do now. Further, front loading is not entirely eliminated in any system that separates the contests widely; in some years unrepresentative, less populous regions would be the leaders by virtue of timing.

Those who object to primaries, generally those who take the organizational view of the nominating system, of course find the same problems in the regional primary proposals as they do in the current system. In part they feel that voters without strong party ties—who may well vote in primaries for reasons other than party loyalty—will give undue advantage to flashy, ideological candidates who look good on television.

Even supporters of the participatory systems may feel that it is unwise to take more power from the states; the regional primaries would play down the role of the states, though to a lesser degree than would national primaries. Dividing the country into regions is essentially an arbitrary way of sequencing the nominating season. The regions would be heterogeneous and large; to administer contests in these groups of states Congress might well have to intervene in the nominating process, a development many would not welcome.

Because the changes required to institute regional primaries would not be as radical as for a national primary, these proposals have received a good deal of attention. Even a presidential commission recommended the shift to regional primaries as a means for avoiding "the excessive emphasis given the earliest primaries" and for strengthening the party system and ties between Congress and the White House through encouraging the participation of party professionals.[15] Recently, however, there has not been much pressure to adopt regional primaries, although this proposal would probably receive more attention than the national primary proposals if change were to become likely.

Approval Voting

The proposals we have discussed so far in this chapter have been concerned with the broad structure of the primary system. Approval voting could be added to any nominating system, since it addresses how votes are cast. Steven J. Brams is the foremost proponent of this notion.[16] Under approval voting, as applied to primaries or national conventions, voters would cast ballots for *all* the candidates they liked or felt that they could support. The candidate with the most total votes—presumably the most widely acceptable candidate—wins the primary or the nomination. The method was tested in the 1976 Pennsylvania presidential primary, in which over 70 percent of those participating voted for between two and four candidates. The objective of approval voting, which it does seem to accomplish, is to identify centrist candidates who could win elections (that is, a voter could vote for the candidate, although he may not be the voter's first choice) while discouraging fringe or radical candidacies. In the convention, Brams writes, "The main effect would probably be to give comparatively more support to moderates that most delegates find acceptable, comparatively less to extremists who are only acceptable to ideological factions in their party." [17]

Indirectly the plan might help revitalize the parties by reinforcing their consensus-building functions and by providing representation for the mainstream base of their coalitions. Although factional candidacies and protest voting would remain possible, Brams argues that the outcomes would be legitimate because moderates are favored and a majority winner is likely. The plan has clear merits for party supporters. Nevertheless, the approval voting plan appears to be different enough from current practice to make passage by either Congress or the state legislatures unlikely in the near future.

Standardizing Nominating Procedures

Even though major changes may not be on the horizon, many feel that the current nominating system needs some improvement because it is so grueling and costly that the best candidates can be discouraged from even entering the race. Morris Udall, a onetime contender for the Democratic presidential nomination, has voiced the frustration many candidates feel with the nominating process they encounter:

> Lacking uniform rules and procedures, the primaries are not a reasonable yardstick of a candidate's potential support in a general election.
> Depending on where he or she chooses to run, the candidate may be a contestant in a beauty contest meeting all others head-on; in an election in which delegates pledged to a candidate are selected; or in a primary that blends both approaches. If the rules vary, so do the prizes. A victory in Illinois does not guarantee the candidate one delegate; 50 percent in Florida could theoretically yield little convention support if the candidate does not win a majority in each of the State's Congressional districts; a plurality in Indiana will assure him of the backing of that State's delegates for one ballot; a similar showing in Oregon will lock in delegates until victory or the bitter end. A candidate who can do well in New Hampshire or Wisconsin, but is unknown elsewhere, may

want to dodge primaries on the west coast. Yet he may be listed on the Oregon ballot anyway, particularly if he is a promising Democrat and the controlling State official a Republican, or vice versa. . . .

A candidate's future is in the hands of a hodgepodge of laws, regulations, and faceless officials over whom he has no control or recourse.[18]

Udall and other members of Congress have proposed a number of refinements to the present nominating system in an effort to smooth the way for candidates. The standardization proposals would limit the dates for preconvention contests, to three dates or to a single month, for example; but a national primary would not be encouraged. They would encourage major candidates and would see that primary votes were rewarded with committed delegates. Rules regarding filing deadlines and qualification requirements, delegate commitments, in-state national convention vote distributions, and the like would be standardized on a national level. To enforce the rules, the proposals call either for a federal commission to be named by Congress or for authorizing the Federal Election Commission to assume this function. State and national parties would relinquish that responsibility.

The value of the approach is that it does equalize the hurdles faced by the candidates; it preserves many of the better aspects of the reforms; and it introduces uniform standards into delegate selection. But the changes may be more radical than they first appear. The proposals would introduce a more active federal presence in the process, thus further undercutting the political parties' control over presidential nominations. Many believe that a shorter season does not necessarily shorten campaigning time, as we have mentioned in connection with other proposals. And these proposed rules changes perpetuate a faith in the power of rules that has not been supported to any great degree by the experience of the reform era. We have no evidence that the changes would accomplish their goals, and we do have reason to believe that the party system would be damaged.

Conclusion

Before instituting further change in the nominating system, Congress and the parties must consider the potential consequences of new processes. By adopting the most radical of the proposals we have reviewed, reformers would risk dismantling the party system entirely. Some versions of the proposed national primary intentionally eliminate the party label; others ostensibly maintain a party presence in the nominating system—though state and federal control of the process would downgrade the parties' role. Some believe that the parties have too much power over the presidency, but the national primary would be perhaps too drastic a solution of that problem.

The other proposals, modest as they may seem in contrast to the national primary, hold hidden costs for the party system. Each of the proposals requires the introduction of a federal presence into national party affairs, which works to make the political parties less relevant to the nominating system. Many critics feel that the party organizations have been severely damaged over the past two decades, and these proposals would accelerate that trend. Social needs and party needs both might be better served by efforts directed toward finding ways to improve party performance and toward helping the parties adjust to a rapidly changing social and technological environment.

As we see it, these efforts should begin with encouraging the parties—especially the more centralized Democratic party—to allow greater state autonomy within the current nominating system (with guarantees of fairness to all who choose to participate) and building up the strength of both the state and national party organizations. Rather than always competing, the two levels should complement each other. In contrast, the Republicans are stronger and much better financed at the national party level, but they have paid little attention yet to broadening their coalition by encouraging minorities and women to play a more active role in the nomination process. In sum, the two parties' strengths and weaknesses are mirror images. Each national party would be strengthened by adopting some of the other party's major strategy for rebuilding.

Political parties have functions that are crucial to the performance of a democratic political system. Parties can provide a degree of order and rationality in creating coalitions and establishing policy themes; within the nominating system they can select candidates who are broadly representative of their constituencies and accountable for their actions. Actually, few people would intentionally do away with the party system. Most observers would prefer to encourage the ideal functioning of the parties, changing the nominating processes in the direction of encouraging the parties' role rather than playing it down.[19]

Throughout American history political elites have freely tinkered with the electoral machinery in response to crises of various kinds (Chapter 1), and the American public is quite willing to experiment with further changes.[20] In light of our broadening expectations of the presidency, it is not surprising that the workings of the nominating system have received a good deal of attention in recent years. When voters are dissatisfied with the actions of incumbent presidents and with the parties' election-year offerings, they demand that the machinery be fixed. When political elites and disappointed office seekers are dissatisfied with the rules, as they often are, they have the resources to seek to change the system. And so bills are introduced in Congress; the parties appoint yet another commission to review their nomination and convention rules; the national media write editorials and present special reports on what's wrong with the nominating system, the conventions, or the presidency.

Yet the American political system has been remarkably stable. Perhaps one of the keys to this fundamental stability is the willingness Americans have shown to experiment. Presidents can be driven from office. Rules can be modified to accomplish social and political ends. Demands of disadvantaged groups can be met. The flexibility of the electoral system has been critical in maintaining the stability of the political system as a whole.

The question remains of whether further reform is likely in the near future. If future elections result in widespread dissatisfaction, and especially if controversy along the lines of the problems of 1968 ensues, there will be pressure for change. Chances are that greater pressure will result in more radical changes, such as the institution of a national primary. Meanwhile, as Donald Bruce Johnson points out, "Many persons believe that in spite of the confusion and complications, the system generally works about as well as the American people expect it to work." [21]

NOTES

1. Stephen Hess, *The Presidential Campaign*, rev. ed. (Washington, D.C.: Brookings Institution, 1978), 1.
2. See William Crotty, " 'Improving' Presidential Selection," *Commonsense* 4 (1981): 5-12.
3. Hess, *The Presidential Campaign*, 25-37.
4. James David Barber, *The Presidential Character* (Englewood Cliffs, N.J.: Prentice-Hall, 1972), 6.
5. Ibid., 10.
6. Ibid., 13.
7. Nelson W. Polsby, *The Consequences of Party Reform* (New York: Oxford University Press, 1983), 168-169.
8. Robert T. Nakamura and Denis G. Sullivan, "Party Democracy and Democratic Control," in *American Politics and Public Policy*, ed. Walter Dean Burnham and Martha Wagner Weinberg (Cambridge, Mass.: MIT Press, 1978), 26-40.

9. See the argument in William Crotty, "The Philosophies of Party Reform," in *Party Renewal in America,* ed. Gerald M. Pomper (New York: Praeger, 1980), 31-50.

10. These plans are discussed in Donald Bruce Johnson, *Selection of Delegates to National Conventions* (New York: Robert A. Taft Institute of Government, 1980) and William Crotty, *Political Reform and the American Experiment* (New York: Thomas Y. Crowell, 1977), 228-235.

11. "Majority of Americans Seek Campaign Reforms," *Gallup Opinion Index,* 183 (December 1980): 58-61.

12. Thomas Cronin and Robert Loevy, "The Case for a National Pre-Primary Convention Plan," *Public Opinion* (December/January 1983): 50-53.

13. Ibid., 53.

14. See Johnson, *Selection of Delegates,* 25-27, and "Presidential Primaries: Proposals for a New System," *Congressional Quarterly Weekly Report,* July 8, 1972, 1652.

15. President's Commission for a National Agenda for the Eighties, *A National Agenda for the Eighties* (New York: Mentor, 1981), 107-108.

16. Steven J. Brams, *The Presidential Election Game* (New Haven: Yale University Press, 1978), 193-229.

17. Ibid., 221.

18. Quoted in Crotty, *Political Reform and the American Experiment,* 231.

19. Johnson, *Selection of Delegates,* 27.

20. "Majority of Americans Seek Campaign Reforms," 58-60.

21. Johnson, *Selection of Delegates,* 27.

Appendix

Table A.1 Democratic Presidential Primary Winners, 1972-1980

Primary	1972	1976	1980
N.H.	Muskie (46%)	Carter (28%)	Carter (47%)
Mass.	McGovern (53%)	Jackson (22%)	Kennedy (65%)
Vt.	—	Carter (42%)	Carter (73%)
Ala.	Wallace	Wallace	Carter (82%)
Fla.	Wallace (42%)	Carter (34%)	Carter (61%)
Ga.	—	Carter (83%)	Carter (88%)
Puerto Rico	—	—	Carter (52%)
Ill.	Muskie (63%)	Carter (48%)	Carter (65%)
Conn.	—	—	Kennedy (47%)
N.Y.	McGovern	Jackson	Kennedy (59%)
Kan.	—	—	Carter (57%)
Wis.	McGovern (30%)	Carter (37%)	Carter (56%)
La.	—	—	Carter (56%)
Pa.	Humphrey (35%)	Carter (37%)	Kennedy (46%)
Texas	—	Carter	Carter (56%)
D.C.	Fauntroy (72%)	Carter (32%)	Kennedy (62%)
Ind.	Humphrey (47%)	Carter (68%)	Carter (68%)
N.C.	Wallace (50%)	Carter (54%)	Carter (70%)
Tenn.	Wallace (68%)	Carter (78%)	Carter (75%)
Md.	Wallace (39%)	Brown (48%)	Carter (48%)
Neb.	McGovern (41%)	Church (38%)	Carter (47%)
Mich.	Wallace (51%)	Carter (43%)	Uncommitted (46%)
Ore.	McGovern (50%0	Church (34%)	Carter (57%)
Ark.	—	Carter (63%)	Carter (60%)
Idaho	—	Church (79%)	Carter (62%)
Ky.	—	Carter (59%)	Carter (67%)
Nev.	—	Brown (53%)	Carter (38%)
Calif.	McGovern (44%)	Brown (59%)	Kennedy (45%)
Mont.	—	Church (59%)	Carter (51%)
N.J.	Chisholm (67%)	Carter (58%)	Kennedy (56%)
N.M.	McGovern (33%)	—	Kennedy (46%)
Ohio	Humphrey (41%)	Carter (52%)	Carter (51%)
R.I.	McGovern (41%)	Uncommitted (32%)	Kennedy (68%)
S.D.	McGovern (100%)	Carter (41%)	Kennedy (49%)
W.Va.	Humphrey (67%)	Byrd (89%)	Carter (62%)

Note: Primaries are listed in the order they were held in 1980. Where no preference vote was taken, the candidate who won the most delegates is listed. A dash (—) indicates that no primary was held.

Source: Congressional Quarterly Weekly Report, December 10, 1983, 2603.

Table A.2 Democratic Campaign Calendar, 1984

Date	Primaries	Caucuses
Feb. 20		Iowa (58)
Feb. 28	New Hampshire (22)	
March 4		Maine (27)
March 10		Wyoming (15)
March 13	Florida (143)	Washington (70)
	Massachusetts (116)	Oklahoma (53)
	Georgia (84)	Hawaii (27)
	Alabama (62)	Nevada (20)
	Rhode Island (27)	American Samoa (6)
	Democrats Abroad (5)	
March 14		Delaware (18)
March 15		Alaska (14)
March 17		Michigan (155)
		South Carolina (48)
		Mississippi (43)
		Arkansas (42)
		Latin America (5)
March 18	Puerto Rico (53)	North Dakota (18)
March 20	Illinois (194)	Minnesota (86)
March 24		Kansas (44)
		Virginia (78)
March 25		Montana (25)
March 27	Connecticut (60)	
March 31		Kentucky (63)
		Virgin Islands (6)
April 3	New York (285)	
April 7		Wisconsin (89)
April 10	Pennsylvania (195)	
April 14		Arizona (40)
April 16		Utah (27)
April 18		Missouri (86)
April 24		Vermont (17)
April 28		Guam (7)
May 1	Tennessee (76)	
	District of Columbia (19)	
May 5	Louisiana (69)	Texas (200)
May 7		Colorado (51)
May 8	Ohio (175)	
	Indiana (88)	
	North Carolina (88)	
	Maryland (74)	
May 15	Oregon (50)	
	Nebraska (30)	
May 24		Idaho (22)
June 5	California (345)	
	New Jersey (122)	
	West Virginia (44)	
	New Mexico (28)	
	South Dakota (19)	

Source: Congressional Quarterly Weekly Report, February 11, 1984, 252.

Table A.3   Democratic Presidential Primary Vote Summary, 1984

State	Estimated turnout	Hart	Jackson	Mondale	Others	Uncommitted
N.H.	101,131	**37.3%**	5.3%	27.9%	29.5%	
Vt.[a]	74,059	70.0	7.8	20.0	2.2	
Ala.	428,283	20.7	19.6	**34.6**	24.1	1.0
Fla.	1,160,713	**40.0**	12.4	32.1	15.5	
Ga.	684,541	27.3	21.0	**30.5**	20.8	0.4
Mass.	630,962	**39.0**	5.0	25.5	29.7	0.8
R.I.	44,511	**45.0**	8.7	34.4	10.9	1.0
Puerto Rico	143,039	0.6		**99.1**	0.3	
Ill.	1,659,425	35.2	21.0	**40.5**	3.3	
Conn.	220,842	**52.6**	12.0	29.1	5.4	0.9
N.Y.	1,387,950	27.4	25.6	**44.8**	2.2	
Wis.[a]	635,768	**44.4**	9.9	41.1	3.5	1.1
Pa.	1,656,294	33.3	16.0	**45.1**	5.6	
D.C.	102,731	7.1	**67.3**	25.6		
Tenn.	322,063	29.1	25.3	**41.0**	2.5	2.1
La.	318,810	25.0	**42.9**	22.3	3.7	6.1
Ind.	716,955	**41.8**	13.7	40.9	3.6	
Md.	506,886	24.3	25.5	**42.5**	4.6	3.1
N.C.	960,857	30.2	25.4	**35.6**	4.2	4.6
Ohio	1,444,797	**42.1**	16.4	40.3	1.2	
Neb.	148,855	**58.2**	9.1	26.6	3.0	3.1
Ore.[b]	377,939	**58.9**	9.5	27.3	4.3	
Idaho[a]	54,722	**58.0**	5.7	30.1	2.2	4.0
Calif.[b]	2,724,248	**41.2**	19.6	37.4	1.8	
N.J.[b]	678,893	29.5	23.6	**45.1**	1.8	
N.M.[b]	186,635	**46.5**	11.9	36.2	4.6	0.8
S.D.[b]	53,155	**51.2**	5.2	38.5	2.6	2.5
W.Va.[b]	359,744	37.1	6.7	**53.7**	2.5	
N.D.[a]	29,584	**88.0**			12.0	
National primary total	17,814,392	36.2	18.3	38.6	6.2	0.7

[a] Nonbinding primary. Delegates selected by caucus process.

[b] Unofficial results.

Note: Boldface indicates winner of each primary. California's total based on aggregate of vote for each candidate's most popular delegate in each congressional district. North Dakota figures based on 88 percent of precincts.

Source: Congressional Quarterly Weekly Report, June 16, 1984, 1443.

Table A.4 Democratic Presidential Primary Recap, 1984

	Primaries on ballot	1st	2d	3d	Total vote	Percentage
Walter F. Mondale	28	11	16	1	6,885,241	38.6%
Gary Hart	29	16	10	3	6,447,671	36.2
Jesse Jackson	27	2	1	21	3,266,781	18.3
John Glenn	17	0	1	2	520,703	2.9
George McGovern	17	0	0	1	265,174	1.5
Lyndon LaRouche	13	0	1	0	122,353	0.7
Reubin Askew	13	0	0	0	52,759	0.3
Alan Cranston	15	0	0	0	51,380	0.3
Ernest F. Hollings	12	0	0	0	33,684	0.2
Others		0	0	0	50,826	0.3
No preference	14	0	0	0	117,820	0.7

Note: Cumulative totals and aggregate number of first, second, and third place finishes. Based on data available as of June 15, 1984; some states' results were unofficial.

Source: Congressional Quarterly Weekly Report, June 16, 1984.

Table A.5 Democratic Delegate Selection Methods, by State, 1984

State	Method	State	Method
Alabama	PR primary	Montana	Bonus caucus
Alaska	PR caucus	Nebraska	PR primary
Arizona	PR caucus	Nevada	PR caucus
Arkansas	Bonus caucus	New Hampshire	PR primary
California	Direct primary	New Jersey	Direct primary
Colorado	Bonus caucus	New Mexico	PR primary
Connecticut	PR primary	New York	Bonus primary
Delaware	PR caucus	North Carolina	Bonus primary
D.C.	PR primary	North Dakota	PR caucus
Florida	Direct primary	Ohio	Bonus primary
Georgia	Bonus primary	Oklahoma	PR caucus
Hawaii	Bonus caucus	Oregon	PR primary
Idaho	Bonus caucus	Pennsylvania	Direct primary
Illinois	Direct primary	Puerto Rico	Bonus primary
Indiana	PR primary	Rhode Island	PR primary
Iowa	PR caucus	South Carolina	PR caucus
Kansas	PR caucus	South Dakota	PR primary
Kentucky	Bonus caucus	Tennessee	PR primary
Louisiana	PR primary	Texas	PR caucus
Maine	PR caucus	Utah	PR caucus
Maryland	Direct primary	Vermont	PR caucus
Massachusetts	PR primary	Virginia	PR caucus
Michigan	PR caucus	Washington	PR caucus
Minnesota	PR caucus	West Virginia	Direct primary
Mississippi	PR caucus	Wisconsin	PR caucus
Missouri	PR caucus	Wyoming	PR caucus

Note: PR stands for proportional representation.
Source: Congressional Quarterly Weekly Report, January 28, 1984, 131.

Index

Accountability, of candidates - 9, 64, 65
Accountability, of delegates - 41
Adams, John - 9
Affirmative action - 33-34, 47
Agnew, Spiro - 203
Aldrich, John H. - 150, 154, 158
Alexander, Herbert E. - 186
Almond, Gabriel A. - 209
Amateurs - 119, 120, 122, 124
Anderson, John
  campaign financing - 163t, 164, 165t,
    168t, 169t
  campaign spending - 182t
Antidiscrimination rules - 31, 33-34
Anti-Masonic party - 11
Approval voting - 228-229
Arterton, F. Christopher - 77, 79
Asher, Herbert - 101, 185
Askew, Reuben - 152
Association of Community Organizations
  for Reform (ACORN) - 112
At-large delegates - 39

Bain, Richard C. - 24, 137, 209
Baker, Howard H., Jr.
  campaign financing - 163t, 164, 165t,
    168t, 169t, 170t
  campaign spending - 182t
Baker, James - 183
Barber, James David - 79, 148, 158, 209,
  210, 214-215, 232
Beveridge, Albert J. - 78
Bibby, John F. - 78
Bicker, William E. - 209
Black delegates - 196
Black voters
  Democratic party reform - 28, 31, 33-34
  representation - 107, 108-109, 110
Blanket primary - 19

Bode, Kenneth A. - 102
Bositis, David - 102, 131, 138, 139, 158
Brams, Steven J. - 157, 228-229, 233
Broder, David S. - 63, 65, 79
Brokered conventions - 18, 41
Brooke, Edward - 134
Brown, Barbara L. - 102, 131, 138, 139, 158
Brown, Edmund G., Jr.
  campaign financing - 163t, 164, 165t,
    168t, 169t, 170t
  campaign spending - 182t
Brown, Jesse C. - 139
Buckley v. Valeo - 161, 183
Bull Moose party - 15
Bumpers, Dale - 152
Burnham, Walter D. - 138
Bush, George - 97, 130, 151, 202
  campaign financing - 163t, 164, 165t,
    166-167, 168t, 169t, 170t
  campaign spending - 170, 172t, 174,
    178, 182t

Campaign Finance Study Group - 185
Campaign financing - 156, 159
  candidates - 167-168
  contribution limits - 180
  federal funding - 160-162, 179-180
  fund-raising difficulties - 180-181
  geographical sources - 166-167
  individual contributions - 161, 164-167
  political action committees (PACs)
    161, 168-169, 169t
  prenomination campaigns - 160-161,
    162t
  proposals for change - 185
  reform legislation - 160-162, 179-184
Campaign, prenomination. See Prenomination campaign
Campaign Reform Act of 1974 - 160

Campbell, Angus - 142, 147, 157
Candidates - 3, 5
  accountability - 9, 44, 65
  convention caucuses - 195-196
  convention role - 199-201
  delegate selection - 39-40
  ideal - 213, 214-216
  ideology - 146-149
  image - 67, 75, 95, 142, 144, 145-146, 148
  peer review - 35
  personal financing - 167-168
  quality - 20, 64-65
  strategy - 94-95, 149-155, 174
  success factors - 17, 156
  See also Prenomination campaign; Vice
    presidential candidates
Carter, Jimmy - 205, 210
  campaign financing - 163t, 164, 165t,
    166-167, 168t, 169t, 170
  campaign spending - 171, 172t, 178,
    182t
  convention delegates - 38, 66, 96, 131,
    153
  image - 146, 150, 151
  prenomination campaigns - 67, 200
  vice presidential selection - 203
Casey, Carol F. - 102
Caucuses - 5, 50, 52
  origins - 10-11
  representativeness - 95
  timing - 41-42, 154
  versus primaries - 95-97
  voter participation - 84
  See also Congressional caucuses; Con-
    vention caucuses
Ceaser, James W. - 24, 100, 102
Center for Political Studies - 90, 132, 144
Chambers, William N. - 9, 24
Charles, Joseph - 9, 24
Charter Commission. *See* Sanford Com-
  mission
Chisholm, Shirley - 196
Citrin, Jacob - 157
Civil rights movement - 28, 31, 33-34, 51
Clark, Ed - 163t, 164, 165t, 167, 168t, 169t
Clark, Peter B. - 121
Clarke, James W. - 120, 124, 138
Closed primaries - 19, 43, 85
Commission on Delegate selection and
  Party Structure. *See* Mikulski Commis-
  sion
Commission on Democratic Participation
  - 32
Commission on Low and Moderate In-
  come Participation (Leland Commis-
  sion) - 32, 33

Commission on Party Structure and Dele-
  gate Selection. *See* McGovern-Fraser
  Commission
Commission on Presidential Nomination.
  See Hunt Commission
Commission on Presidential Nomination
  and Party Structure. *See* Winograd Commission
Commission on Rules (O'Hara Commission) - 31
Commission on the Democratic Selection
  of Presidential Nominees. *See* Hughes
  Commission
Congressional caucuses - 10, 23, 196
Connally, John
  campaign financing - 162, 163t, 164,
    165t, 168, 169t, 170t, 179
  campaign spending - 178, 182t
Conservatives
  amateur vs. professional - 120, 122
  factions - 130
  self-identification as - 117, 118t, 118-
    119, 128t
Convention caucuses
  definition - 209
  general purpose - 195-196
  special purpose - 196-197
Converse, Philip E. - 138, 142
Conway, M. Margaret - 186
Coolidge, Calvin - 205t, 215
Corporations
  campaign contributions - 161, 169t, 170,
    171t
  convention role - 194
Coter, Cornelius - 78
Cousens, Theodore W. - 25
Cousins v. Wigoda - 57
Crane, Philip - 152
  campaign financing - 163t, 164, 165t,
    168, 169t
  campaign spending - 182t
Cranston, Alan - 152
Crawford, William - 11
Credentials committees - 58, 191-192
Cronin, Thomas - 224-225, 233
Cronkite, Walter - 192
Crotty, William - 53, 54, 78, 79, 100, 102,
  186, 210, 232, 233
Crouse, Timothy - 209
Cultural conservatives - 126
Cultural liberals - 126, 128
Cunningham, Nobel E., Jr. - 24

Dahl, Robert - 137
Daley, Richard J. - 57, 191
David, Paul T. - 24, 106, 137, 209

Davis, James W. - 25
Delegate selection
  affirmative action - 33-34
  candidate right of approval - 39-40
  caucus vs. primary - 95-97
  direct election - 37, 38, 99
  discrimination outlawed - 28, 31, 33
  national party influence - 40, 57-59
  proportional representation - 36-39, 50, 57
  rules and procedures - 5, 17
  state conventions - 11-12, 15
  See also Caucuses; Primaries
Delegates
  amateurs vs. professionals - 120-122
  at-large - 39
  behavior types - 193-194
  caucus membership - 195-197
  commitment - 34, 35, 40-41, 62, 224
  credentials - 58, 191
  disputed - 57-58, 209
  ex officio - 34-35, 46
  goals - 197-199
  representation - 103-106
  representativeness - 103, 106-113
  superdelegates - 35, 115-116
Delegates and Organizations Committee. *See* DO Committee
Democratic Compliance Review Commission (CRC) - 38, 60
Democratic National Conventions
  public and party officials - 34-35, 113-116
  reform commissions - 31-44
  1964 - 28, 107, 120
  1968 - 29-31, 107, 120
  1972 - 33, 39, 57-58, 120-121, 191
  1980 - 121
Democratic party
  demographic representativeness - 107-109, 136
  factions - 88, 129-131
  ideological identification patterns - 87, 117-119, 132, 133t, 134
  nationalization - 56, 60-61
  political base - 21
  reform - 27-28, 31-44
  socioeconomic representativeness - 111-113
Democratic Party of the United States v. La Follette - 43, 57, 59-60
Democratic-Republican party - 9-10, 22
Dennis, Jack - 79, 157
Descriptive representation. *See* Representation, Standing For
Devries, Walter - 157

Di Clerico, Robert E. - 79
Direct election primaries - 37, 38, 99
Dixon, Julian - 116
DO Committee - 46-47
Dole, Robert
  campaign financing - 163t, 164, 165t, 168t, 169t, 170t
  campaign spending - 182t
Due process rules - 43-44

Eagleton, Thomas - 202
Edelman, Murray - 158
Educational level
  of Democratic convention delegates - 112t
  demographic changes - 69, 70t
  and party loyalty - 69-71
  and primary turnout - 90-91
Eisenhower, Dwight - 17, 205t, 209
Elitism - 52. *See also* Party elite
Epstein, Leon - 25, 86, 100, 101
Equal Rights Amendment (ERA) - 197
Everson, David H. - 210
Ex officio delegates - 34-35, 46

Factionalism - 18
  Democratic party - 88, 129-131
  Republican party - 130
Federal Campaign Act Amendments of 1974 - 160
Federal Election Campaign Act (FECA) of 1971 - 160
Federal Election Commission (FEC) - 160, 230
Federalists - 9-10, 22
Fernandez, Benjamin - 163t, 164, 165t, 168t, 169t
Ferraro, Geraldine A. - 71, 116, 201, 202
Flanigan, William H. - 157
Ford, Gerald - 192, 201, 202, 205
  1976 prenomination campaign - 199-200
  primary performance - 97, 154
  supporters - 130, 151
Fraser, Donald - 32
Front loading - 42, 65-68, 76, 174
Front-runners
  delegate assignment - 36, 37, 38
  early primaries - 68
  strategic environment - 155
Fund for a Conservative Majority - 180, 184

Gamson, William A. - 158
General elections
  campaign spending limits - 181
  voting behavior - 84, 141-143

Germond, Jack - 209
Glenn, John - 151, 152, 154, 203
Goldman, Ralph M. - 24, 137, 209
Goldwater, Barry - 150, 202
Goldwin, Robert A. - 102
Graber, Doris A. - 209
Greenstein, Fred J. - 157

Hacker, Andrew - 71, 79
Hadley, Charles D. - 138
Harding, Warren - 215
Hargrove, Erwin C. - 79
Harmel, Robert - 78, 210
Harris, Fred - 102
Hart, Gary
  delegates - 39
  image - 146
  platform strategy - 200-201
  primary performance - 68, 96, 154
  supporters - 43
Hempstead, Ernest - 25
Hennessy, Bernard - 78
Hershey, Marjorie Randon - 186
Hess, Robert D. - 157
Hess, Stephen - 214, 232
Hill, David B. - 157
Hitlin, Robert A. - 138, 210
Hoffman, Paul J. - 139, 158
Hofstadter, Richard - 24
Hollings, Ernest - 152
Hoover, Herbert - 15, 205t
Hughes, Harold - 32, 33
Hughes, Richard - 32, 33
Hughes Commission - 32, 33
Hughes Committee - 32, 33
Humphrey, Hubert H. - 96
  campaign financing - 159
  supporters - 87, 124, 125, 126, 127t, 130
  1964 Democratic convention - 28
  1968 nomination - 29
Hunscher, William - 163t, 165t, 167, 168t, 169t
Hunt, James - 32
Hunt Commission - 32, 33, 34, 35, 36, 37, 38, 39, 40, 42, 50, 67, 115
Hyman, Herbert - 157

Ideology
  candidate strategy - 149-152
  cycles - 148, 210
  issue-based - 123, 124, 127t
  party orientation - 128-131, 137
  representation - 116-117
  self-identification - 87, 117-119, 131-136
  voter participation and - 92-93, 94, 99
  and voting behavior - 146-149

Illinois
  delegation selection - 57-58
  primaries - 19, 38, 66
Image, candidate - 67, 75, 95, 142, 144, 145-146, 148
Income level
  affirmative action - 33-34
  demographic changes - 70, 73
  1984 Democratic delegates - 113
Incumbency
  campaign contributions and - 170-171
  renomination and - 205
Independents - 19, 45, 142-143
Inkeles, Alex - 74, 79
Interest groups - 6
  convention caucuses - 195-197
  overrepresentation of - 99
Iowa - 15, 42, 66
Irish, Marian - 188, 209
Issues - 117, 125-126, 129
  as ideology base - 123, 124, 127t
  voter participation and - 93-94, 95
  voting behavior and - 143

Jackson, Andrew - 11
Jackson, Henry - 130, 131
Jackson, Jesse - 57
  convention delegates - 36-37, 108
  platform strategy - 200-201
Jackson, John S. III - 102, 131, 133, 134, 137, 138, 139, 158, 210
Jacksonian Democrats - 11
Jacobson, Gary C. - 157, 186
Jagoda, Barry - 75
Janda, Kenneth - 78, 186, 210
Javits, Jacob - 134
Jefferson, Thomas - 9, 10
Jewell, Malcolm E. - 54, 143, 157
John, Kenneth E. - 138
Johnson, Donald Bruce - 233
Johnson, Lyndon B. - 28, 29, 201-202, 205, 215

Kayden, Xandra - 186
Keeter, Scott - 144-145, 157, 158
Kefauver, Estes - 204
Kelley, Stanley - 157
Kelley-Mirer rule - 144
Kelly, Peter - 112
Kennedy, Edward - 150, 152
  campaign financing - 163t, 164, 165t, 166-167, 168t, 169t, 170t, 171
  campaign spending - 171, 172t, 178, 182t
  convention delegates - 96
  1980 presidential bid - 146, 200
Kennedy, John F. - 17, 202, 204

Kennedy, Robert - 29, 87, 150
Kessel, John - 101
Key, V. O., Jr. - 25, 56, 78, 86, 87, 91, 92, 100, 134, 139, 207, 210
King, Martin Luther, Jr. - 29
Kirkpatrick, Evron - 210
Kirkpatrick, Jeane J. - 99, 102, 117, 125, 126, 138, 139, 208, 210
Kritzer, Herbert - 88, 89, 92, 101

Labor unions
  campaign spending - 161, 169t, 170-171
  convention role - 194
  primary turnout - 89
Ladd, Everett Carll - 101, 128-131, 138, 139
La Follette, Robert - 98
LaRouche, Lyndon - 163t, 164, 165t, 168t, 169t
Lederman, Susan L. - 209
Leland, Mickey - 32
Leland Commission - 32, 33
Lengle, James I. - 87, 88, 91, 92, 100-101, 102
Leuthold, David A. - 157
Levitin, Teresa - 138
Liberals
  factions - 130
  self-identification as - 117-118t
Lipset, S. M. - 79
Local parties. *See* State and local parties
Loevy, Robert - 224-225, 233
Longley, Charles - 56, 78
Loophole primary - 38
Luetscher, George D. - 25
Luttbeg, Norman R. - 157

McCarthy, Eugene - 29, 87, 124, 130, 150
McClosky, Herbert J. - 25, 126, 132, 139, 158, 207, 210
McGovern, George - 32, 151
  image - 146
  1972 prenomination campaign - 96, 202-203
  supporters - 87, 125, 126, 127t, 130, 131, 150, 196, 197
McGovern-Fraser Commission - 31-37, 39, 42, 44, 107-109, 120
McGrath, Wilma - 120, 121, 138
McKinley, William - 205t
Malbin, Michael J. - 186
Manatt, Charles - 189
Marshall, Thomas R. - 18, 25, 50, 54, 95-96, 100, 102, 158, 179, 186
Master cue function - 147
Matthews, Donald R. - 158
  campaign spending on - 183
  candidate image - 67, 146

Media
  influence of - 50, 64, 69, 74-78
  national convention coverage - 192-193
  and national primary proposal - 222
  use in campaign strategy - 155
Merriam, Charles E. - 25
Mikulski, Barbara - 32, 33
Mikulski Commission - 32, 34, 38, 39, 43, 107
Milbrath, Lester - 193, 209
Miller, Arthur H. - 157
Miller, Warren E. - 138, 142
Miller, William - 202
Minnesota - 15, 95-96
Minority rights - 6, 35-36
  affirmative action - 33-34, 47
  representation - 36-39, 50, 61
  See also Blacks; Women; Young people
Mirer, Thad - 157
Mississippi Freedom Democratic Party (MFDP) - 28
Moderate conservatives - 130
Moderates - 117
Mitofsky, Warren J. - 111, 137
Mondale, Walter - 151, 152
  convention delegates - 36-37, 96, 108
  image - 148
  1984 prenomination campaign - 68, 200-201, 202
  regional primary plan - 225
  selection as vice president - 203
  strategy - 155
  supporters - 43
  vice presidential selection - 203
Montjoy, Robert S. - 132, 139
Moral Majority - 180
Muskie, Edmund - 203
  primary performance - 154
  supporters - 125, 126, 127t

Nakamura, Robert T. - 217, 232
National Conservative Political Action Committee (NCPAC) - 180
National Conventions - 5, 23, 187-188
  brokering - 18, 41
  candidate role - 199-201
  caucuses - 195-197
  committees - 190-192
  demographic composition - 108t
  functions - 188, 207-208
  goals - 41
  history - 11-12
  media coverage - 192-193
  order of business - 188-189
  public officials and party professionals - 21, 34-35, 113-116

reform commissions - 31-44, 46-49, 113-114
revitalization - 206-208
sites - 189-190
socioeconomic makeup - 111-113
See also Delegate selection
National Education Association (NEA) - 194
National Organization for Women (NOW) - 196
National parties
authority over state law - 44, 56, 60-61
centralization - 43, 44, 49, 51, 55-61
and delegate selection - 40, 57-59, 224
effect of primaries on - 18
importance of unity - 204-206
structure - 217
See also Democratic party; Party leadership; Republican party
National primary, proposed - 221-223, 230
implications of - 222
procedures - 221-222
Negative campaigning - 184
New class Democrats - 129
New Hampshire primaries - 42, 66
New liberals - 130
Nie, Norman H. - 157
Nimmo, Dan - 157, 158
Nixon, Richard - 48, 189, 201, 205
image - 146
party leadership - 45
personality - 215
primaries - 17
supporters - 126
vice presidential choice - 203
Nofziger, Lyn - 74-75

O'Hara, Rosemary - 139, 158
O'Hara Commission - 31
Old class Democrats - 129
Old fashioned liberals - 130
Old party system - 21-22
brokered conventions - 41
party strength - 56
presidential nominations - 29-30
primaries - 62
Olson, David N. - 54
Open primaries - 19, 63
representativeness - 85
Supreme Court decisions - 59-60
versus closed - 42-43
Oregon primary - 14, 21
Organizational party model - 217-219
Orren, Gary R. - 180, 182, 184, 186
Orthodox conservatives - 130
Overacker, Louise - 25

Packwood, Bob - 225
Page, Benjamin I. - 101
Parris, Judith H. - 24, 209
Participatory party model - 217-219
Party elite - 216
ideological identification - 131-136, 137, 150, 152
nomination role - 21-22
organizational hierarchy - 216-219
postreform - 99
Party identification - 88, 91-92, 118, 134, 142, 147
Party leadership
hierarchy models - 217-220
ideological self-identification - 131-136
nomination role - 131, 217
representation - 113-116
Party loyalty
education and - 69, 71
open vs. closed primaries - 42-43
voter turnout - 91-92
Party strength
effect of primaries - 18, 63-64
old party system - 56
Pateman, Carole - 102
Peer review - 35
Pennsylvania primaries - 13, 14
Personality factors - 214-215
Petrocik, John R. - 157
Pitkin, Hanna F. - 104, 137, 152
Platform drafting - 5, 190
Plissner, Martin - 111, 137
Political action committees (PACs) - 161, 168-169, 169t, 184
Political activism
amateur vs. professional - 119-123, 124, 128t, 129
incentives - 121-122
Political culture index - 126
Political cycles - 7, 148, 210
Political parties
early organization - 9-10
function - 18, 231
nationalization - 44, 49, 55-56
See also National parties; State and local parties; *and* individual parties, by name
Polsby, Nelson W. - 24, 101, 102, 198, 210, 216, 232
Pomper, Gerald M. - 25, 143, 157, 190, 209, 210
Postconvention primary proposed - 223-225
Prenomination campaign spending
independent - 183-184
on media - 183
timing of - 175, 178-179

Prenomination campaign spending limits - 171-183
Prenomination campaign strategy - 149, 152-155, 174
Prenomination campaigns
  cost - 18, 20, 183
  financing - 160-161, 162t
  length - 67
  media influence - 67, 74-78
  winnowing role - 67, 215-216
Pre-party era - 7-9
Presidential nominating systems
  context - 3-5
  democratization - 6, 12-13, 22
  goals - 216-217
  mixed - 51
  old party system - 29-30
  reform - 5-7, 27-53, 63, 220-230
  self-nomination - 8-9, 22
  standardization - 229-230
  See also Delegate selection; National conventions
Price, David E. - 53, 54
Primaries
  blanket - 19
  campaign costs - 18, 20, 183
  and candidate quality - 64-65
  closed - 19, 43, 85
  direct election - 37, 38, 99
  effect of reform on - 50
  front loading - 65-68, 76, 174
  history - 13-18, 23, 62-63
  loophole - 38
  media coverage - 74-77
  old party system - 21
  open - 19, 42-43, 59-60, 63, 85
  presidential 1912-1980 - 16t
  problems - 18-20
  representativeness - 84-91, 94
  rules setting - 5
  timing - 41-42, 65
  versus caucuses - 95-97
  voter participation - 18, 20, 28, 84, 87, 88-89
  voter qualifications - 19
  voting behavior - 143-145
  winner-take-all - 37-38
  See also National primary, proposed; Postconvention primary, proposed
Procedural rules
  enforcement - 60-61
  interpretation and review - 60
  reform - 31-44, 46-48
Professionals - 119, 122-124
Progressive movement - 12-13, 14, 15, 18, 23, 49

Proportional representation (PR) - 36-39, 50, 57
Prothro, James W. - 188, 209
Proxy voting - 44, 46
Public officials, convention role of - 34-35, 113-116
Pulley, Andrew - 163t, 164, 165t, 168t, 169t

Ranney, Austin - 25, 84, 86, 92, 99, 100, 101, 102, 120, 138, 210
Reagan, Ronald - 48, 146
  campaign financing - 163t, 164, 165t, 166-167, 168t, 169t, 170t, 180
  campaign spending - 171, 172t, 174, 175, 182t, 184
  1976 presidential bid - 46, 96-97, 152, 199-200
  nomination 1980 - 147, 151
  primary performance - 66, 154
  supporters - 130, 150
  vice presidential choice - 202
Reed, Roy - 25
Regional primary proposals
  implications - 227-228
  Mondale plan - 227
  Packwood plan - 226-227
Representation - 103-106
  Acting For - 105-106
  demographic - 107-110, 136
  issue-oriented - 117, 125-126, 129
  of mass voters - 35-39, 65
  of party leadership - 113-116
  quotas - 107-108
  socioeconomic - 111-113, 136-137
  Standing For - 104-105, 116-117, 152
Representation, proportional. *See* Proportional representation (PR)
Representativeness - 99, 219
  of caucuses - 95
  demographic - 106-113, 136
  of primaries - 84-91, 94
Republican National Committee (RNC) - 46-47, 49
Republican National Conventions
  delegate apportionment formula - 59
  demographic representativeness - 109-111, 136
  1952 - 209
  public officials at - 114
Republican party
  factions - 48, 130
  ideological self-identification - 117-119, 132-134
  minority representation - 47, 61
  national party vs. state laws - 61
  political base - 21, 45, 47, 48

primaries - 16t, 60
reform - 44-49, 61
state autonomy - 61
Revenue Act of 1971 - 160
Roback, Thomas - 121, 138
Roberts, Steven V. - 138
Robinson, Michael J. - 76, 79
Rockefeller, Nelson - 17, 134
Roosevelt, Franklin D. - 205t
  personality - 215
  primaries - 15, 17
Roosevelt, Theodore - 205t
Rubin, Richard L. - 74, 79, 88, 89, 92, 101
Rules committee - 47, 191

Sabato, Larry - 158
Sait, Edward McChesney - 8, 24
Sanford, Terry - 6, 24, 32
Sanford Commission - 32
Savage, Robert L. - 157
Schneider, William - 79
Schumpeter, Joseph - 208, 210
Schweiker, Richard - 199
Shafer, Byron - 53
Shaffer, William R. - 132, 139
Shriver, Sargent - 202
Singer, William - 57
Slatemaking - 39, 57
Smith, Al - 15, 17
Socioeconomic factors
  education - 69, 70, 90
  income - 70, 73
  representation - 90, 111-113, 129-130
  voter participation - 94
Sorauf, Frank - 106, 137, 209
Soule, John W. - 120, 121, 124, 138
Special Equal Rights Committee (Hughes
  Committee) - 32, 33
Split-ticket voting - 143
Starr, Joseph - 78
Stassen, Harold - 163t, 165t, 167, 168t, 169t
State and local parties
  declining influence - 41, 56-59, 61
  delegate selection - 15, 30, 57-59
  ideological orientation - 132-136
  and national convention delegations -
  195
  national sanctions - 44, 60-61
  primaries - 13-14, 23
State conventions - 11-12, 15
Steiger, William A. - 47
Stevenson, Adlai - 203
Stokes, Donald E. - 142
Strategic political environment - 3-5, 7
  attitude changes - 73-74
  economic changes - 73
  media - 74-78

population changes - 69-72
Structural-functionalism - 209
Sullivan, Denis G. - 196, 197, 210, 217, 232
Sundquist, James L. - 64, 65, 79
"Super Bowl" primaries - 66, 68
Superdelegates - 35, 115-116
Supreme Court
  and independent campaign spending -
  161, 183
  party nationalization - 43, 56-60
Sussman, Barry - 138

Taft, Robert - 17, 209
Taft, William H. - 205t
Taft regulars - 14, 15
Tarrance, V. Lance - 157
Ticket balancing - 201-202
Torney, Judith V. - 157
Truman, Harry S - 201, 205t

Udall, Morris - 152, 154, 229-230
Unit rule - 35
Uslaner, Eric M. - 79

Verba, Sidney - 157
Vice presidential candidate selection -
  201-204
Vietnam War and nomination politics -
  28, 29, 31, 51, 124, 125
Voter participation - 83, 97-98
  advantages and disadvantages - 95-100
  biases - 86-87, 94
  caucuses - 84
  demographic factors - 90-91
  and ideology - 92-94, 99
  party identification - 88, 91-92, 147
  primaries - 18, 20, 84, 87-89
  See also Representativeness
Voting behavior
  candidate ideology - 146-149
  candidate image - 145-146
  general election - 141-143
  party identification - 147
  primaries - 143-145
  and voter education - 144-145

Wallace, George - 126, 127t, 150
Walzer, Michael - 64, 65, 79
Warren, Earl - 19
Wattier, Mark - 143, 144, 147, 157
Weaver, David H. - 209
Weber, Ronald E. - 132, 139
Wekkin, Gary - 54
West, Darrell M. - 186
Westin, Av - 209
White, Theodore H. - 209
Wildavsky, Aaron - 101, 120, 138, 198, 210

Wilson, James Q. - 119, 120, 121, 122, 138
Wilson, Woodrow - 205t
Winner-take-all primaries - 37-38
Winograd, Morley - 32, 33
Winograd Commission - 32, 34, 36, 38, 40, 42, 43, 67, 108
Wisconsin primaries - 14, 19, 21, 43, 59-60
Witcover, Jules - 209
Women
   affirmative action - 33

   convention caucuses - 196, 197
   representation - 6, 50, 107-110
Women's movement - 28, 51, 71

Young people, representation of - 107, 108t, 109, 110

Zingle, Nancy - 157
Zukin, Cliff - 144-145, 157, 158